PRAIS

The Greatest Stock Picks

"An Asian wise man used to ask the Deity in his prayers to spare him from living in an interesting era. But Jones won't allow it. He makes the reader a co-pilot on a journey through the 1920s, the 1990s, and points in-between, unfolding in the sagas of twenty-five fascinating companies that were among the great stock picks of their day. Readily accessible and highly recommended."

—DR. MICHAEL J. BOSKIN, Professor of Economics and Senior Fellow, Hoover Institute, Stanford University; Former Chairman of the Council of Economic Advisers

"This timely book proves that very few American corporations of any size, any quality, any management dominate for an indefinite period of time. Ultimately market events, consumer needs, and technological changes take over. The only certain thing in life is change. And Jones shows the investor how to recognize that change in order to recognize a portfolio gain. Read this and reap."

—GERALD TSAI, JR., President, Tsai Management

"Read this book and let Randy Jones's spellbinding business stories create a happy ending for your portfolio."

—TODD BUCHHOLZ, Economist, Managing Director of Enso Capital Management, and author of *New Ideas from Dead Economists*

"This is a really worthwhile tome. . . . I don't know how I ever did without it."

—LIZ SMITH, *New York Post*

THE
Greatest
Stock Picks
OF ALL TIME

*Lessons on Buying
the Right Stock
at the Right Time*

W. RANDALL JONES
WITH JULIE M. FENSTER

A BYRON PREISS BOOK

THREE RIVERS PRESS
NEW YORK

Copyright © 2002 by *Worth Magazine* & Byron Preiss Visual Publications, Inc.

All rights reserved. No part of this book may be reproduced or transmitted in any form or by any means, electronic or mechanical, including photocopying, recording, or by any information storage and retrieval system, without permission in writing from the publisher.

Published by Three Rivers Press, New York, New York.
Member of the Crown Publishing Group, a division of Random House, Inc.
www.crownpublishing.com

THREE RIVERS PRESS and the Tugboat design are
registered trademarks of Random House, Inc.

Originally published in hardcover as *Worth's Greatest Stock Picks of All Time* by Crown Business, New York, New York, in 2002.

Printed in the United States of America

Design by Robert Bull Design

Library of Congress Cataloging-in-Publication Data available upon request.

ISBN 1-4000-5141-X

10 9 8 7 6 5 4 3 2 1

First Paperback Edition

For Connie, Cole, Chancellor, and Chip.

Contents

THE
Greatest
Stock Picks
OF ALL TIME

INTRODUCTION: MAKING THE CUT

Nothing in life is to be feared. It is only to be understood.
—MARIE CURIE

For many, the thought of picking stocks engenders ferocious fear, but to paraphrase Madame Curie, stocks are not to be feared, they are to be understood.

One reason I founded *Worth* magazine was to learn how to make the markets work for me. I had always been reasonably good at making money and extraordinarily good at spending it, but not nearly as proficient at investing it properly. When I was in my early thirties, I was the publisher of *Esquire* magazine when it was sold. I enjoyed a "liquidity event," or flush of cash, which even I knew shouldn't languish in a savings account earning 3 percent interest. I realized then that I had to take control of my financial life with the same vigor with which I had taken control of my business life. I had to learn the way the markets worked and how best to profit from them. So I sought that understanding and became a student again—a student of investing. The result was *Worth* magazine.

The first thing my new education taught me was that personal finance is a broad subject, yet every investor, new or old, has the same basic fantasy: to pick the right stock at the right time. Ever since the first brokers started hanging around the curb on Wall Street in the 1810s, trading certificates back and forth, some stock picks have been better than others. But even the greediest robber baron of the nineteenth century would have gasped at the gains to be made in our own gilded era.

The momentum of the bull market spoiled us all—changing our perceptions, and for most of us (thankfully), our bank balances. Even people who weren't trading knew that if a stock had merely doubled in value over five years, it was practically pathetic.

Stocks that increased 1,000 percent in the same time were just barely CNBC newsworthy. If a stock grew by 5,000 percent, then it became slightly interesting, although that was hardly the limit in a heady decade of 10,000 percent increases.

The 1990s were unique, but there is probably something unusual about every bull market, when, by definition, stock prices grow faster than the overall economy. (Likewise, there is something exaggerated about any bear market, when stock prices put on the brakes ahead of the real business cycle.) Big, galloping bulls may make things easier for investors looking for a hot stock pick, but no single method of selection will succeed in all stock climates. And since that up-up-uppity market of the 1990s is over, stockpicking has become a high art again.

This is the first book published under the *Worth* banner. Fittingly, it is also the first to create a fascinating list: the twenty-five greatest stock picks in Wall Street history. For each of the twenty-five stocks profiled, we analyze how an average investor could have recognized the potential of "the right stock at the right time." With thousands of stocks to choose from at any given time (3,000 today on the New York Stock Exchange alone), we sought to uncover the signs that made General Motors in 1924 or IBM in 1953 or Intel in 1992 the BEST picks any investor could have made. We will also detail how those same signs will benefit us today as we evaluate stocks for our own portfolios. What are the right indicators to be looking for? Which are the opinions to ignore? What, if any, are the signs to sell? Is management all-important? Or should you do as Peter Lynch says, "Invest in companies that any old fool could run, because one day—one will"?

Worth's Greatest Stock Picks of All Time covers the whole modern era, defined from the point of view of common stocks and the way investors use them. In the 1920s, individual investors danced into the market by the millions, their new money and new expectations transforming the market. Part of the shift was caused by an author named Edgar Lawrence Smith, who proved conclusively that in the long run, common stocks were better investments than bonds (which had long been the choice of sensible, conservative investors). Drawn along by Smith, investors began to recognize that good companies in growth sectors would provide a much better return than bonds—and with less risk than was formerly associated with common stocks.

Early in the modern era, the dividend rate was the most important element of a stock's appeal. The early emphasis on dividend rates helped ease the transition from bonds. However, picking out a bond was a relatively organized process, akin to taking a book out of the library, in the sense that you normally have an idea of what the book is going to be about. When individuals began to trust their money to common stocks, they were faced with a swirling bazaar, not the predictability of the trusted library.

As so often happens in bazaars, items seem beautiful until they fall apart on the way home. Such is the way with many stocks. Slowly but surely through the decades, individuals have learned to pick stocks, taking more and more responsibility for their choices. In the new millennium, that choice is usually about growth and capital appreciation, with the dividend now reduced to a secondary role. Those of us picking our own stocks today—even if it's only managing our 401(k)s—are part of a revolution that was a century in the making.

If Edgar Lawrence Smith implanted the idea in investors' minds that vigorous stocks outperform the economy in the long run, individuals have increasingly taken his words as a mantra for stocks: seek them and buy them. With rising passions, each generation has created a whirlwind around such stocks known in different times as glamour stocks, highfliers, the nifty fifty, or just plain growth stocks.

Accompanying each stock profiled in this book is a timeline of key corporate events, and, best of all, a few themes that will endure for your own selections. The one cautionary note is that most of the stocks in this book aren't necessarily recommended for the present time. In fact, some of the companies mentioned, such as Dr. Henry Singleton's imperturbable Teledyne, aren't even in business any longer. Stock picks don't last forever, but the knowledge behind them is your arsenal for the future. May *Worth's*

Greatest Stock Picks of All Time help turn any fear you might have into true understanding.

BUILDING THE TOP 25

If we had chosen *Worth*'s greatest stock picks of all time solely in terms of their percentage increase, this book would have been a whole lot easier to write. All we'd have to do is revisit the technology rally of the 1990s, which convinced millions of new investors that they were masters in the art of stockpicking.

Indeed, if economic conditions remained fixed just as they were in the 1990s, then those high-flying computer and Internet stocks would be the only models you'd ever need. Dell . . . AOL . . . Intel . . . Oracle. Isn't the air getting exhilarating already? Alas, the market doesn't stay the same, and never has. For a century now, Wall Street has been a new world every morning.

Taking literally thousands of stocks over the last hundred years and choosing only twenty-five that we deemed the best was a Herculean task. But we arrived at the greatest stock picks of all time both quantitatively and qualitatively. To give you the benefit of a lifetime of investing experience, we looked back through bull markets and stubborn bear years, through times of national crisis and times of technological advances. Once you grasp the reasoning behind the twenty-five stock picks in this book, your investing strategy will be set to respond to any market condition . . . including the one that's coming next.

Some of the picks reflect companies positioned as long-term investments—insurance giant AIG or General Electric, for example. Others required good timing to get in a quick bounce, such as Paramount or L-T-V, the aerospace conglomerate of the 1960s.

Because it's so much easier to be smart when the whole market is going up, we especially liked bear-beaters: GM and Coca-Cola, which fared well in the midst of the Great Depression; Teledyne, which soared in the dull market of the 1970s; and Krispy Kreme, which sailed through the downturn of 2000–2002.

When a company dominates its sector, you have to gauge both that sector and the ability of the king to remain standing. Gillette showed how tricky that can be, and shows, too, that a company caught napping can be an opportunity for wide-awake investors. Reynolds, on the other hand, was the upstart of the aluminum business. Alcoa, the overlord of the industry, was a good investment in the 1950s, but as we see, Reynolds was an even better one.

Of course, as long as there is a stock market, investors will be looking for "another Xerox" or "another Polaroid," so both of these onetime glamour stocks were automatic additions to our list. On the other hand, we also wanted to show you how to see the potential in the un-glamour stocks of any market. We chose Chrysler, which was given up for dead at its low point, and Fannie Mae, a company about which most investors were making fundamental mistakes.

Technical indications aside, when you invest in a stock, you have to look at a company as though you were the very first investor—understanding its business and the way it makes money. Avon, Home Depot, and Amgen are examples of companies with unique business plans that the investor had to fully understand.

Finally, we thought it was important to include one stock that was a great pick even though its price didn't go up in a remarkable way. Today, share price seems like the only way to judge a stock, but there is another. We included AT&T, whose rise was unspectacular until you realize that it returned a steadily increasing dividend for most of the twentieth century.

To help guide you through this book, our twenty-five featured stocks are broken into categories that illustrate common features. We quickly learn that the factors that make a great stock can be shared by companies in entirely different industries. It's easy to group Xerox and Polaroid, because both companies revolutionized their respective fields. But some of the groupings might surprise you.

Dell Computer and Avon Products, for example, share virtually nothing at first glance, until you realize that what made both companies special was the *way* in which they sold their products, not the products themselves. Similarly, Fannie Mae and Intel are worlds apart, but each company made a fundamental change that simultaneously avoided disaster and set the stage for a glorious future. GM and Gillette, Reynolds Metals and Oracle—this book is filled with strange bedfellows. Even our "takeover trio" of L-T-V, Teledyne, and Paramount Communications were stocks that excelled for completely different reasons. The point of this mixing and matching is that any one stock can possess a variety of investment-worthy qualities, and it's important to see as many as possible.

We recognize that it's always possible to look at a historical stock price chart and start playing the game of "coulda, woulda, shoulda." If you always bought and sold at the right time, you could have gotten rich even with such utter disasters as Sunbeam or Enron. That's why the stocks in this book are featured over eras: years, not days.

In reviewing *Worth*'s greatest stock picks of all time, we try to cover the purchase decisions through the investor's eye rather than just the lens of history. You'll find that the stories don't always begin at the lowest possible share price, because real life rarely allows us to buy in such a timely and prescient way. With Polaroid, Home Depot, and AOL, we have deliberately chosen time frames that excluded years of growth, to focus on the indicators that average investors could have noticed.

No stock goes up forever, so we also provide clues on when to get out. Again, though, we've tried to avoid 20/20 hindsight. We look for indicators that investors could have actually used had they owned the stock at the time in question. And the ownership periods we suggest aren't intended to be absolutes: Coca-Cola may have been a star during the Great Depression, but it's been great over the past sixty years as well.

Finally, after each of the twenty-five picks, you will find two or three major investment lessons that emerge from the story. The book may cover the past, but these lessons should help us to pick the right stock at the right time today and in the future.

ONE
THE LINK BETWEEN GREAT MANAGEMENT AND BOTTOM-LINE PROFITS

ETERNALLY YOUNG: AMERICAN INTERNATIONAL GROUP (1988–2000)

A GROWTH STOCK AT ANY AGE—OR SIZE: GENERAL ELECTRIC (1951–1959)

CHANGING WITH THE TIMES: INTERNATIONAL BUSINESS
MACHINES (1956–1971)

Louis Rukeyser has said that evaluating a corporate management in isolation of the company it leads is every bit as difficult as evaluating the director of a Broadway play. He's right. We tend to evaluate managements and directors backward; if they produced a hit, they must have been pretty good, and if they didn't, well, you can draw your own conclusions. But a backward conclusion isn't worth much in the stock market, because you can't invest in the past.

Yes, investors should demand strong management from companies whose stock they own. But how can you tell? Wasn't Enron once the most admired company in America? Certainly an investor's job is made easier when a company has a visible leader at the helm whom investors can get to know and trust. If Warren Buffett weren't leading Berkshire Hathaway, you can bet that the annual meeting would be considerably less crowded—and that his company's approach to business would be less widely understood.

In the absence of a charismatic personality to deliver the corporate message, you as an investor must do some legwork. You can begin by reading the annual report to see the human faces behind corporate performance. When you read on, you hope to find more than glossy pictures. You're looking for a clear link between the actions and philosophy of management and the bottom-line profitability of the company. Above all, the question you should be asking is "Has this company distinguished itself from its competitors?" If the answer is no, then management hasn't made its case.

In this chapter we see that three outstanding companies— AIG, GE, and IBM—were more than just a sea of initials; they were great long-term stock selections. Investing for the long haul requires unusual confidence, and those investors who truly understood the management teams behind the scenes were the most confident of all.

ETERNALLY YOUNG

American International Group

1988–2000

> *AIG was that actuarial's complaint—the statistical anomaly. It was a big insurance company that was still growing at a gallop, making money in good times and bad. Not many insurance companies could say the same over the last quarter of the twentieth century, which is what made AIG so cool and consistent. In other words, it was an investor's dream.*

When analyzing the quality of a company's management, it's natural to start at the top. Not every CEO gets to be a national media star, so it can take a bit of legwork to learn how a company is run. The process is certainly easier when there's continuity in the executive suite.

Investors who prize continuity hit the jackpot with American International Group. What has set it apart over the years has been management's insistence that growth take place away from the commodity segment of the business. Every single CEO of AIG felt the same way: both of them, that is.

Two Strong Leaders = One Great Company

From 1919 to the present day American International Group (AIG) has had only two CEOs, Cornelius "Neil" Starr and Maurice Greenberg, and it's been the better company for it. The latter is bombastic and the former was reticent, but outward personalities aside, their philosophies have reflected the same values, and given AIG a distinct corporate culture. Most of all, the romance of the insurance giant, incongruous as that phrase may be, is a deep involvement in business all over the world. Since the day AIG opened its first two-room office in Shanghai in 1919, overseas revenues have been central to the business, and accounted for about 50 percent of operating income from 1988 to 2000. The company stock was not only an insurance play, but for an individual portfolio, it also offered one-step global diversification.

Both Starr and Greenberg were alike in believing that every center in the business is a profit center, or should be. One arm could not be expected to make up for another. Greenberg in particular has long believed that innovation is essential to AIG's growth. The company, therefore, cast a wide net, including the more mundane property-and-casualty, marine, life, and auto insurance, of course, but it also would offer the more exotic, such as insuring children in day care against kidnapping and Internet websites from hackers. With so many types of policies and different entities to sell them, "innovation" has translated into a corporate structure so complicated that AIG could be called a corporate spiderweb, woven of as many as 300 subsidiaries.

To say that Greenberg wanted AIG to grow would be an understatement; by his own confession, he has thought nothing else ever since he took over in 1968. One year into his tenure, he oversaw AIG's first public offering of shares. The stock thrived on Greenberg's dictum for the company—earnings growth of nearly 20 percent per year. It was easier to say than to do, but from 1968 to 1998 AIG found ways, ridding the books of lagging businesses and starting or acquiring ones with glowing potential. By the mid-1980s, the company easily hit Greenberg's target, as assets grew by an average of 34 percent from 1984 to 1988, while in each of the four preceding years growth in earnings followed at an average clip of 27 percent. During that time, the stock price languished, due to the pessimistic perception of the whole property/casualty sector. Smart investors may have been accumulating AIG stock, but the price didn't really start to move until 1988. That year, with Asian markets booming, Wall Street looked for companies poised to benefit. AIG was belle of the ball.

Americans were hearing a great deal about the accelerating overseas economies of the Pacific Rim and AIG offered a ride along with those "tiger" economies. The stock, which had made precious little progress between 1985 and 1988, burst out, showing that insurance could still be a high-growth industry when it encompassed practically the whole world.

From 1988 to 2000, AIG stock increased from a price (adjusted for splits) of $4.85 to $110. A $10,000 investment would have been worth $226,804 after a dozen years. Even more intriguing for investors, AIG was surefooted. The stock moved upward without a noticeable downturn or even a plateau. In that sense, it only reflected the company, which turned a profit even in years when the earnings reports of other property-and-casualty companies were laid waste by hurricanes or other natural disasters. While AIG stock easily outstripped the S&P 500 (average of large companies), as well as its own brethren in the insurance sector, it also stayed ahead of the NASDAQ average. AIG was one of the anomalies of the 1990s bull market, which was largely propelled by nascent high-tech companies: it was old company, old economy, but decidedly high-growth nonetheless.

Blatant Opportunist

One of the things that helps distinguish AIG is its origins. In 1919, fresh from service in World War I, twenty-seven-year-old Berkeley grad and lawyer Neil Starr went to Shanghai looking for opportunity. He found it, all right, in a nation of millions unable to buy their own life insurance.

The Chinese people were going uninsured because the British companies that dominated the business in China wouldn't consider selling life insurance policies to native Chinese. The only logical reason for the English position was that actuarial tables (which predict average life spans) did not yet exist for the Chinese population. These tables are key, because normally the people who issue policies depend on tables in order to set rates. So, Starr saw quite a business. He founded American Asiatic Underwriters (AIG's predecessor) and established a pattern when he extended his company to include life insurance for Chinese nationals, estimating longevity and setting rates that ensured a profit.

Another hallmark of Starr's young company was that its staff was exclusively Chinese. Foreign companies in China nearly always employed their own imported managers and salesmen. Starr hired locals. As his company expanded into other Asian nations and into other types of coverage, he continued the practice of relying on native-born employees. In the late 1920s, Starr, by then married to the daughter of a Canadian missionary, returned to the United States to build up the center of his empire. He purchased several of the insurance companies that his agency represented and started new firms, too, most of them with an overseas connection. During World War II, he was especially aggressive in South American markets previously dominated by German and Italian firms. Privately held, the burgeoning insurance conglomerate made a millionaire of Neil Starr, but he began to neglect it somewhat in the late 1950s, when he had a personal crisis. (He was devastated when his wife left him for a Russian painter.)

Neil Starr's companies, which would assume the name American International Group in 1967, were global long before most other American financial firms started to look overseas. The difference was patience, as Starr and his colleagues learned the intricate art of insurance on a mosaic of more than a hundred countries. They took the time to understand local customs and to navigate regulations that baffled many U.S. firms. One of the toughest challenges was retaining sharp employees in developing economies, where AIG training often made a worker worth more than even AIG could afford to pay.

The Next Generation

Even though AIG had thousands of policies, offered by hundreds of subsidiaries, the man Neil Starr tapped to replace him believed that the behemoth was basically quite simple. Maurice Greenberg, nicknamed "Hank" after the Detroit Tigers ballplayer of that name, grew up on a farm in upstate New York. He earned a law degree between stints in the army during World War II (in which he landed with the Rangers during the D-Day invasion) and the

Korean Conflict. After distinguishing himself in a domestic insurance subsidiary, he was picked as president of AIG. "Sometimes I find a man who has an inner fire, a man who is perfectly in his métier, his orbit," Starr once said of his ability to choose executives, "and when I do, I back him."

Hank Greenberg's zeal for new businesses led AIG to pioneer coverage in many new areas. It insured satellites, offshore oil rigs, and computer networks; it protected companies against the cost of environmental cleanup and corporate directors from shareholder lawsuits. A subsidiary called AIG Political Risk wrote insurance against kidnapping and extortion. With the help of consultants such as Henry Kissinger, AIG continued another tradition, pushing across forbidding political boundaries.

AIG sought permission in 1992 to stage a homecoming and reestablish operations in mainland China, from which foreign businesses had been barred when the Communists took power in 1949. Hank Greenberg stepped up as the lead salesman and worked the prospect tirelessly. Meanwhile, his company quietly cultivated favor by investing heavily in a Shanghai office complex. AIG also took the initiative to locate a set of windows stolen long before from the Summer Palace in Beijing, buying them for $500,000 from a European collector and restoring them to the palace as a gift to the Chinese people.

"It took almost a decade and a half to open China for AIG," Greenberg wrote. "It took dozens of trips. Most CEOs I know who want to open a foreign company want to meet with the leader of that country once. After that, they believe they've done all that's required. It doesn't work that way."

Net income, which was $17.2 million when Greenberg took over in 1968, grew to $50 million in 1975. By 2000, it was $5.64 billion.

INVEST IN SKIING?

Anyone looking over the long list of assets of American International Group (AIG) might wonder why one of the world's

*most potent insurance companies owned a ski resort in Vermont.
However, this was no investment fad: AIG had owned Mount
Mansfield in Stowe for more than forty years. The reason was
twofold: first, Cornelius Starr liked to ski. Second, Maurice
Greenberg liked to ski.*

The AIG Decision

The value in AIG stock was its record of growth. In financial terms,
the company was the eternal youth of the industry, chalking up each
new record as though it was only just starting. The decision points
for buying the stock in 1988 related to the future and just how long
the company could continue its insistent rate of expansion.

Overall, the property/casualty industry stagnated in 1986–
1987, but not AIG. Some investors noted that it was writing fewer
policies and worried about its growth slowing in the future. That
idea was blown away in 1988 when AIG continued to record
increased earnings on its crafty strategy.

"We look for markets without a lot of competition," said AIG's
longtime vice chairman, Thomas Tizzio. The company's philosophy was to actively seek areas in which it could offer coverage that
was otherwise unavailable. Furthermore, it simply left fields that
were overcrowded. Investors could see the effect of the company's
choosy standards in the margins it was able to maintain. Investors
who picked AIG out of the pack were rewarded with a stock that
increased by more than twenty times from 1988 to 2000.

Acquisitions extended the types of businesses in which AIG
was engaged, but insurance remained the most important revenue
stream. The deterioration of Communism in the Soviet bloc
enhanced prospects for the expansion into Eastern Europe and
Central Asia. At the same time, the Asian market was more entic-
ing than ever, especially with a return to China in the offing. In
the two fastest-growing Asian nations, the Philippines and Japan,
AIG subsidiaries either led the market or came up second.

"Entrepreneurial" is an expression often used to imply a certain autonomy of the divisions; at AIG, it has gone much further ever since the reorganization of 1967–1968 when Greenberg took over. At any given time upper management in effect owns at least 30 percent of the company. It is a unique arrangement, giving AIG some of the best characteristics of a professional partnership. AIG's top 300 employees receive the right to buy dividend-rich shares in a related company that holds, among other things, a substantial stake in AIG. Meanwhile, the top 40 employees are offered similar shares, but of a much higher grade—each block yields dividends of over a half-million dollars annually. The bonus shares, which have to be surrendered when the employee leaves, represent holdings of almost one-third of AIG's stock. Significantly, the company is always in the hands of people with a real stake in its performance.

At Home Abroad

The factors ruling against the purchase of AIG in 1988 were led by a general uncertainty about the insurance sector. However, as is often the case, the dullness of a sector isn't necessarily a bad thing and does not affect every stock within it. AIG was different from most other insurance companies: at once more daring in its pursuit of uncrowded businesses and more conservative in its own money management. In addition, AIG was assiduously steering clear of insurance that it considered overregulated, notably health insurance.

Smart investors judge stocks in a sector as much by what makes them different as by what makes them similar. AIG was a case that rewarded people who took the trouble to learn why it *was not* like other insurance companies.

The AIG formula made a clear profit on underwriting. That is, it managed to earn money on that basic insurance business of selling policies and paying claims. Surprisingly, AIG is one of the few companies that does so consistently. In the 1980s, U.S. property-and-casualty insurers as a group paid out much more money in claims than they took in through premiums. Their idea, which worked most of the time, was that investment profits on accumulated premiums would more than make up for underwriting losses.

AIG, on the contrary, considered that its revenue would expand in a more stable way if it made a profit at each end of the insurance business: underwriting and investment. Rough stretches are inevitable in the investment climate (making for setbacks in a company's portfolio), as well as the earthly climate, causing natural disasters such as hurricanes that result in losses in the underwriting business. Because the company scrutinized claims closely, sometimes withholding payment, it has occasionally been charged with skirting obligations on technicalities. However, financial conservatism on all fronts consistently earned AIG the highest possible ratings from agencies that grade insurance companies.

One cloud that hovered over the decision to buy AIG stock in 1988 remained for the entire span through 2000. As of this writing, it is talked about still. Hank Greenberg has never indicated any plans to retire or name a successor. "There is only one Royal Highness around here," said vice chairman Tizzio, referring to Greenberg. Like monarchs who live long lives, condemning the eldest heir to a life of harrowing boredom, Greenberg has watched a whole generation of likely successors move on to leadership at other companies. Greenberg's vim is as legendary as his highly effective management. However, investors worried about the overall leadership of a company as powerful as AIG resting so precariously on the shoulders of one man.

Epilogue

The rise in AIG's stock price that started in 1988, or indeed with the IPO nineteen years before that, stalled for the first time in 2000. The price-to-earnings ratio, which was running about double the industry average as it grew to 16 in 1996, soared to more than 20 in 1998 and past 36 in 2000. It was a heady ratio for a financial company, where a number under 10 would be more typical. Over a long span, AIG justified investors' faith, but a change in conditions was inevitable.

A high price-to-earnings ratio is a hungry number that must be fed with great news every year, if not every single quarter. In the bearish market of late 2000, AIG's stock couldn't push higher, even while the company posted another year of double-digit growth at 11.5 percent: great for any other big insurer, only *good* for AIG. Investors were also cautious because of AIG's exposure to the slumping Asian market. Ironic, since Asia was once what made investors run to the stock.

Another factor in AIG's pause was an acquisition spree in 1999–2001. Investors tend to be petulant and expect companies to keep making money without ever spending any of it. AIG's purchases were widely praised for their strategic value, especially in bolstering the company's presence in the lucrative business of financial planning. In the long range, AIG was undoubtedly better off. However, the market moves on short headlines, not long reports. So in 2000, though AIG was still a healthy company, inviting to long-term investors, it was not perceived as a growth stock.

Lessons

Ensuring future profits . . . *Even a competitive, price-oriented business such as insurance can have pockets of profitability. Make sure to hook up with managements intent on finding those niches.*

Variety is the spice . . . *AIG is constantly coming up with new product offerings. You can't get 20 percent growth by standing still.*

When in Rome . . . *Both CEOs believed in the importance of understanding local economies.*

Management . . . *Only two CEOs, both great. The big question mark: Who will take over next?*

TIMELINE

1919 Neil Starr founds American Asiatic Underwriters in Shanghai.

1926 Starr establishes a base in the United States.

1950 China operations cease.

1967 Company renamed AIG.

1968 Hank Greenberg succeeds Starr as CEO.

1969 Initial public offering.

1975 Net income $75 million.

1987 Net income $1 billion.

1993 Returns to business in China.

1994 Net income $2.17 billion.

2000 Net income $5.64 billion.

A GROWTH STOCK AT ANY AGE—OR SIZE

General Electric

1951–1959

*"I'm GE through and through," said an investor who attended
the annual shareholders' meeting in 1949, the eve of what
was unquestionably the company's greatest period of growth.
Loyalty and pride had always run deep for the General
Electric investor, who felt that the company represented a
world of stable profits and tidy dividends. Both had been a
central part of the GE investment profile in every single year
of the twentieth century. Now, however, as the 1950s
approached, the aging company was entering a new era. GE
dared to completely break down and then rebuild—no, completely reinvent—its whole management structure. (No blasé
if-it-ain't-broke-don't-fix-it strategy for them.) The effect? A
revolutionary style of business administration that has filled
management textbooks with barrels of ink since. The smart
investor saw the changes begin, knew the company was on the
move, and bought the stock. But hats off as well to the longtime shareholder, like our friend from 1949, who may not have
been entirely comfortable with such sweeping reforms, but had
enough faith in management to hang on. And get rich.*

Is bigger better? It depends on the way size has been achieved. The
leader in a small niche business is apt to be more profitable than
the number four player in a much bigger market. And owning a
vast collection of number fours won't create economies of scale; it
will simply leave investors confused.

For a big company to succeed on Wall Street, it must balance
the streamlining of existing operations with its forays into new
fields. Concentration among a manageable number of component
businesses not only gives each component a better shot of succeeding on its own, it also gives shareholders a clearer picture of
what they're getting. As the second half of the twentieth century

began, General Electric became the master of balancing big and small—and got much bigger in the process.

The Company's Roots

In 1950 General Electric was putting out close to 200,000 products. These ranged from tiny lightbulbs to massive gas turbines and a Comstock lode of home appliances and medical devices in between. A prime government contractor during World War II, GE was poised in the years afterward to create new businesses ranging from silicone plastics to synthetic diamonds, over-the-horizon radar to turbojet engines, heat pumps to microwave ovens and television sets. And nuclear power plants. And computers. And aerospace programs. And electric knives. And self-cleaning ovens. Each year brought even more new products from a wider range of sciences than ever. In the laboratory, General Electric's research methods merged the pure sciences with unspoken and yet recognized needs of the market. At GE, however, business has tended to grow like kudzu—a beautiful weed, to be sure, but one that has the potential to run amok. Products were springing up from all parts of the vast empire. Despite its obvious success—how many companies would love this degree of invention?—GE was in need of some serious organization.

The management of the company was overwhelmed and knew it. Admitted it, too. During a transition period from 1948 to 1952, the company applied its sense of science to its own problems in management, re-creating itself with room to grow in all directions at once. The president no longer had to, or even could, understand every business GE was involved in—there were too many. Instead, the company redrew its structure from the ground up and installed training programs that would instruct people in the responsibilities of the new, "no excuses" management. GE's most vital product, surely from the point of view of the stockholder, became a new type of manager, trained in the methods that would make the far-flung enterprises meet on one very handsome balance sheet.

This manager needed to be very capable indeed, since the company had such a huge array of products. And investors had nearly the same concern—gauging GE's strength by a different standard from that used for other companies, with their handful of products and occasional research breakthroughs. Growth, for one thing, has not been the issue with GE. At the start, General Electric was mainly in the business of building power plants and its ubiquitous lightbulbs, of course, though it soon developed electric stoves and other appliances as a means of promoting the use of electricity during the daytime, when the lightbulbs weren't burning. Not surprising, then, that with only minor exceptions over the past sixty years, its annual gross revenues have grown at a healthy rate or better. The key to keeping GE flourishing, however, comes back to how well its varied businesses are understood by management and how fully its potential is realized. In the early 1950s, investors were at a crossroads. They had to decide whether the company was capable of pursuing all of its proliferating options without falling down on its most basic business: earning money.

Management already knew the direction in which it was headed. General Electric's transformation from a steady "widows and orphans" stock to one of the stellar growth holdings of the 1950s—rising on a split-adjusted basis from $20 in 1953 to $100 six years later—was no accident. It was certainly appreciated by those average folks who were the majority of the company's shareholders. They saw a $10,000 investment grow to $50,000—even as they received dividends of $667 to $1,000 each year. A stock like GE can make you rich.

A NOT-SO-BRIGHT IDEA

Although no one times the market perfectly, nearly everyone who has ever sold a share of GE stock has probably done so too soon, since the overall trend has been upward. One GE stockholder who definitely sold out too soon was Thomas Edison. The General Electric Company was incorporated in 1892 on the basis of a business he started, but two years later Edison sold his holding. All those who sell a good stock think they have a better way to make money. Edison did, too: motion pictures.

Science as Applied to Management

General Electric's vitality flowed from its research labs, where brilliant scientists came up with discoveries like harnessing X rays for the use of medicine (1913) and tuning in to FM radio as an improvement on AM (1936). But company affairs were another story: they were controlled by a dynasty of strong-willed presidents. Gerard Swope, who ran the company from 1922 to 1940, was a quintessential GE president of the first epoch. He directed all operations from the company headquarters in New York City, giving the impression that he knew everything that was going on, everywhere within his realm. He was a regimented man, not only arriving at the same exact time for work every morning, but leaving without fail during the first commercial break of the 5 P.M. radio news broadcast.

Swope had an expansive mind and was able to micromanage GE into one of America's five largest corporations. However, one of his strengths was his objectivity, which he proved by recognizing that many of the operations were actually quite inefficient. For example, components for appliances were manufactured in outdated factories in five far-flung cities before final assembly in Erie, Pennsylvania. Even if the appliances made money for the company, the transportation costs and logistics problems were unnecessary. Another example of underlying problems that caught Swope's eye: company revenues were 50 percent greater in 1940 than in 1920, with basically the same facilities and workforce. To some executives, that may have suggested an improvement. Not to Swope. For him it meant that 50 percent of those facilities had been unnecessary in 1920.

To his credit, Swope set the stage for GE's fantastic growth by knowing when to say "when." Like the old baseball umpire who retired the day that, for the first time, he wasn't *sure* of every call, Swope had that moment in 1942. He knew it was time to make changes but was just not clear on how to do it. With its expansion during World War II, GE was going in a dozen high-tech directions at once. Swope couldn't be sure of all of them and GE was too big not to be absolute about everything within it. During the war, General Electric's sales revenue quadrupled, adding more than $1 billion to the bottom line as revenues grew from $233 million in 1939 to $1.377 billion in 1943. To the surprise of nearly everyone, sales held that level even after the war, when military expenditures subsided. Yet the imperative for change in management was greater than ever. In 1945, a veteran executive named Ralph Cordiner was given two years to design a reorganization plan. (It was then tested for several years at subsidiary companies.) On the strength of his strategy, Cordiner was named president of GE in December 1950—the same year when restructuring began at the parent company.

Cordiner was a student of organization, analyzing organizations such as the Roman Catholic Church, the U.S. Navy, and Standard Oil of New Jersey. In the end, he submitted a plan not unlike longtime General Motors chairman Alfred P. Sloan Jr.'s widely respected structure for the automaking company. Following Sloan's blueprint, GE was separated into fifty-four operating departments, each one sovereign unto itself, under the administration of an independent manager. The executives at headquarters were no longer supposed to give orders. They were supposed to serve, helping departments to meet goals. The plan, implemented in 1948 and finished in 1952, disrupted many careers and even ruined a few, as new paths to the top were rolled out right over the old ones, leaving many old-timers stranded.

The result, however, was an exacting methodology for business: marketing, cost analysis, logistics, and most of all, planning. Once Cordiner's decentralization was in place, though, GE was ready to live by his guiding edict: to remain in a position to greet all coming business conditions. Or, in his own words, to stay "out ahead of an explosive period and able to plan for it."

Turning Point for Investors

Potential investors evaluating whether to put their money in GE during the years leading up to the 1950s already knew a few things about the company. It was one of the bluest of the blue chips, held not by speculators in any sense of the word but largely by the type of investors who judged the prosperity of the company, as well as their own, by the size of the quarterly dividend. (An aggressive investor, on the other hand, often interprets a fairly big dividend to mean that, in the judgment of the board of directors, investors will be able to make better use of the money than the company would. In other words, avenues for growth are few and far between, so the shareholders may as well have the cash.) That was not at all the case with GE, but the very reliability of its dividend made some analysts argue that the company was not growing as fast as it could. By long tradition, GE was regarded as a safe stock—too safe, some thought, to be capable of any sharp rise in the share price.

The decentralization of GE's management was well publicized and widely praised. Even the most aloof of investors were aware that the old giant was stirring, and many took a fresh look. The reorganization was exciting, but it carried a risk, signaling either the dawn of a new era or the demise of a productive old one. While investors could not be sure what the decentralization would bode, they had to appreciate that it was intended to prepare the company for that welcome word . . . growth.

Some Bumps

Despite extraordinary changes—as well as fervor—sweeping the company, it wasn't all easy during the 1950s. In one bump in the road, GE became entangled in a PR nightmare over labor relations. In the postwar era, the company became widely known for its unusually rigid attitude in this area. From the GE management point of view, it was simply good business to calculate the best pay and benefits that it could afford, make an offer, and then refuse to negotiate. Period. End of story. After all, the calculation represented its best offer, right? The company assumed that to agree to more would certainly be bad business. However, and not so surprisingly, this was not exactly the way the union members saw things. They felt that GE was a little too high-handed. The company, which already had an ultraconservative reputation thanks to official remarks made at the time of the Communist witch-hunts, now had an image problem on its hands. Solution? A little spin control! A public relations office was created for the first time in 1954—a rarity in those days for corporations outside of Hollywood—and the prescient company hired none other than Ronald Reagan as its spokesman. The Gipper helped save the day and the share price. (If you want to find an upside to the controversy, however, GE's stance on dealing with unions spotlighted just how independent it was from the day's prevailing trends in management.)

Bump no. 2: Uncle Sam. In 1951, the corporate tax rate amounted to a staggering 70 percent of earnings; this included the Excess Profits Tax levied to help pay the cost of World War II. "Such taxes are approaching confiscatory levels," wrote GE president Ralph Cordiner. He warned that the remaining profit no longer justified the assets at risk. Relief arrived not a minute too soon with the inauguration of Dwight Eisenhower as U.S. president in 1953 and his promise of reduced corporate taxes.

What the Government Taketh . . .

The only thing Ralph Cordiner disdained more than high taxes was big government spending. Ironically, though, GE was the single biggest beneficiary of new government spending during the ten years after World War II. The three primary areas, all new and all very large-scale, were nuclear energy, aerospace, and electronic defense systems. Even GE's core business was growing: electrical manufacturing accounted for 1.2 percent of the gross national product in 1935 and had more than tripled to 3.8 percent by 1950. To meet demand and continue the creation of new products, GE in 1952 came up with a plan to invest some $125 million per year on new facilities and expansion. That amount, roughly equivalent to the company earnings, was certainly a vote of confidence that the company expected income to grow substantially. As it turned out, the company went on to spend even more than the original projection. On what exactly? New labs, payroll, and plants such as Louisville's renowned Appliance Park, which was opened in 1954.

By 1952 GE was the country's fourth most widely held stock and was third on the Vickers list of mutual fund holdings, which showed that the stock was also popular among professional managers. As investors watched in the 1950s, the share price rose even more steeply than did the earnings per share. While they just about doubled between 1951 and 1959, from $1.51 (on a split-adjusted basis) to $3.19, the stock went up by four times, and even five times as of one heady month at the end of '59. Obviously, this situation caused the price-to-earnings ratio to rise to 27. During the initial rebuilding years, 1948–1952, the price-to-earnings ratio was generally under 10. The p/e ratio for GE would not stoop to that level again for twenty-five years, until the stock's dull stretch in the late 1970s. Both periods of sub-10 p/e ratios were buying opportunities.

A Growth Stock Must Keep Growing

Decentralization allowed General Electric to become vastly bigger during the 1950s, without becoming equally more complicated. Because it was involved in more than twenty separate businesses—and climbing—the tendency was to consider GE practically a one-company mutual fund, or, as a 1955 business magazine article put it, "a share in an investment trust engaged in manufacturing." The perception was that GE was so deeply ensconced in American industry that it could have gone out of business, shut its doors, and *still* reported record sales and a profit for at least a few years. For the company to maintain its identity as a force in the marketplace, and not just a reflection of it, GE had to grow faster than the rest of the manufacturing industry, or even than the economy as a whole. That was the test that has been attached to GE ever since.

While the rebuilding years started with Cordiner's decentralization efforts in 1948, the momentum continued straight through the mid-1950s. From these beginnings, GE has undergone a "complete" restructuring about every fifteen years. Part of that is a natural realignment; a bit is grandstanding for the investors. Either way, GE takes management more seriously than nearly any other company. The periodic restructuring is another means of modernizing. And all the while, new parts of the company rise alongside old ones.

Epilogue

In 1960, GE was hit with a scandal that affected the company, its stock price, and its very profitability. That year the company was found guilty of price-fixing. Three of its executives went to jail and the government levied million of dollars in fines. GE maintained its innocence. Cordiner denied—quite vehemently, in fact—that the pressures on departmental managers had driven GE employees to cut illegal deals with competitors. No matter what the cause was, the effect was clear: the price-fixing stopped GE's rising share price in its tracks. The reason, however, had little to do with the stain of an ultra-American institution caught cheating. Instead, the stock skidded for the simple reason that earnings did. What happened? Did people avoid GE's products because of management's character? No, profits cratered for three years because GE had to pay restitution equivalent to approximately 50 cents per share. (When earnings became whole again the stock price bounced back to its former perky state throughout the 1960s.)

The next decade wasn't so kind to investors: GE's flat years in the late 1970s reflected a perception that GE was growing, sure—tripling sales during that decade alone—but it was not growing any *faster* than the U.S. economy as a whole. Oddly enough, GE was such a big company that its only "competitor" *was* the United States economy. At that time, when the issues of stagnation, recession, and whipping inflation all darkened the outlook for the general economy, investors wanted GE to be more independent, more vibrant and aggressive. Enter Jack Welch. Under the storied leadership of this chief, a product himself of the company's training programs, which he entered right out of college in 1960, GE and its stock entered a new era of growth. It was a more modern one to be sure, but a legacy built right on the playbooks of Ralph Cordiner in those heady days of 1951 to 1959.

Welch and his "Six Sigma" pursuit of error-free manufacturing are now part of American business history. So is his insistence that GE exit any business in which it wasn't either number one or number two. Peter Lynch was a big Welch fan during his last years running the Magellan Fund, talking up the company at every opportunity and devoting 2 percent of his fund to GE shares. Until, that is, Lynch's heir Morris Smith pointed out that GE accounted for an even bigger percentage of the major stock averages with which Magellan was competing. It was yet another form of GE versus the economy, and there was only one response: buy more shares.

Lessons

Never say never . . . *No company is too big, too old, or too "safe" to become a growth company—with the right changes.*

Gotta have faith . . . *If you like the management and believe in them, stick with the company. Trust that they will execute a plan for profits, just as CEO Ralph Cordiner did with his reorganization.*

If the big boys like it . . . *It's a good indication when a large company is even more popular among professional managers than among individual investors. For most of its history, GE made it through a demanding level of analysis without a scratch.*

When everyone's fleeing, think twice and maybe even consider whipping out your wallet . . . *The costly judg-*

ment against GE in 1960 made droves of investors take their
profits and run to other stocks. However, investors willing to
wait out GE's penalty—or buy more shares—were rewarded.
The fines were temporary, while the company's outlook in the
long term was as bright as ever.

TIMELINE

1892 The General Electric Company is incorporated on the basis of a business started by Edison.

1905 The first kitchen appliance, a toaster, is marketed.

1912–1919 Experiments in radio lead to the availability of AM frequency and the start of broadcasting.

1913 GE research results in the "Coolidge" tube, which harnesses X rays for medicine.

1922 Gerard Swope becomes president of the company.

1936 FM divined as an improvement on AM.

1941–1945 Company revenues quadruple during World War II.

1945 Ralph Cordiner is given two years in which to design a restructuring plan.

1950 The company is making close to 200,000 products—and growing.

1951–1952 GE adopts a decentralized management structure.

1953 Eisenhower is sworn in as U.S. president, promising to reduce corporate taxes.

1954 Opens Appliance Park, an integrated consumer goods plant, in Louisville, Kentucky.

1960 Stock price peaks at a price of $100; GE investigated in price-fixing probe.

1961 A $50.5 million judgment is levied against GE for price-fixing.

CHANGING WITH THE TIMES

International Business Machines

1956–1971

Some unsuspecting investors in 1956 bought stock in a profitable tabulating company and ended up owning the reigning computer giant. Others—that is, the ones who actually understood the new technology and believed in its potential— were far less numerous, but they were the predecessors of today's high-tech investor. Because IBM attracted both conservative and high-risk investors, it was an anomaly: a growth stock that people bought for safety. Whatever the reason for buying it, there was a bundle to be made in IBM, as the stock increased from a split-adjusted $20 in 1956 to $350 in 1971.

The most difficult challenge a corporate management can face is how to respond when a market changes underneath it. Turning your back on what got you there is never easy. Some managements set their sights on new markets but don't give their middle managers the incentive to change. Others milk their cash cows for all they're worth, only to find them ending up worthless.

Today it seems hard to believe that IBM could have been the victim of market transition in the 1950s. Certainly the company's name was an advantage: International Business Machines was inherently more flexible than "International Tabulators" would have been. Ultimately, though, the task of transition was left to top management, and they responded brilliantly.

Revolutionary

In the mid-1950s, International Business Machines was already regarded as the grand old paragon of the high-growth, high-tech stock. Ask anyone who still had 100 shares of IBM purchased in 1914 if they could provide a fairly succinct definition of *high-growth*. After paying $2,750 and then exercising rights given to investors to buy more stock for another $3,614, the long-term IBM investor would have a stake worth $2.5 million in 1956. Meanwhile, the stock would have paid out a total of $209,000 in dividends during those same forty-two years, increasing continually until it provided what amounted to an upper-middle-class living.

Thomas J. Watson Sr., the man who created IBM out of a collection of small manufacturing firms, had made a practice of advising practically everyone he met to buy his company's stock. Lucky for the generations of employees who grew rich with the company that he was so persuasive. Even the cooks and waiters in the diner on the ground floor of IBM world headquarters in New York heard Watson speak about the stock, many eventually joining the ranks of IBM millionaires.

A virtuoso salesman, Watson was impressive, but what was even more so was the company's record. Since 1916, IBM had never missed a dividend. And though profits did dip during the Depression, the company had never reported a loss. It hadn't issued new stock since 1925, concentrating the value within the shares already on the market. By 1956, IBM controlled an astonishing 90 percent of the $250 million market for tabulating machines (those devices for sorting data that were considered vital to sizable businesses and government agencies). Yet anyone who bought IBM for only those reasons in 1956 would have been on the wrong track—for the tabulating machine was headed for oblivion.

IBM was at a turning point, one that could just as well have killed as kindled the company. And yet, most people who bought IBM from 1954 to 1956 probably did so because the stock had a stellar history and the market for tabulating machines was then booming. Both IBM's stock and its business were about to change, however. They had to, really. If not, there might not be any IBM at all today.

Over the next fifteen years, both IBM's stock and its business were all about computers, of course. An investment in Big Blue (blue is IBM's corporate color) was nothing less than a vote of confidence in the broadening scale of the computer revolution, but over the years, that decision was harder to make than it might appear in hindsight. Every pause seemed to be the final step in the revolution. IBM was charging forward at breakneck speed—that much was clear. But investors in the days of the slide rule had to decide just when Big Blue would overshoot the vaunted potential of the electronic computer.

Creative Choices

When Thomas Watson took charge of the Computing-Tabulating-Recording Co. in 1914, the name described the firm's activities in a succinct, albeit clunky, way. C-T-R had three divisions that made mechanical devices ranging from time clocks to scales to mechanical calculators. Watson concentrated on the tabulating machines, which performed the timesaving miracle of reading punch cards, which processed thousands or even millions of separate pieces of information in a single operation. Watson soon changed the name of the company to reflect his own expansive plans: International Business Machines.

Magazine publishers used IBM machines to keep track of subscribers; insurance companies stored information on policyholders; and the government generated information on taxpayers. Once IBM salesmen had plumbed all of the most obvious uses for tabulators, though, they learned to become creative, studying individual businesses in order to suggest uses in new industries. Before the end of the process, the salesman was likely to know as much about a business's operations as the manager, since the two of them worked with an IBM engineer to implement tabulating machines successfully.

IBM's domination of the market stemmed in part from its engineering, which was traditionally aggressive in refining its machines. The only thing more aggressive was the sales force, which pressed IBM into first place—and kept it there—by teaching one customer at a time how to reap the potential of the new office machines. The quality of service after the delivery became a prime IBM selling point. The thoroughness of IBM sales as an educational effort was fundamental to the company's next phase: computers.

THE POWER OF LEASING

Because IBM leased machines to customers, a salesman remained within earshot, solving problems and, of course, introducing upgrades. Watson later admitted that he'd borrowed the idea of leasing the machines rather than selling them from AT&T, the phone company that initially rented telephone equipment to its customers. Likewise, Xerox would borrow the same idea from IBM.

During World War II, IBM had cooperated in a U.S. Navy project that used a series of IBM tabulators in the construction of America's first modern computer. The machine successfully calculated missile trajectories; it led to several increasingly powerful versions even after the war. In the 1940s, the prevailing verdict was that computers might have some limited uses in the military or academia but none in business. However, the pioneering Eckert-Mauchly Computer Corp. continued development work, and in 1951, its parent, the powerful Remington-Rand Corp., introduced the first electronic computer suitable for business, UNIVAC. Known popularly as an "electronic brain," it received a tidal wave of publicity. In fact, for a long time "UNIVAC" was a generic name for computers.

Few people at IBM were interested in the computer at that time. Its practical use was still largely an abstraction, while the ever-profitable tabulating machine was already whittling away work in thousands of American businesses. Thomas Watson Jr., the son of the president, led a largely frustrating effort to organize a computer division at IBM. But with the start of the Korean War in 1951, the company received so many advance orders—eighteen, to be exact—from military contractors in need of computers that it finally produced its own first model, the 701, in 1952. IBM was now officially in the computer business.

"I think what chased us along very rapidly were two things," Watson said later. "First, every time we built a computer, or announced we were building one, we got a lot more orders than we expected. Second, I visited a few customers—aircraft plants, Atomic Energy Commission installations—and everyone said: 'God, we've got to have better, faster computers.' So it was obvious to me and my associates that the need was much beyond anything we had imagined."

IBM was not first in the business of computers, but by the mid-1950s it was coming on strong. When *Time* magazine decided to publish a major article on the newfangled machines, IBM was the only company that cooperated enthusiastically. As a result, Tom Watson Jr. and a model 702 were featured on *Time*'s cover in March 1955—both looked bright, representing the future. It was a moment Watson remembered ever after as symbolic of his company's arrival: IBM was in the computer business and everyone knew it. Whether or not that was a good place to be was the question facing investors.

Time to Plug In?

Today it is so obvious: computerization is the revolution by which the last half of the twentieth century will always be remembered. Any sharp investor who could manage it would go back in time and invest in computers. But high technology—the very business of imagining the future—is never as easy as it seems in retrospect. Not even in the case of that gold mine called IBM in 1956.

In fact, in 1949, John Mauchly (cofounder of Eckert-Mauchly) assessed the American business scene and concluded that, at the most, five companies in the United States would buy computers. Even though estimates continually rose from there, investors were long aware that the whole phenomenon might just be a fad. A study by McKinsey & Co. as late as 1963 found that two out of three computers operating in business were not being used enough to make them pay for themselves. A New England mill owner had admitted as much a few years before: "We use ours just an hour or so a week. The rest of the time it just sits there looking pretty." The investing world was long divided between those with sanguine predictions for the computer and those who believed it would never gain widespread acceptance.

Despite the doubts about the future of computers, IBM had plenty of competition. Remington-Rand was first in computers in the early 1950s, and by the time IBM entered the fray, several large companies, including General Electric, RCA, and Burroughs, were already committed to the business. Other companies were in a better position to develop the science side of computers, but no one was better positioned than IBM to put the machines into offices. "It doesn't do much good to build a better mousetrap if the other guy selling mousetraps has five times as many salesmen," said the president of the Rand's UNIVAC division.

IBM acknowledged its late start and made up for it. "We went from almost none to nearly five hundred electrical engineers in about two years," Thomas Watson Jr. said of the initial expansion in 1953–1954. People who knew IBM's ways were aware that the company, which maintained a policy against layoffs, was likely to be in the computer business to stay.

If an investment in IBM was a vote for the computer age, the credit lay with the company's management: namely its young president, Thomas Watson Jr. More than anyone else of his generation, Watson staked his reputation and his own future on the computer business. In interviews and decisions—words and deeds—he pointed IBM toward a transition unthinkable at the beginning of the decade. Under Watson, the company began to drift away from punch cards and focus itself on computers. Had they been nothing but a flash in the pan, Watson would not have lasted to the end of the decade as president of IBM, no matter who his father was.

Financially, IBM's business was humming in the mid-1950s. Earnings per share, which had meandered downward in 1951–1952, were at 36 cents in 1953, about where they had been in 1950. Then they began to jump . . . 49 cents (1954) . . . 59 cents (1955) . . . 72 cents (1956). By that time, 10 percent of IBM's revenues were derived from its computer business. Some investors appreciated that old Tom Watson Sr. was a conservative money manager who carried a low debt ratio and who all but refused to issue new stock. However, more impatient investors worried whether IBM could take advantage of the potential of the computer business without raising extra capital, through much more creative financing than IBM was used to.

Cementing Its Place

Nearly six thousand electronic computers were installed in offices as of 1958, according to a survey by John Diebold, and 80 percent were IBMs.

Even more encouraging was that 88 percent of new orders belonged to Big Blue. The company had doubled its sales over only four years and the pace was accelerating, thanks almost entirely to the computer division. Earnings followed sales and the stock price started to jump, doubling from mid-1956 to the end of 1958.

IBM's success in the computer age could be traced to two factors: a way in which it didn't change from the old days and a way in which it did. The first IBM advantage was that its sales army had had real expertise in both their products and their clients' needs. Four decades of teaching individual businesses to embrace tabulators had more than prepared the sales force for the task of introducing electronic computers, which were even more daunting from the customer's point of view. "If you really look at the history of IBM," Thomas Watson wrote in 1987, "technological innovation wasn't always the thing that made us successful. Unhappily there were times when we came in second. But in the game I knew, that was less important than sales and distribution methods. We consistently outsold people because we knew how to put the story before the customer, how to install the machines successfully, and how to hang on to customers once we had them."

Investors would have had to read IBM's annual reports to recognize that the company's success was also due to its admission that even it couldn't take advantage of vast new opportunities without finding vast new sources of money. The company increased its level of borrowing, derived from Prudential Insurance, to $500 million (up from $30 million in 1945). And in another break with tradition, IBM began to place stock offerings on the market. In the span of one year, between 1956 and 1957, the number of shareholders nearly doubled. While the new shares diluted the value of the old ones somewhat, the cash generated soon made up for it by adding value to the company and so to all of its stock.

By 1963, IBM's 80 percent share of the computer market hadn't grown—but the market certainly had, to $1.5 billion. Even as the company's revenues increased by an average of 20.8 percent since 1956, its earnings were out in front of that, at an average of 22.8 percent. There are few indications of corporate health more convincing than earnings growth outpacing hefty revenue growth. (This indicates that sales are not being "purchased" at a premium, but rather that they are actually increasing the overall efficiency of the operation.)

Investors who put their money in IBM stock as a prediction that the computer revolution would continue unchecked were proved right. Computer sales in the 1960s were increasing at the rate of 20 to 22 percent per year, a mark with which IBM kept abreast, even building up a two-year backlog of orders. The automobile industry, the second most expansive sector of the decade, was growing at only 7 percent.

Even as IBM dominated its 80 percent share of the computer industry, it took nearly all of the available profits. Of the companies scrapping over the remaining 20 percent of the computer market, only one (Control Data) posted a profit. Competitors, however, accused IBM of maintaining its share by using some disingenuous practices. For example, they complained that IBM was letting small companies introduce breakthrough products, only to then sweep into the opening with a similar product all ready to go. When even tougher competitors planned product introductions, on the other hand, IBM would "scoop" them, announcing comparable products so far in advance that customers were inclined to wait before buying anything. "IBM has got where it is, because it *is* what it is," explained an electronics stock specialist in 1967. "And it's going to stay where it is. We're telling our people to buy."

With so many believers, IBM stock shot upward, doubling in one year, 1967. By 1968, its market value was worth more than the *combined* value of twenty-one of the thirty stocks on the Dow Jones Industrial Average. Then, in 1971, IBM suddenly stumbled, reporting second-quarter earnings that hadn't grown. Not even a little. Wall Street was aghast. The stock fell, and though it managed to recover by the end of the year, it was no longer considered invincible. The bear market of the 1970s, the threat of antitrust lawsuits, and the specter of new competition from personal computers dogged the stock and kept its price within a trading range throughout the rest of the decade. Phase I of the revolution was over. People knew the computer had a permanent place in business life. And IBM, which had helped to speed that realization, had a permanent place in the business of computers.

Epilogue

It is probably no coincidence that the next great phase for IBM shares coincided with the advent of the personal computer in the early 1980s. Transforming a mainframe mentality to the PC age was by no means automatic, but Big Blue quickly became the market leader. Portfolio managers had seen a decade of uninspired performance, but IBM was one of the leaders in the first phase of the great bull market.

To many onlookers, IBM's PC dominance was to be expected. Those who understood the difficulty of transition could better appreciate the accomplishment—and that group would include some once major competitors. Stocks such as Digital Equipment and Data General had their days in the bull market, to be sure, but neither could achieve second- and third-generation successes as competition in computers intensified. Small wonder. Transition is the toughest time in business, and IBM did it better than anyone.

Lessons

Visionary management . . . *Thomas Watson Jr. was a capable leader who was able to guide the company on to the next big thing. He realized that tabulating machines were on the way out and boldly attached the company to the new trend of computing.*

Product shift . . . *Dominance can never be taken for granted. Success in one product line is not necessarily an advantage in achieving success in another line, and sometimes prevents it.*

Use what you've got . . . *This was a nimble company. IBM was able to effectively train its veteran sales force to sell a brand-new product. IBM's dominance in computers proved that while tabulating machines weren't a perpetual advantage, an established, knowledgeable sales force was.*

TIMELINE

1953 The 650 Magnetic Drum Calculator is introduced.

1956 Thomas J. Watson Sr. dies at age eighty-two, six weeks after handing the title of chief executive officer to his son, Thomas J. Watson Jr.

1956 RAMAC magnetic hard disk storage introduced.

1956 Revenue is $892 million and net earnings are $87 million.

1957 FORTRAN (FORmula TRANslation), a scientific programming language available to consumers, is introduced.

1964 Introduction of the System/360, the first large "family" of computers to use interchangeable software and peripheral equipment.

1969 Marketers "unbundle" computer components and offer them for sale individually.

1969 Gross income grows to $7.19 billion and net earnings increase to $934 million.

1971 Thomas J. Watson Jr. steps down as CEO.

TWO
PATHBREAKING PRODUCTS

THE VERY PICTURE OF PROFITS: POLAROID (1958–1970)

TAKING A RISK: XEROX (1959–1972)

PRESCRIPTION FOR PROFITS: AMGEN (1990–2001)

Perhaps the most exciting form of investing is catching a revolutionary new product at the early stages. We're not talking about building a better mousetrap. We're talking about building something that no one else has built before.

As investing strategies go, the approach of seeking out new inventions is riskier than most, because the list of failed product launches is inevitably longer than the list of successes. But those risks are hardly a reason to stay on the sidelines. As any venture capitalist can tell you, you can make a lot of money even with a low success ratio, because even the worst failures go only to zero, whereas the hits just keep on going.

From the consumer's point of view, inventions enable us to do things we could never do before. Depending on what point in history we're talking about, that activity could be reading by an electric lightbulb or clicking on a personal computer. In either case, we marvel at the newfound convenience and productivity. From the businessperson's point of view, the rollout of a new invention means something else. Above all, it is a time when competitors are nonexistent and profit margins are luxurious. If the product is special enough and the barriers to entry correspondingly high, the company's heyday can last for years.

Three of the biggest hits of the twentieth century came from three legendary companies: Polaroid, Xerox, and Amgen. The first two of these companies transformed American lives in a most visible way. The third's successes were less transparent to the public, but no less impressive. We will discover that the products that seemed to be overnight sensations were in fact developed over many, many years, giving investors plenty of lead time. Better still, we will discover that even when the pathbreaking products hit the market, it's still not too late to place your bets.

THE VERY PICTURE OF PROFITS

Polaroid

1958–1970

Of the so-called glamour stocks of a postwar generation, there was no question that Polaroid was the most glimmering. Composed of the high-tech industries of the day, including electronics, rocket development, and photography, glamour companies moved fast and so did their stocks. Polaroid shares were flying high—at $100 in 1958—making it easy to see how some skeptics, thinking the stock had run its course, could decline the invitation to snap up shares. Big mistake. Polaroid's share price increased by 780 times over the next twelve years, meaning a $1,000 investment in 1958 would be worth $110,000 in 1965 and $780,000 in 1970. Not too shabby. So sometimes what's considered an "overpriced" stock is still a bargain.

By definition, if you invest in a good company at the very first moment the blockbuster product hits the market, you will do brilliantly. But suppose you're late to the party. If a company's stock has already gone up by a factor of eight, won't you feel like an idiot if you buy at the top?

But wait a minute. Just because a stock goes up by a factor of eight, who says you've reached the top? Revolutionary products don't play by the same rules as conventional ones, and ditto for their stocks. To prove the point, we'll set the clock back to 1958, several years after Polaroid's instant cameras turned the photography market upside down.

Not by the Book

It wasn't until Polaroid transformed the idea of making instant photography a reality that it really had sustained growth, driving sales from $1.5 million in 1947 to $65 million (and climbing fast) in 1958. By that year, investors could look at an impressive three-year record of growth. Starting in 1955, Polaroid stock had risen from $12 to $100, based largely on the company's eye-popping sales growth for the same years: 31 percent (1956), 41 percent (1957), and then 36 percent (1958).

The sales growth may have been fantastic, but in the manner of classic growth stocks, the stock price had nonetheless managed to outpace it. By 1958, Polaroid's price-to-earnings ratio was sailing past 50. What that meant, in the plainest terms, was that it wasn't easy for an investor to decide whether or not to buy Polaroid stock in 1958.

Earnings, however, are what form a floor under stock prices in all but the most panicked of markets. When the stock price floats high above what it "should be" according to a rational earnings ratio—the average price-to-earnings ratio in 1958 was 10; the Dow Jones stocks had an average of just over 20—many conservative investors turn away. To them, everything above about 20 is water, meaning that in Polaroid's case, its 50-plus P/E ratio looked like a flood.

Other investors, however, are drawn to that very same heady price-to-earnings ratio. They want to see what all the excitement is about and, sure enough, in every case the excitement is about the future. As one observer pointed out, should Polaroid's annual growth rate continue indefinitely—as many investors were certainly telling each other it would—then in A.D. 2090, Polaroid would be the only corporation left in the United States.

Another evaluation method usually cruel to growth stocks is the comparison of a company's current selling price to its book value. The book value is calculated by dividing the assets of the company by the shares. In other words, should the company go out of business and sell off everything, the book value reflects the amount that would be returned for each share. A conservative investor would like the market value and the book value of a company's stock to be the same. That's very rare, but it can be a comfort to think that they are close. Just take Polaroid in 1958: its book value was $9.00 while a share of its stock cost $99.88. Hardly a match. Yet, in a growth stock the present tense is the least important factor. The future is all and it is reflected in the past.

How the Picture Developed

Polaroid was incorporated in 1937, built as a gleaming skyscraper, so to speak, over a modest brownstone of a partnership started by Edwin Land and George Wheelright III, both formerly of Harvard. Land was a prodigy who had invented a polarizing material while still an undergraduate; Wheelright, one of his instructors, provided some of the capital needed to produce the new product commercially.

Land-Wheelright's specialty was taming light, whatever the source. It dutifully developed its polarized material for a study lamp that reduced eyestrain. Polarized sunglasses also generated steady income, as much as $1.5 million annually, but sunglasses were not the fashion they are today; anyway, polarized ones were expensive. Polaroid's best customer, and corporate mentor, in the early days was industry giant Eastman Kodak. However, it wasn't until Land developed a system for eliminating the glare of automobile headlights, with its market potential of an estimated 30 million autos in the United States alone, that Wall Street came calling, in the form of a gaggle of Harrimans, Rothschilds, and Rockefellers. The men who vied for the chance to give the new company money may have had decades of experience—centuries, if it were all added together—but they had never seen anything on Wall Street like Edwin Land.

Land absolutely insisted that scientific research had to be the real impetus of the company, christened Polaroid after the name Land had given his polarizing material. As a guiding philosophy, he wouldn't allow it to produce any item for which a market already existed. First and foremost, there was pure science. Worthwhile experiments would probably, but not necessarily, lead to commercial products. Such talk may have been sacrilege on Wall Street, yet on that basis, the high-powered investment group capitalized Polaroid with $750,000—a breathtaking sum at that time when the Depression had just renewed itself in 1937–1938.

Polaroid's newborn stock fell from a high of about 60 just after it was issued to a low of 9 in December 1941. The calamity had nothing to do with the attack on Pearl Harbor—which affected the Dow Jones average negligibly—but rather with the fact that no one in Detroit was interested in Polaroid's system for glare-free headlights. It was and still is a viable solution to the problem of blinding headlight glare, but it required an industry-wide changeover in order to work. Car companies decided that the cost (about $8 per car) was more than the public would accept.

Polaroid and its stock recovered somewhat on the influx of military contracts, but when war work receded in 1945, it left an uncertain future at Polaroid. A study by Harvard's School of Business Administration suggested that the wisest course, financially, would be the sale of Polaroid to a larger company. "Polaroid," according to the report, "has repeatedly invested funds in research—often remotely related to its principal business where the apparent prospects of commercial profit in the foreseeable future were slight, but where the research was considered scientifically or socially important." No problem there for Edwin Land—that was exactly how he wanted it.

Land was on vacation with his family in 1943 when one of his daughters, a three-year-old, demanded to know why she couldn't see a picture he'd just snapped. Not in days or weeks but right then. The impatience of a three-year-old, of course, would become the clarion cry of the late twentieth century. Land threw himself and his research team into the challenge of instant photography. In only three years, the product was ready for stores.

Take the Picture?

"Marketing is what you do when you don't have any ideas," Edwin Land once said. Never mind his words, though. Polaroid was the master of marketing. In fact, the reason the science behind the cameras was so exciting was that the company managed to bring the public in on the excitement. Polaroid's formula called for the introduction of an expensive version of any new technology, followed by increasingly affordable editions: a simple recipe, but one that Polaroid simmered to perfection. In 1948, Land cameras produced sepia prints, tones of brownish red on white paper. In 1952, the first black-and-white photography was introduced. In 1954, a less expensive version was introduced. Color came in the 1960s. During the heyday of instant photography, Polaroid managed to put research and marketing onto a seesaw that lifted each one higher and higher with each passing year.

The shares of consumer products companies are often given a real push from marketing because broadcast advertising simultaneously reaches two very important customers: those for its products and those for its stock. Polaroid fit into that category. In addition, the unique company and its admired president became darlings of the financial press. From any angle, Polaroid told an interesting story. Most of all, though, Wall Street itself kept a sharp eye on Polaroid. According to Peter C. Wensberg, an executive who wrote an engaging memoir called *Land's Polaroid* in 1987, about fifty Wall Street analysts closely followed the company. However, the glamorous Polaroid Corporation didn't deign to stoke this interest—it just wouldn't cooperate with analysts in any way. And so it was that analysts hated the company, but loved its stock.

One thing the analysts appreciated was that Polaroid was definitely capable of servicing its debt load. That is because the company never borrowed money, maintaining a firm policy against it. Land wanted no financial exigencies to pressure the course of his company.

And what a great course, with all its wide-open potential. Amateur photography, which accounted for 97 percent of Polaroid's revenues, was a $1 billion market and growing in 1958. Within families or business cycles, two factors instigate camera sales. The first is the presence of a baby within aperture range. The second is vacation travel. Both were more common than ever in the postwar years.

Despite the treacherous competition offered by Kodak within the overall field of amateur photography, Polaroid had no competitors within its niche of instant photography. That alone generated more confidence in its stock from 1958 to 1970 than any other factor. Indeed, "Polaroid" became synonymous with the instant photograph. "We took Polaroids at the party" was something people might say and—lucky for shareholders—would actually do. Knock-off cameras didn't materialize. Why not? The first reason was the technical sophistication of the Polaroid processes: "elegant" was the term Edwin Land liked to use. But the cameras boasted nothing compared to the technical sophistication and sheer elegance of Polaroid's vaunted patent protection. By 1958, Land and the company already had over two hundred U.S. patents on instant photography. Polaroid's secret garden did have one ominous shadow, however. The original patents for the Land camera were due to expire in 1965.

Instant Gratification

Shielded by patents and adored by customers, Polaroid Corporation was the quintessential great stock pick in 1958. Sales increases continued during the early 1960s and profitability kept pace as well, with the company reporting after-tax profits of 12.5 percent in the middle of the decade. That's high, especially for an outfit with a hefty commitment to research.

The price-to-earnings ratio could be viewed as more worrisome than ever, though, rising sometimes over 80, making it the highest among U.S. corporations over the course of the 1960s. But, nonetheless, Polaroid was still a great stock—and a great company—going forward. In terms of research, the Colorpack camera was the hit of the decade because it made instant pictures in color. In marketing, the inexpensive Swinger, at $19.95, was the headliner because it was especially popular among teens. The stock price went even higher even faster when, all at once, institutional investors discovered Polaroid, or inundated it. In 1963, the stock wasn't even in their top 50 holdings, as charted by Vickers Group, a market research company. By 1967, Polaroid stock was the second favorite holding of institutional investors, behind only IBM, a much larger company.

Epilogue

By 1970 the ride was nearly over. Although the stock would nominally hit new highs at several points in the middle of the decade, none of the peaks was enough above its 1970 price to compensate for the deep chasms in between. The characteristics that made Polaroid a growth stock had begun to erode.

"In three years," said an analyst at Oppenheimer in 1969, "Polaroid's sales of color film will be greater than Kodak's." That was not hard to fathom at the time, because by then camera sales were nearly equal between the two firms. News like that should have been a cause for celebration, but the specter of Polaroid encroaching on old, hard-won turf was untenable to Eastman Kodak, which had dominated sales of standard film since inventing it in the previous century. In 1970, it abruptly ended a long-standing truce between the two firms, giving Polaroid an extra poke in the eye by announcing that it was developing its own instant photography system. Polaroid retreated behind its patents, over four hundred in number, and waited for the fight. Investors were shaken by the vision of the two companies squaring off face-to-face for the first time.

In 1976, Polaroid's former friends at Kodak did introduce an instant camera, though one that was never really accepted by customers. Eventually, after a protracted infringement suit, Kodak was forced to pay Polaroid over $900 million. But the distraction of the ill-timed brawl between the two companies kept them both from recognizing that instant photography was no longer a "growth" segment, anyway.

The crucial decision point surrounding Polaroid stock in the early 1970s was the potential market, which was changing rapidly with the advent of 35mm photography. Polaroid had considered entering the field in the mid-1960s, but Land decided that since 35mm cameras had already been invented, they were of no interest to Polaroid. Above all, he liked to be alone in a market. Unfortunately, the surging interest in 35mm photography did indeed leave Polaroid all alone. The company was also on the sidelines during the advent of digital photography in the 1990s. By the end of that decade, the stock price was sinking toward penny-stock status. Finally, in 2001, the Polaroid Corporation was forced to seek bankruptcy protection.

For more than a dozen years, Polaroid basked in a niche that it had invented scientifically, delineated diplomatically, and protected legally. In its heyday under Edwin Land, the company proved that just because a company isn't the biggest in its industry, it doesn't mean it can't have a swinging little monopoly just the same.

Lessons

A consumer product with a huge market potential and a patent, too . . . A very clear profit picture is presented. These opportunities don't come around too often, so take advantage when you can.

Just because a stock looks expensive . . . Don't dismiss it on that basis alone, because the shares may have a long run ahead. "Expensive" doesn't automatically mean "overpriced."

Watch out when a company sticks too stubbornly to its old formulas . . . It may end up missing key opportunities, as Polaroid did with 35mm and digital photography. What got you on top needn't keep you on top.

TIMELINE

1957 Listed on the New York Stock Exchange.

1960 The Model 900 with electric eye, Polaroid's first automatic exposure camera, is introduced.

1962 The MP-3 Land, a copystand camera with macro- and microphotography capabilities for use in research labs, hospitals, universities, is introduced.

1963 Instant color film introduced.

1964 Stock split, 4-for-1.

1964 The five millionth instant camera is produced.

1965 Net sales: $204 million. Net earnings: $29 million.

1969 The Colorpack II camera is the first nonfolding, plastic-bodied camera for pack film and the first low-priced camera that uses both color and black-and-white instant film.

1969 Net sales: $536 million; net earnings, $71 million.

TAKING A RISK

Xerox

1959–1972

"I keep asking myself," said Joseph Wilson in 1962, "when are you going to wake up? Things just aren't this good in life." Wilson was speaking about his role as president of Xerox Corporation, a company where gross revenues had tripled since 1959 and profits had jumped from $2.5 million to $13.8 million, but he could have just as easily been speaking for one of his stockholders. From 1959 to 1972, Xerox stock rose almost 700 percent. Customers weren't exactly unhappy, either, since the company's product made their business lives all that much happier, too.

Some "new" ideas have been around a lot longer than we think. When singer Tommy Edwards took "It's All in the Game" to the top of the Billboard charts in 1957, who knew that the song had been written by former U.S. vice president Charles Dawes—in 1912! So when people tell you they got in at the very beginning of a hot stock, don't believe them, and above all, don't think it's necessary to do so.

The story of Xerox was decades in the making by the time the company "came out of nowhere" in the late 1950s. If you bought shares while it was still called Haloid Company, congratulations are in order. But Haloid-Xerox, and, finally, Xerox, still had a long way to go.

Copying Its Success

The very name Xerox had become a catchphrase in the investing community, a word synonymous with *hot pick*. It was a huge growth stock, practically as good as a rigged slot machine for generating yearly gains. That was the stellar record that Xerox Corporation compiled, every year but one during the 1960s.

The company had been wending a quiet path through the photographic industry since 1906, but it burst on the national scene in 1959 with the introduction of the 914 photocopier. The desk-size machine revolutionized office routine around the world because it was so easy to use—almost too easy. (To the consternation of office managers everywhere, clerks began producing perfect copies of their hands and faces.) One 1964 television advertisement showed a little girl Xeroxing her rag doll. When the Federal Trade Commission protested that it must have been a setup, since no copier could be that simple to use, Xerox produced another commercial, entirely under the scrutiny of an FTC official, showing a chimpanzee making copies on a 914.

With each copy, be it for work or fun, a counter on the back of the machine would click off another number, to the delight of Xerox. The company charged a basic rent for its machines, along with a charge of a few cents each for copies over the contracted amount. While a 914 cost Xerox $2,500 to manufacture, it gave the company an average annual return of $4,000 in sales revenue. Even at that, however, the amount of money Xerox made depended only on its inclination and ability to build more 914s, and in the early 1960s there was a three-month wait on delivery. With earnings doubling in the years 1960–1962, the stock began to move—dramatically.

National publications gushed over the new leader on Wall Street. The *New York Times* called it "the perennial favorite of the glamour stock set." *Fortune* described it as an elevator that only went up. *The New Yorker* agreed with the common opinion that the 914 was "the most successful commercial product in history." Investment letters, which existed to generate new ideas and knock down old ones, were typically filled with commentary on the phenomenon known as Xerox. The only question that loomed over the new giant was whether it could continue its spectacular success.

Investors who looked at the numbers in a new way saw that Xerox was applying the best of old-style business to its pioneering new enterprise. The formula worked: XRX climbed more than sixty-six times between 1959 and 1972, while providing an ever-rising dividend throughout. Yet even Joseph Wilson, one of the most astute businessmen of the postwar era, was at a loss to explain the heady jet ride taken by Xerox stock. "I have long since given up trying to explain it," he said early in the rise, in 1961. "Frankly, I'm as mystified as Wall Street—more so, in fact, because I'm living closer to the trees."

The Storied Story

Xerox began in 1906 as the Haloid Company, manufacturing specialized papers and other photographic supplies. Its Rochester, New York, location was no coincidence since several of the founders had defected from Eastman Kodak. Just as in the case of another postwar wunderkind, Polaroid, giant Kodak cooperated with the upstart during its early years, only to take it head-on much later. Haloid meandered along, a medium-size company even for Rochester, until Joseph Wilson was named president in 1945. Wilson, whose grandfather was one of Haloid's founders and whose father was a company president, heard from an employee about a process known as *xerography*, a word derived from the Greek for "dry writing."

The man who invented that word, as well as the process, Chester Carlson, was a Long Island patent attorney. Using some of the knowledge he picked up from working as a printer, in 1938 Carlson discovered a way to use electricity in conjunction with a light-sensitive element called selenium and powdered ink. Result? Clean, clear reproductions on plain paper. There had been photocopying processes before, but they were difficult to master and rarely used. Carlson's process was perfectly suited to office work, where duplication was delegated to battalions of typists and reams of carbon paper. Yet for more than ten years, no company took any interest in xerography. Things changed, however, in 1947 when Wilson and John Dessauer, the head of Research and Engineering, saw the potential and secured the rights for Haloid.

In a good year, Haloid earned $500,000 on its photographic business, yet over the next five years it borrowed over $1 million a year to spend on preparing xerography for the commercial market. Wilson drew praise for financing the new arm of the company without issuing new stock, but he was largely alone in his belief in xerography's future. He kept calling it "a whole industry," but others were unconvinced.

The company's 2,800 stockholders recognized along with the rest of the financial community that Haloid was risking its future on the future of xerography. Most were dubious, making Haloid's over-the-counter stock quiet during the 1950s. At one point Wilson decided that the task of Xeroxing the world, so to speak, was too much for his tiny company—he offered IBM the rights to the process. The computer giant in turn enlisted a consulting firm to study the prospects. Its conclusion? Photocopying did not have much of a future.

IBM turned away from Haloid, but not before Joseph Wilson decided to copy it, in one crucial respect. IBM had long depended on a policy of leasing machines, both as means of controlling its products after they left the factory and also in financial terms, as a way to stretch profits out into the future. When Haloid-Xerox introduced its landmark 914 office model, it also specified a lease arrangement. Wilson later called that the "the most important decision we ever made—except for backing xerography itself."

The Xerox Decision

The launch of Xerox as a stock market favorite began with the explosion of interest in the company's first office copier, the 914, in 1959. While executives adjusted their sales projections upward, Xerox became more than a company—it took its place in the English language as a verb meaning "to copy." Very few businesses have become legends in such a short time.

During the 1950s, the overall copying industry grew at an even faster clip than the red-hot electronics field. The prediction for the future was that sales would double between 1959 and 1965. By then, office copy products, Xerox's target niche for the 914, were expected to make up half the overall market. In addition, Xerox had an international market plan in place, due to a partnership with Britain's Rank Organization, a British conglomerate. Best known for its production of movies, Rank had connections in an array of businesses and was well positioned to distribute the Xerox idea in all regions except North America.

Xerox had no competition in the dry-copy field; a wall of 332 patents protected its process. However, four other methods were on the market, promoted by giants including Eastman Kodak and Minnesota Mining and Manufacturing. Other copy machines, which were sold, not leased, were less expensive to operate in moderate use. The 914 was attractive for businesses making one hundred or more copies per day. Today, that does not seem like much, but in 1959 only 10 percent of the businesses then using copiers would have qualified.

Fresh ideas are integral to a growth company. That's why the research and development budget at Xerox was a generous 8 percent of sales. As a rule, 5 percent of sales reflects a robust R&D budget. The effect of Xerox's lab work was reflected in the 84 percent of Xerox's revenue in 1959 derived from products developed during the previous nine years. This was remarkable in those days of slower development since today aggressive companies are known to shoot for one-third of sales from products introduced in the previous three years.

The Lease on Profits

In July 1961, Xerox stock moved to the New York Stock Exchange. It seemed to flourish in its new setting, with shares rising by more than a third in the first month. Though earnings were on track to double that year, the price-to-earnings ratio still outran the stock, reaching 196 in September. At the time, IBM was considered heady with its p/e of 90. Compare that with the average for the blue chips in the Dow Jones Industrial Average: 9.

Conservative investors dismissed Xerox as a frenzy doomed to peter out, as they thought all overpriced stocks (those with p/e ratios higher than about 25) must someday do. However, because a stock as exciting as Xerox normally comes along only a couple of times each decade, investors couldn't help but become fascinated. In turn, they began looking for other ways to judge the company, its stock, and the price.

What they found was Xerox's business of leasing. When a business makes outright sales, every year is, on the books at least, a brand-new year. The strongest of the broad measures of success is naturally profit and loss. However, when a company leases its products, it defers its full profits, even while accumulating depreciation credits on those products. It is a method of business that tends to average out both growth and reversal in future years. The best gauge by which to judge the outlook of such companies is not necessarily profit and loss but cash flow.

DETERMINING VALUE

Although the profit is always of interest, the real level of business activity can be seen when depreciation on each leased machine is included. Investors who were watching Xerox carefully noted that cash flow was increasing even faster than earnings growth in the 1960s. Moreover, it was increasing even faster than the share price, which gave investors another encouraging measurement of Xerox's long-range value.

Xerox was a star performer by any measure, with return on stockholders' equity in the range of 35 percent. That figure held steady as demand outstripped even the optimism of Joseph Wilson. By the mid-1960s, the United States was in the grips of a full-fledged love affair with photocopying. *Newsweek* estimated that 10 billion copies were made in 1963—Mobil Oil alone made 30 million per year. Xerox controlled 65 percent of the office photocopy market as of 1965 and was in the oddly enviable position of wondering about charges of monopoly.

Xerox had only one real problem: how to grow beyond photocopying. "The market has valued us at two billion," said company vice president (and later president) Peter McColough in 1964. "Investors haven't done it because they like the way we stand pat." Wall Street expected Xerox to grow into a real asset value (not merely a market value) of $2 billion and more.

Epilogue

Xerox didn't rest on its laurels; it regularly bolstered its share of the office market with new copiers. But it needed to expand its empire, and it certainly had the wherewithal to do it. Growing by acquisition posed one unusual problem. As *Forbes* magazine pointed out, there were only three major companies that would not dilute Xerox's remarkable earnings. The three that were even more profitable on a percentage basis than Xerox were Avon (see chapter 3), Gillette (see chapter 4), and Smith, Kline and French.

Grooming, razors, and pharmaceuticals were not tempting targets for the copy king. Nonetheless, Xerox did try to grow through acquisitions, purchasing a whole slew of educational companies in the late 1960s. At the same time, its research and development budget rose to well over 10 percent of sales. Smartly, Xerox considered that its primary product was not the ubiquitous photocopy machine, but rather information in the broadest sense and the means to process it. Sad to say it never quite made good on that vision.

Xerox was creating personal computers ten years before Apple, icon-based operating systems fifteen years before Microsoft, and Internet service twenty years before Netscape. Yet it bypassed these opportunities and others in the high-tech arena. Computer operations were money losers for Xerox in the late 1960s and 1970s. For a company boosted into the stratosphere by savvy risk-taking, Xerox was reluctant to continue expensive operations. While it is hard to say that Xerox's head starts would have definitely led to further success, it is tragic that the company gave up on so many high-potential fields.

Lessons

Businesses that revolutionize the way we do things . . . *These companies are worth at least a once-over. Ask any venture capitalist: the ones that pay off will more than make up for any that fizzle.*

Creative financing techniques . . . *Leasing instead of outright sales can project growth into the future. Look at cash flow figures to see if momentum is building. When you're selling to bean counters, make sure they don't have to count too many beans.*

If learning is good for people shouldn't it be good for companies? . . . *A high R&D budget is more than okay if it is funding the products of tomorrow.*

When a company stops taking risks . . . *As Xerox did by not fully embracing new inventions like the personal computer, it may be time to look elsewhere.*

TIMELINE

1906 The Haloid Company is founded in Rochester, New York, to manufacture and sell photographic paper.

1936 First public offering of Xerox stock.

1947 Haloid acquires license to Chester Carlson's basic xerographic patents from Battelle Development Corp. of Columbus, Ohio, a subsidiary of Battelle Memorial Institute.

1949 The first xerographic copier, the Model A, is introduced.

1956 Rank Xerox Limited is formed as joint venture of the Haloid Company and the Rank Organization.

1958 The Haloid Company changes name to Haloid Xerox, Inc.

1959 The Xerox 914, the first automatic, plain-paper office copier, is announced.

1961 Haloid Xerox, Inc., changes name to Xerox Corporation.

1961 Xerox is listed on the New York Stock Exchange, July 11. Some 7,700 shares are traded, and the stock closes at $104 for the day.

1962 Fuji Xerox Co., Ltd., is launched as joint venture of Rank Xerox Limited and Fuji Photo Film Co., Ltd.

PRESCRIPTION FOR PROFITS

Amgen

1990–2001

*Investors were beginning to wonder whether biotech compa-
nies, the talk of high-growth investing in the 1980s, could
actually deliver products and make money. That was before
Amgen pulled to the front of the pack for good in 1989. After
that year it was an earnings machine, and whatever the news
the numbers were nearly always on Amgen's side.*

Polaroid's camera and Xerox's copier were both revolutionary and
visible throughout the land. Not all inventions are that way, especially in the field of health care. That's where investors have to do
their research even in the absence of firsthand experience, lest a
laparoscopy be a prerequisite for an investor in surgical supplies.

The biotech companies were doubly behind the scenes,
because their handiwork often applied to future medical
processes. The field took off in the early 1990s, and the stocks
were pushed up enthusiastically. Many companies fell by the way-
side, a reminder that biotech investing is risky indeed. One company that endured was Amgen, a pioneer and a super stock for the
decade.

A Story (Stock) Comes True

Many prudent investors won't go anywhere near a stock with a
high price-to-earnings ratio. As they can explain quite convinc-
ingly, absolutely anything over 25 or 30 is precarious and overpriced. Not surprising, then, that a lot of people looked on Amgen
stock as an untouchable. More than a few said, "Thanks, but I'll
pass," in 1987 when its p/e was 400. (At the time, the average p/e
ratio on the Standard & Poor's 500 was 15.)

But then, in 1987, Amgen, located in the Thousand Oaks sub-
urb of Los Angeles, was nowhere close to the S&P 500. It was a

fledgling entry in the brutally difficult business of drug development. Moreover, its mission was to become a bona fide pharmaceutical company. Worldwide, only one biotech company, Syntex Lab, had grown from start-up to full integration since the end of World War II. However, Amgen was hustling hard, hoping to squeeze through an unexpected opening in the walls surrounding the drug industry. Biotechnology, the emerging art of creating organic substances such as hormones or proteins within altered cells, presented new opportunities for creating lifesaving drugs—and start-up businesses. In 1987, after seven years in business, Amgen was still hovering on the verge: no products, scant income. Nonetheless, investors were hearing a lot about Amgen—so were doctors. *Science* magazine, *Chemistry News,* and the *New England Journal of Medicine* had all carried articles about the company, details about an impressive new breakthrough, the isolation of the gene that creates erythropoietin (EPO), a hormone that stimulates the production of red blood cells. If genes could be altered to create this hormone, the world would have a new and viable treatment for anemia.

"EPO builds red blood cells. And it could build Amgen into a major drugmaker," said a prescient *Business Week* in March 1987. As that article and others implied, EPO could just as easily flop in clinical trials. But investors believed. They picked Amgen out of the pack, calculating that if its manmade miracle worked, the company's revenues could increase from $23 million per year to $2 billion, making it easily the biggest company in all of biotech.

In the late 1980s, the stock price rose or fell on every piece of news regarding Amgen and EPO. Most of the news was good, lifting Amgen's stock price, giving it a market capitalization (based on the worth of all outstanding shares) of more than $700 million—rather steep for a company that still didn't have any products. To be sure, it was a play for the speculative investor but no real basis for investment. Buying into an unproven laboratory based on one or two promising drugs is an act of blind faith. Because of all the pitfalls involved in bringing a drug to market, it's not merely high risk. It's all risk.

A large part of the suspense at Amgen was finally over in June

1989 with the Food and Drug Administration's approval of EPO. The victory already seemed to have been built into Amgen's share price, however, but the stock doubled nonetheless in the following year. With shipments of about $15 million per month, Amgen reported an eleven-fold increase in earnings in 1990 over 1989. Because of the flow of profits, and even with the increase in stock price, the p/e ratio fell to 55. That was more rational than 400, but it was still more than three times the average on the S&P 500.

"Way undervalued," insisted Stanley Goldring, an analyst at Ladenburg Thalmann. "The best in the Amgen story is yet to come." Mr. Goldring was not alone. Once Amgen graduated into the category of *producing* biotechs—the first of its class to do so— it gained a new group of fans. Among them were institutional investors, who had anted up for a relatively light 39 percent of Amgen shares before the FDA announcement. The stock market would prove just how undervalued Amgen stock was in 1990; it rose during the decade from a split-adjusted 3 1/2 to 80. In 1990, Amgen was a great stock pick. Before that it had only been an adventurous one.

The investor who bought Amgen before its first drug was proven probably bought thirty or forty other speculative stocks with the same criteria: news but no numbers. That sweepstakes approach to stock selection has exploded the prices of start-ups in various sectors from time to time: electronics in the late 1950s, franchise restaurants in the 1960s, personal computers in the 1980s, and Internet stocks in the 1990s. Anyone who could pick one winner out of the pack of promises was lucky and well rewarded.

Five-Step Program

In the early 1980s, Amgen and about seventy other companies followed the path of Genentech, the first of the biotechs, which had been founded in 1976. Genentech became one of the world's leading biotech companies by marketing and manufacturing nine protein-based products for serious or life-threatening medical conditions. The odds of any of these biotechs succeeding in the market with a new drug was equivalent to their shooting an arrow through six bull's-eyes, one lined up behind the other. The first of the long shots depended on executives making the right decision as to the research to pursue. Matching what was needed with what was possible and fitting it to the particular researchers on hand was crucial. The safest course was to develop improved versions of existing pharmaceuticals. Amgen's management was bolder, choosing instead to try to produce EPO in part because success would put the company alone in a niche.

The second step was easy to say but painstaking in practice: deciphering genes, reconfiguring them, and then coaxing them to produce the desired hormone, EPO. For almost three years the scientist leading Amgen's EPO effort, Fu-Kuen Lin, labored without results. Other biotechs were working on the same problem and occasionally the rumor would drift to Amgen headquarters that one or another had succeeded. Lin and his team kept at their own experiments. As it turned out, none of those pesky rumors were true. Late in 1983, the Amgen team was first in replicating the DNA structure responsible for EPO.

The patent process is as sensitive to the origination of a new drug as the most complex chemistry. In this third step toward realizing EPO as a product, Amgen wasted no time in applying for a patent. Unbeknownst to the management, another company had applied for a related patent only months before. In the meantime, Amgen started the fourth step, clinical testing of EPO. It is not at all unusual for a drug with a perfect pedigree from the laboratory to fail in actual use. For example, in the mid-1990s, Amgen would develop production of a hormone that made fat mice slim down and remain trim. When testing began of the human version, hopes soared with investors *and* flabby people everywhere. In clinical tests, though, nothing happened. The company was left with little except a miracle cure for fat mice.

The process used to make EPO was so delicate that a single pound had a projected value of $100 million. Many experts within the pharmaceutical industry were skeptical that Amgen could even complete the fifth step in the realization of EPO: mass production.

The company had an unexpected advantage, however. Like other biotechs, it had survived its early years through partnerships and other arrangements with outside firms. Kirin Brewery, the Japanese beer company, had one such joint venture with Amgen, giving it the future right to make and manufacture EPO in Japan.

BOTTLING PROFIT

When Amgen needed custom-made bottles and special equipment with which to handle them, its partner came to the rescue. "Kirin knows bottles," quipped Amgen's chairman, George Rathmann, speaking of Japan's leading beer producer.

Because the clinical trials were a complete success, Amgen filed an application with the Food and Drug Administration. The final submission stretched to 19,000 pages. The announcement that Amgen had received its patent may have fanned excitement, but the June 1989 announcement of FDA approval shifted Wall Street into overdrive. Amgen was finally a real company; within days it was in production and making shipments.

Amgen's success with EPO faced one more hurdle, unfortunately common to the process of drug introduction, and this one was as tough as any before: legal action. For four years Amgen battled the biotech company that had taken out a related patent on EPO (without having actually isolated the gene or the process responsible for making it). Amgen eventually prevailed in large measure, but it lost its second major litigation. That was a suit brought by Johnson & Johnson, which had given Amgen working capital in the mid-1980s in exchange for certain marketing rights to EPO. The lawsuits cost millions of dollars in addition to the attention of top executives, but they became part of the news stream at Amgen, and investors grew used to reports of judgments, filings, and petitions. As Edmund Andrews, patent correspondent for the *New York Times,* wrote, "Good science isn't much good without good lawyers." That was especially true at feisty Amgen.

Concern that Amgen would stumble in at least one of the major steps in the development of EPO made its stock flighty. Short positions rose sharply on even tepid news—at times more than 2 percent of the outstanding shares were connected to people who believed and hoped that Amgen would crash.

SHORT POSITION

In taking a short position, *a person borrows stock from a brokerage and sells it, with plans to replace it at some point in the future when the price is lower.*

Amgen's Makeup

As it turned out, Amgen hit all six bull's-eyes with its new drug, EPO. It was an amazing accomplishment for any new company, but especially for one in a brand-new industry. For serious investors, 1990 was the real birth of Amgen: the year when the business plan was overwritten by actual events. The facts were finally on the table.

In July 1990, Amgen reported first-quarter earnings of 57 cents per share, up from 5 cents the same quarter during the previous year: the last one before EPO production began. After the initial jump, the company continued to report sales increases of more than 100 percent per year in the early 1990s. They were outstripped only by profits, which grew at an annual average of 184 percent. It is always a good sign, with a new company or an old one, when profits grow at an even faster rate than sales.

In 1989–1990, Amgen executives followed up the instant success of EPO, the hormone that increased red blood cell production, by describing Amgen's next product, a substance called G-CSF that selectively stimulates the growth of infection-fighting white blood cells known as neutrophils. Under the name Neupogen, it is used in the cancer chemotherapy setting to decrease the incidence of infection associated with some forms of chemotherapy. Because neither product had direct competition from any other drugs, they were not under pricing pressure.

Even while Amgen was beginning the process of bringing EPO to dialysis patients, the company was exploring other indications for it. Though Johnson & Johnson retained the right to market EPO in any cases except kidney dialysis, Amgen received a royalty on those sales. In addition, analysts estimated that the company's second product, G-CSF, could generate sales of $500 million per year.

Blockbuster

Amgen stock doubled in 1990, the first full year after the EPO introduction, as the company's revenues soared to almost $200 million, based on production of *seven ounces* of the new drug. On the practical side, the company impressed the pharmaceutical industry with its instant mastery of the complex business, selling its new product and completing deliveries like an old pro. Amgen stock tripled in 1991, as G-CSF received FDA approval. Investors who thought Amgen could repeat its success were right. Within two days of the government's green light, 50 million dollars' worth of the new drug was in shipment. By then, the market value of Amgen was $7 billion, more than that of venerable Upjohn, for example, with its long history and full array of products. The *Overpriced Stock Service* calculated that the stock market's valuation rated Amgen at $10 million per employee. Perhaps that was not as outrageous as it sounded. Chairman Rathmann once acknowledged that "Our assets walk out of here every night in tennis shoes."

Yet it is arguable that Amgen's growth justified both the swelling price and a p/e ratio hovering around 100. Net profits were up over 2,000 percent in 1992, despite the fact that the markets for EPO and G-CSF were not yet fully tapped.

Amgen stock slowed in 1993, however, when the company claimed about a quarter of the potential markets for its two drugs. It reversed the following year, but investors fretted that the company was unable to follow up its first two successes. EPO and G-CSF were phenomenal. However, the company needed "a third home run," said Evan Sturza of *Sturza's Medical Investment Letter,* repeating what Amgen's friends and foes alike were thinking. The conclusion was that it had successfully avoided becoming a boutique drug research lab by moving into production and sales. The new danger was even worse: it was beginning to look like a mere drug packager. The p/e ratio of about 16 reflected that new perception. Whatever Amgen was, it was still a profitable company.

Though Amgen continued to fund extensive research, major new drugs failed to materialize in the 1990s. Nonetheless, the company proved canny in developing new revenue streams from its two franchise products, and earnings continued to increase through the decade. When biotechs returned to favor as a sector, Amgen, the elder statesman of the group, enjoyed a steady price rise. By the end of the decade, the stock was still headed up, and so were earnings.

"Amgen demonstrated that it's not how many drugs you come up with that counts," noted Michael Gordon in 1991, when he was biotech-fund manager at Fidelity. "It's how many you get through clinical trials, the FDA, and onto the market." The same comment still held true a decade later. Two drugs and the savvy to develop them into blockbusters were enough to give Amgen the tenth-best appreciation of any stock in the 1990s.

Epilogue

The fundamental strength of Amgen—its two start drugs—remains consistent at the turn of the new millennium, but without fresh news of the long-awaited third, fourth, and fifth breakthroughs, the stock was prone to the great bear market that began in 2001. For an innovative stock like Amgen, hard news is the turbo charge that lets it set its own pace. Amgen continued to hold its own in a dismal market but by comparison to its heyday in the 1990s it was adrift.

It should be noted that many biotech investors prefer to invest via funds, taking the reasonable view that a diversified approach is best for such a risky field. If you prefer that course, fine. If your fund is like most health care or biotech funds, it has Amgen in it already.

Lessons

Don't bet on a pipe dream . . . *Wait until a company has had solid success before you put money on it. Good general advice, and nowhere more important than in biotech.*

Have a pipeline . . . *Amgen had G-CSF to follow up on EPO. Even the most adventurous companies can benefit from diversification.*

Huge market and no competition . . *Can't beat those two for a successful company. But don't expect the stock to be cheap, and don't shy away just because it isn't!*

TIMELINE

1980 Incorporated as Applied Molecular Genetics, Inc. (Amgen).

1983 Initial IPO.

1989 Food and Drug Administration approves EPO.

1989 Added to NASDAQ 100 Index.

1991 Food and Drug Administration approves G-CSF.

1992 Added to S&P 500.

1992 Achieves more than $1 billion in product sales.

1999 G-CSF sales are approximately $1.2 billion.

1999 EPO sales are approximately $1.8 billion.

THREE
THE INNOVATIVE BUSINESS MODEL

DOOR-TO-DOOR PROFITS: AVON PRODUCTS (1958–1973)
BILLIONS AND BILLIONS EARNED: McDONALD'S (1966–1972)
HARD DRIVE: DELL COMPUTER (1990–1999)

Everyone knows that investors like companies that can increase their earnings by 20 percent per year. But finding great growth companies is more than a numbers game, because behind most great earnings reports there is a corporate strategy. The plain truth is that some strategies are better than others. Many companies made stock market history for the simple reason that they had brilliant business models.

A business model isn't something that's put together with glue, clay, or papier-mâché. A model is in essence a corporate decision about how a business should be structured. Once upon a time, the brokerage industry operated on a model based on high commissions: give your customers service and a smile, and charge through the nose when they want to make a trade. When those nice, fluffy commissions were legislated out of existence, a whole new model was born—the discount broker, lean on service but terrific on price. Meanwhile, the old-line firms moved to alternative profit centers such as underwriting, derivatives, and a host of others. The point is that the word *broker* could suddenly mean many different things, and investors had to appreciate those differences.

If you can't answer the question "Where does a company's money come from?" you won't be much of a investor. More optimistically, when you lay out a business according to its most basic components, you'll go a long way to understanding its strengths and vulnerabilities. What you'll discover is that some business models are better than others, and that some models are absolutely ideal for their times. In that delightful latter category are three of our twenty-five picks: Avon Products, McDonald's, and Dell Computer. In the tradition of this book, that's an odd trio. But when you've finished reading about the innovative business models that made them famous, they'll seem closer than ever before.

DOOR-TO-DOOR PROFITS

Avon Products

1958–1973

By the late 1950s personal grooming products were all the rage. Sales zoomed throughout the industry. Avon Products, however, outpaced them all. A household word in more ways than one, Avon was a high-growth company at the ripe old age of seventy-five. Thanks to its loyal devotees—both product users and investors—shares grew by almost 900 percent during the Swinging Sixties.

The word *innovative* typically refers to something new and fresh. But it's possible for an innovative business strategy to peak years after its formulation.

Avon Products was one of the biggest stars of the go-go markets of the 1960s, a company whose strategy perfectly fit the times. Who knew that the strategy of going door-to-door had been brewing since the nineteenth century?

Reflecting the Times

The history of Avon is very much a social history. Its growth in the postwar era was accelerated on the customers' side by a new emphasis on appearance and by the increase of leisure time for housewives. Likewise, its female representatives signed with the company because they had extra time, though due to scheduling conflicts or a lack of experience, they were not willing to take a conventional job. The cycle on which Avon thrived continued, because in a status-conscious society, many women became Avon reps to earn money for household appliances—which, in turn, gave them more leisure time.

The relationship between Avon and the changing role of the housewife could be the subject of a major sociological study. In business terms, there are companies such as Ford, IBM, or Apple that create an era. Avon is an example of a company that *was created* in its vast success by an era: the suburban postwar years were a time when a whole generation of housewives were starting to redefine themselves.

Ugly Duckling

In 1966, newsmagazines and newspapers were tickled by the fact that the most profitable company in America was Avon, the door-to-door cosmetics company. Most of the other companies bearing down on it represented, predictably, the star industries of the day: airlines, pharmaceuticals, electronics companies, and military contractors. Gillette (see chapter 4), at number five in the rankings, was also in the personal products industry, but Gillette counted on stores to do business. Avon had only people.

In the 1960s Avon relied on independent contractors, all of them women, to sell its two hundred products door-to-door. A standout "Avon lady" would sell $4,000 worth of cosmetics in a year, taking $1,600 for herself and sending $2,400 back to the company's New York headquarters. Perhaps figures like these are what made some investors think of Avon as a penny-ante enterprise. After all, Gillette sold its products in lots of hundreds of thousands of dollars, not one dollar at a time. However, Avon Products, a company considered quiet even within the cosmetics industry, had ranks of more than 200,000 sales reps. There was nothing demure, however, about the $400 million in perfume, makeup, and sundries they sold in 1966. Year in and year out during the 1960s, Avon earned its reputation for profitability, delivering stellar figures for return on equity. A chart of Avon's stock price from 1958 to 1973 shows how well investors were paying attention. During those fifteen years, Avon rose in price from 5 to 140 and the company's performance record was as consistent as the rise in the stock price. The only investors to lose money on Avon were the ones with foolishly short time frames, since the stock's few downward slides lasted months, not years.

RETURN ON EQUITY

The return-on-equity figure is useful because it indicates whether the earnings, however large they may be in dollars, reflect the full potential of the corporation. It is calculated by dividing a company's annual earnings by its net assets: everything the company has with which to make money, as described in the annual report. Generally, companies are happy if they can report return on equity above 10 percent. Many companies that are well touted on Wall Street never report even a 1 percent return on equity. During the 1960s, only two companies used their assets so efficiently as to notch an annual average for the decade of over 40 percent. One was Avon, which posted a return on equity that remained within two points of 41 percent. The other was Xerox, a well-known hero of Wall Street (discussed in chapter 2). In different ways, each was not only growing but also growing more efficient. And that is bound to make investors pay attention.

Because the company's means of distribution was so well suited to the postwar lifestyle, Avon became the biggest "little" company on Wall Street. Its stock price kept rising until the market capitalization, or the total value of all of its shares, was practically stratospheric. In 1973 Avon Products, Inc., was worth more than the entire U.S. airline industry.

The Advantage of a Social Call

Avon was founded in 1886 by David H. McConnell in New York City. McConnell was a door-to-door book salesman with the bright idea to give a small vial of rose-scented perfume to customers willing to hear his presentation. Like William Wrigley Jr. of Chicago, who discovered at roughly the same time that his customers were less interested in his baking powder than in the chewing gum he used to promote it, McConnell decided to abandon his original product. So, with a $500 investment from his friend Alexander Henderson, he moved to New York City and began manufacture of his own perfumes.

Gentle by nature and insistent on respect and ethics throughout his business, McConnell was the antithesis of the aggressive and cynical archetype of a door-to-door salesman. His qualities became a legacy at Avon and contributed substantially to the company's phenomenal success in the 1950s and 1960s.

"Avon isn't a cosmetics company," observed one stock analyst, "but a distribution machine." If that's the case, then perhaps the real founder of Avon was a certain Mrs. P. F. E. Albee of New Hampshire. A family friend of McConnell's, Mrs. Albee at fifty was the widow of a U.S. senator, left with a crop of children to raise. Good thing she was also a latent business genius in need of money. With this in mind McConnell hired her as one of his company's first sales representatives—actually its very first female rep. At the turn of the century, millions of women were in the workplace, but not many were going door-to-door, the bailiwick of rougher characters.

Mrs. Albee changed a lot of mind-sets. She became living proof not only that many women wanted to earn money through sales, but that they were much more welcome than men in the homes of cosmetics customers. She was the one who organized the Avon sales system and made it work, neighbor to neighbor. In her first six months, she had 100 saleswomen working under her tutelage. After twelve years, Mrs. Albee had trained more than 5,000 "Avon ladies." The company was launched in its dual roles: marketer of cosmetics and provider of part-time work for women.

A genuine characteristic of the company was that it welcomed novices into the Avon workforce. And that workforce was by far the biggest bargain in the business world. Since representatives were independent contractors, they didn't receive wages, benefits, expenses, or free samples. Therefore, an Avon lady could be a plus but never a liability.

Taking Stock

The Henderson and McConnell families owned the company outright until the initial public offering in 1946. Even after that, they
retained more than half of the shares. With sales of $18 million in
1947, the company didn't receive much attention for its stock,
traded over-the-counter. Equivalent to today's NASDAQ exchange,
the OTC market was ignored by many investors in those days. At a
time when corporate information was hard to obtain, the cachet of
a listing on the New York Stock Exchange served to validate a stock
and assuage fears of a swindle. Nonetheless, as Avon sales
increased by more than five times through 1958, with earnings following at an even faster clip, the stock became a star of the back-
ground exchange. It would remain a headliner even after moving to
the Big Board in 1964.

When Avon sales passed $100 million in 1957, on top of con-
secutive 2-for-1 stock splits in 1955 and 1956, one analyst wondered why the stock was not better known. A likely reason was
that, as he noted, "while more flamboyant industry members
shout, conservative Avon scarcely whispers about its financial
achievements." Breaking $100 million in sales spoke volumes,
however, since it made Avon the biggest cosmetics company in the
United States, ahead of Revlon, which grossed $95 million. After
that, Avon didn't have to brag loudly, or softly for that matter.
Other people were saying plenty about it, and investors could no
longer plead ignorance of one of the most exciting stocks around.

GETTING COVERED

*The conventional wisdom is that institutional investors—i.e., insur-
ance companies, mutual funds, and pension managers—move
stock prices. While stock markets are created by differing opinions,
institutions are considered the most rational voices. In Avon's last
years as an OTC stock in the early 1960s, it was the second most
popular stock among large institutions (Weyerhaeuser was first). By
the early 1970s, it was among the top fifteen on the NYSE. Typically,*

about 12 percent of its shares were held by institutions, including Morgan Guaranty Trust, which owned 1 percent all by itself.

Investors had their pick of methods of measuring growth, because Avon registered remarkable numbers by any measure. Gross sales, for example, increased at an average rate of 16 percent per year from 1954 to 1963. Net profits were growing even faster—at 19 percent—proving that Avon was growing leaner, not flabbier. Earnings per share, the figure that tells investors whether the profits translate into meaningful gains for the thousands of corporate owners, were growing at more than 20 percent. And within the fast-growing cosmetics industry, Avon was outpacing its rivals by miles. Taking first place in sales in 1958, it was selling more than the second- and third-place companies combined five years later.

Even better, Avon actually benefited from the efforts of its competitors. When retail cosmetics companies, including Revlon, Cheseborough-Pond, and Helene Curtis, promoted a new product, Avon could reap the benefit by bringing its own version of the product right into the customer's living room. As to direct competition, forget it. Several companies tried to follow Avon into the door-to-door cosmetics business, some backed by retail giants of the industry, but all of them fizzled after realizing how long it would take to build a viable sales organization. Avon's three-quarters of a century head start certainly made it hard to catch.

Avon's prices were in line with those of the retail companies, yet its costs were substantially lower. Investors saw that much of Avon's stunning profitability came from three simple tactics:

1. Avon spent less than 3 percent of sales revenue on advertising, while the industry average was 17 percent. (Not only was Avon in the position of benefiting from the advertising of others, as noted above, it also counted on the effectiveness of the in-person advertising of its 150,000 representatives—which, again, cost the company nothing.)

2. The commission for Avon reps was far lower than standard retail distribution costs.
3. Avon had a relatively small number of actual employees. It treated its sales force as independent contractors, thereby reducing payroll and benefits, both of which were on the rise in the 1960s and cut into the profits of other companies.

Mind the P/E

As Avon Products racked up new records in sales and profits, gaining new fans for its stock by the day, the number of shares outstanding remained stable, aside from 2-for-1 splits in 1964 and 1970. Since 70 percent of the stock was closely held by the founding family, directors, and executives, the price of the shares that were available on the market was constantly pressed upward by eager investors. A Wall Street cult grew around the stock, causing the price to rise far in advance of even Avon's ability to generate earnings per share. The price-to-earnings ratio in 1958 was a fair and rational 18.9. Ten years later, however, when the average S&P 500 stock's p/e ratio was in the low teens, Avon's was a sky-high 52.

As has been seen with other stocks in this book, a p/e ratio above the "worry line" of 30 does not mean that the stock can't keep rising. In 1968, people kept buying Avon and they kept making money on it. At a price of about 60 (adjusted for a split) at the end of 1968, Avon continued its breathless climb during the next five years, touching 140 in March of 1973.

In 1973–1974, the Avon stock chart that had once looked so smartly Alpine suddenly looked like the wrong side of the Matterhorn: sloping practically straight down. In ten months, the price declined by 80 percent. The worst of the slide began at 6 P.M., Friday, September 29, 1973, when the company made an announcement. The timing definitely foreshadowed this story. (When companies make announcements after-hours on Fridays they're usually hoping that the weekend will soften the impact of the news they are compelled to deliver.) In the tone of a shamed confession, Avon admitted that its earnings for the third quarter would be "flat." The company would not be able to generate that conspicuous increase shareholders had learned to expect over the previous twenty years, although for 1973 the company was able to use short-term maneuvers—which amounted to little more than window dressing for the books—to salvage an 8 percent increase in earnings. Earnings for 1974 were a lost cause—they were actually *down*. By then, $20 was a good price for a share of Avon stock.

In Avon's case, investors might have predicted the troubles by noticing an unhappy divergence hovering just behind the stock's fat price-to-earnings ratio. In the five years after 1967, the rate at which earnings were growing slid from 20 to 14 percent. As a company grows larger, it is not unusual for its rate of growth to slow. Yet Avon's price actually grew at a *heightened* pace during those same years. It is vital for an investor to understand just where a high p/e ratio has come from, especially when that number is as high as 55—or even 65, which was Avon's p/e during part of 1972.

PRICE-TO-EARNINGS RATIO

The curse of a price-to-earnings ratio above 30 is that the stock will fall hard and fast at the first whiff of bad news. General Electric (see chapter 1) sank from 100 to 60 in 1960–1961 on news of a price-fixing scandal; it was a high p/e of 38 that made it so susceptible to decline. Reason? The premium in the stock price that makes for a high p/e ratio is based on "future" earnings justifying current hopes. Analysts try to make forecasts of earnings, but when a ratio rises above 30, it becomes harder and harder to be specific about when the two will coincide. In 1972, investors looked past Avon's p/e and bought the stock at 120, figuring that sometime down the road—it would have to be the mid-1980s at the earliest—that price would look like a bargain. When the news came through that earnings were going in the wrong direction to meet that goal, shareholders dumped the stock.

Epilogue

While Avon executives offered the high inflation rate as the reason for the slowing growth, analysts looked further. In Avon's down years of 1973 and 1974, the company found itself at the mercy of social conditions, those very same forces that had encouraged its growth over the previous two decades. The early 1970s were a flowering for women's liberation. So not only did the company find fewer customers at home, it found fewer women willing to work for low pay. To make matters worse, the fact that Avon's management was all male and its workforce all female became a sore point.

A final reason for the steep decline in Avon stock was, well, a doozy. During the early part of 1973, Avon insiders sold substantial stakes in the company stock. One of them, a director by the name of Girard Henderson, the son of McConnell's original investor, happened to be asked in July 1973 whether Avon shareholders should sell. He replied, "Hell no!" Unfortunately, it was later reported that he had been selling shares all spring. The number of shares sold by the insiders was not enormous, but the timing and the fact that the company's top officers were involved put the stock in hopeless disarray when those stock sales were made public in October. The SEC has since mandated that insider trades be filed for public inspection.

Avon's stock leveled out and didn't emerge from its doldrums until 1995, when it began a general rise on increasingly active investor interest. New selling methods, like in-store counters and online selling, enhanced the old one-on-one cosmetics business for both the company and its reps, who by then were doing business in 139 countries. Mrs. Albee would be proud.

Lessons

Bring it on! . . . *Avon's "competition" did nothing but increase its earnings. The secret was the business model: for a company whose business was distribution, were the big cosmetics makers competitors at all?*

Fast profits . . . *If investors are happy to find a company enlarging its revenues on a steady basis, they should be thrilled when profits increase at an even faster pace.*

No speeding . . . *If, when the rate of earnings increase slows, the price of the stock accelerates at an even faster rate (yes, it does happen), it means the stock price is becoming unstable. The first signs of weakness will rarely be the last.*

TIMELINE

1886 Founded by David H. McConnell in New York City.

1946 Initial public offering.

1947 Sales of $18 million.

1955–1956 Stock splits 2 for 1.

1957 Sales of $100 million.

1964 Another 2-for-1 stock split.

1968 Stock price of about $60.

1970 Yet another 2-for-1 stock split.

1973 Stock price peaks at $140.

BILLIONS AND BILLIONS EARNED

McDonald's

1966–1972

Sometimes identifying a high-growth sector is easy. Anyone with a car and, perhaps, a few children in the late 1960s could tell by the wrappers piling up on the backseat floor that franchise restaurants were taking over. The trick for the stock market investor was no longer picking a place to eat, but selecting which of the new fast-food franchises would outlast the boom.

Can you imagine investing in a company without knowing where its revenues come from? It happens more often than you might think. When you buy a screwdriver at your local hardware store, how much goes to the store and how much to the manufacturer? Knowing how money flows within an enterprise is an investor's first responsibility.

In the 1960s, a dollar at a fast-food restaurant went a long way. But what happened to that dollar after it left your hands? In the case of McDonald's, that dollar might well have ended up in the hands of a franchisee. Franchising was an innovative model that enabled the company to grow surprisingly swiftly. McDonald's has been a great stock for many years, but the period from 1966 through 1972 was the best time of all.

Franchise on Profits

American roads and restaurants underwent quite a transformation in the mid-1960s. Practically overnight, suburban boulevards were crowded with new, colorful little restaurants, following a century-long run for inns and diners. The new restaurants appeared to be stamped out by the hundreds and lined up like booths at a fair, each one serving something different: chicken, hot dogs, ice cream, pizza, roast beef, fried fish, hoagies, and hamburgers. The best thing about them, from a business point of view, was that a town that had enough restaurants didn't necessarily have enough *franchise* restaurants. Society was changing and the fast-food business was growing, as Ray Kroc, the head of McDonald's, explained. "We're part of the growing leisure-time business," he said in 1968. "Shorter work weeks, more autos, larger and more college areas, and most important of all, more people."

Vance Bourjaily, a novelist, described the new fast-food society differently: "People in the U.S. don't eat for pleasure. To them, eating is just something done in response to advertising." Although he meant this to be a bleak statement, fast food was a booming opportunity for the investor.

To be sure, there was nothing new about the uniformity of franchise restaurants. Harvey Houses, an elegant chain that grew with the railroad, had greeted tourists throughout the West starting in the 1880s. Chain restaurants from Strait's to White Tower had expanded at least regionally in the middle of the century. The problem was that the chains tended to grow slowly, stymied at each new opening by problems of finance and hiring.

The new idea of applying the concept of franchises to the restaurant business changed all that. A form of association used predominantly in automobile dealerships before the restaurant craze, franchising shifted nearly all obligations downward. The parent company entrusted its recipe for success to entrepreneurs who financed individual restaurants and ran them as independent businesses. To the parent corporation, the difference was a matter of pace. Through franchising, a company could spread outlets across the countryside just about as fast as its vice presidents could sign contracts.

In the mid-1960s, when the whole country was convinced that, for better or for worse, franchise restaurants were the wave of the future, investors were inundated with opportunities to buy stock. The way that many of the new companies explained the outlook to potential shareholders was that franchising represented the quickest moneymaking scheme around. With a good recipe and a bright architectural plan, a start-up could reap instant cash by collecting franchise fees, and then look forward to long-term income through annual royalties and profits on wholesale food and equipment sales. All that a franchise needed was a little push: something to draw people with cash and credit into the circle. Celebrities seemed to be the answer. In 1965–1967 many a star matched his or her name to an eatery: Johnny Carson, Joe Namath, Mickey Mantle, Roy Rogers, and Arthur Treacher among them. Even before the first meal was served, many of these companies reported eye-catching profits, just on the initial franchise fees collected from willing entrepreneurs.

The hotter the franchise sector became, the harder it was to select the good stocks within it. For the first year or so, nearly every one of them looked tasty—especially to investors who didn't really understand the accounting behind franchising. The first point of confusion was that growth in a franchise operation is measured differently from that of a standard retail chain. Investors found that out all too soon.

In 1966, when McDonald's was first listed on the New York Stock Exchange, it was just another name in the pack. A $10,000 investment in McDonald's stock that year was worth $513,000 six years later. Contrast that with what a $10,000 investment in competitor Lum's would be worth: $1,800. Unfortunately, for those investors in many of these competitors the direction of shares was more like Lum's than McDonald's. Even as others collapsed, McDonald's remained solid. The reason was in the way that McDonald's was set up for business. Investors who took the time to compare its system to the systems of others knew that its growth was sustainable and its revenue stream remarkably predictable. Because of that, when the rest of the sector froze over in 1970, McDonald's heated up. More investors were finally beginning to understand the economics of successful franchising.

No Fried Balance Sheets Sold Here

The McDonald brothers opened the first of their drive-in hamburger stands in 1948 near Pasadena, California. Four years later they added the distinctive yellow ("golden") arches. The stands were clean and cheery, with low prices on a limited menu of hamburgers and milkshakes. McDonald's was revolutionary in that food was made before the customers ordered it: the opposite of nearly every other restaurant in the country. California had plenty of hamburger joints, but none quite like McDonald's. It was so crazy that folks from around the country were making pilgrimages just to see it. For example, meat wholesaler William Moore Jr. heard about the chain through a friend, who insisted he check it out. "I blew out there," Moore later recalled, "and sure as hell, there were these long lines of people. I couldn't believe it. Of course, this story is practically a legend now, but you couldn't imagine then, back in 1953, what an operation the McDonald brothers had going."

Ray Kroc, a former musician from Chicago, was selling milkshake mixers the following year when he too heard about McDonald's and made a trip to California just to see what all the excitement was about. Kroc's previous claim to fame was serving in the same outfit as Walt Disney during World War I. Wowed by what he saw on his western trip, Ray Kroc eventually contracted to sell franchises for the McDonald brothers. In 1961, he and a small investment group bought them out completely for $2.7 million. "I needed the McDonald name and those golden arches," Kroc said. "What are you going to do with a name like 'Kroc'?"

The reputation of the McDonald's restaurants helped the new corporation arrange financing and sign franchisees. It's hard to imagine getting either would have been easy for a start-up. But Kroc and his early associates, Harry Sonneborn and June Martino, quickly evolved a formula by which they would charge initial fees for new franchises, take a royalty on sales, make money leasing real estate for new restaurants, and finally, charge for ongoing consulting. The last two were what really helped to set McDonald's apart.

Most franchise restaurants made their biggest profits by selling initial franchise fees and also by selling food and equipment to their restaurants. Although McDonald's set standards for such products, it let the restaurants find their own suppliers. That subtle difference was what made its restaurants function as independent businesses, ones that had to succeed in their own right in order for the parent to prosper. In many other franchise operations, the parent could show good figures even when its restaurants were struggling to make a profit. But not for long, however. Many investors learned that lesson in 1969–1971, when the sector gained a reputation for flash-fried balance sheets.

How Not to "Minnie-Pearl It"

McDonald's was listed on the NYSE in July of 1966, one year after its initial public offering. It soon found itself in the company of about sixty fast-food companies with stock on the various markets. The only fast-food franchisers with greater sales than McDonald's were Dairy Queen, based in Canada, and Kentucky Fried Chicken (KFC), which launched its IPO early the same year. KFC was similar to McDonald's in that experienced businessmen had purchased an existing restaurant business and were streamlining and expanding it. However, they did not tweak the basic formula—as McDonald's did—of earning money on franchise fees and the sale of supplies. McDonald's stock was among the many stars of franchising. With the success of more than 700 outlets and earnings per share increasing from 14 cents to $1.80, shares rose from $15 to $45 the first year they were traded over-the-counter, with a pair of splits to boot.

McDonald's stock wasn't quite as spectacular in its first year on the NYSE, however, rising by a *mere* three times. In fact, even more excitement revolved around Minnie Pearl's Fried Chicken, named after a comedienne popular on television's *Hee Haw*. That company's stock became a special favorite on Wall Street, vaulting from less than $5 per share to $68 in about eighteen months. But the company turned out to have a fatal flaw. Minnie Pearl's Chicken Systems was almost entirely dependent on initial franchise fees for revenues. Investors who were impressed by the immediate growth shown on the books were not aware that follow-up supervision of the restaurants was almost nonexistent. As long as the initial fees kept rolling in, the company's numbers were good even as individual outlets failed. That business model, a second-generation Ponzi scheme, was later called "Minnie-Pearling it" within the industry. By then the stock had fallen spectacularly, to just 12 cents per share.

McDonald's had a business model based on the continuing success of its outlets, so it avoided the Minnie Pearl trap. "We don't sell franchises to make a buck," said Fred Turner, who was named president of McDonald's in 1968. "We're a restaurant chain."

McDonald's to Go

In any fast-growing sector, the key to picking a stock is to ignore practically every figure used to measure growth in stabilized industries. After all, companies in a hot sector always deliver sizzling numbers. More important to an investor is the business model—the way the company intends to make and use money—because that will give context to the numbers.

McDonald's, of course, happened to be in a hot sector. The franchise industry was growing by an average of 20 percent per year, as measured by restaurant openings. No one doubted that the habit, once ingrained, would permeate society even more deeply. Certainly not Ray Kroc. At the top of the list of things that annoyed Kroc (the list was a long one) was the idea that McDonald's growth was limited. "I don't believe in saturation," he said, insisting that worldwide marketing and other aggressive concepts left room for the company to extend its 30 percent annual growth long into the future.

McDonald's Corporation differed from others in the franchise boom in that there were no silent partners. The biggest shareholders were officers of the company. As welcome as investment capital can be, it has a tendency to distort the priorities in an evolving company. At competing companies, for example, the sale of new franchises was the most important operation. McDonald's management became known for its relative conservatism, selling franchises only after suitable locations had been selected. Likewise, the company didn't grow so fast that it could leave the reasons for its success behind: "It's not that we're so smart. It's just that this business takes a lot of attention to detail," said Turner, a college dropout who had started at the company as a hamburger cook in 1956.

When investors pondering fast-food companies wondered where the profits came from, as they should do with any new type of business, McDonald's provided the most intriguing answers of any of the franchise restaurant stocks. Beyond collecting franchise fees, the company made money in several different ways from locations already up and running. About one-half of franchisees rented the land and building from the parent corporation. Real estate was McDonald's profit center, initially generating 33 percent of its profits, even while accounting for only 15 percent of revenues. Those figures shifted over the years, but real estate remained, in its quiet way, the factor that separated McDonald's from all the others in the race for profits. On a third tier of revenue creation, McDonald's owned and operated about one-quarter of its restaurants.

Happy Meal

On July 17, 1966, an article in the *New York Times* helped introduce McDonald's to investors with its simple explanation. It said, "A 10-item food menu, with no order costing more than 29 cents, had enabled a roadside hamburger chain to become so successful that it has met the requirements for a listing on the New York Stock Exchange." Investors who read that article or others, did their research, and recognized that McDonald's had a long-range plan in a short-term boom were rewarded with $687,500 by 1972 for every $10,000 invested in 1966. During that span, McDonald's stock grew on a split-adjusted basis from $1.12 per share to $77.

The company's system and its attention to detail were working: from 1966 to 1972, earnings per share grew at an average rate of 36 percent. In 1972, when McDonald's passed $1 billion in sales for the first time, it was opening, on average, a new restaurant every day. The total number of restaurants, 2,500, was still second to those of Kentucky Fried Chicken, but McDonald's was second to none in serving meals: in 1972, it even passed the U.S. Army on that list. That same year, a banner one in the company's history, profits increased at a higher rate than revenues, due in some measure to the real estate end of the business and the fact that as mortgages were paid off, profits on rentals were boosted by about 5 percent. In addition, the introduction of new menu items increased revenues at each restaurant substantially.

Heartburn

From 1970 to 1972, when most fast-food chains were battered by slowing growth and shareholder lawsuits, McDonald's was still perceived as the blue chip stock in the sector. The price of the stock soared until the price-to-earnings ratio was above 70. After that the stock price was dragged down by a series of external factors, starting with an overall market malaise early in 1973. The energy crisis that started that year was particularly hard on the McDonald's stock, causing people to believe that with less driving, there would be less eating out. A spike in the price of beef in the middle of the decade continued the pressure on the stock, which was considered dependent upon the chain's ability to provide inexpensive hamburgers.

And then there was another factor: by 1972, McDonald's biggest competitors had been absorbed by deep-pocketed corporations. Pizza Hut was merged into PepsiCo, Burger King was purchased by Pillsbury, and Kentucky Fried Chicken was part of Heublein (all three chains have changed hands since). To some investors, that isolated McDonald's against tough competition; to others, it made the hamburger chain the most attractive "pure play" available in fast food.

McDonald's stock continued to droop in the mid-1970s, even with profits continuing to grow by 32 percent annually—one point ahead of revenues. Earnings were still growing at a rate above 25 percent annually at the end of the decade, when the price-to-earnings ratio was below 10. The stock was simply out of favor, even underperforming the restaurant index charted by Prudential-Bache. Analysts lined up to label it with "sell" recommendations. "McDonald's faces a relatively stagnant market," said one, and others predicted that people were tiring of hamburgers and would seek out more interesting fare at other new chains. By 1981, the fears subsided, as McDonald's stubbornly continued to report double-digit earnings increases. Investors found it hard to ignore that the company was *still* a growth company. No surprise, however, that once it dislodged, the stock rose steadily through 1992.

Epilogue

It has been said that bull markets "climb a wall of worry," and that same phrase can apply to individual stocks. The most important theme of McDonald's long run has been the worry about saturation—that one day McDonald's would simply run out of places to put its restaurants.

The fact that Ray Kroc heard this fear (and despised it) decades ago makes it laughable now. But it has been earnestly felt nonetheless, and maybe someday it will come true. But the worrywarts underestimated more than just the number of golden arches an area can sustain. In the 1970s, they underestimated how important breakfast was to the overall equation of a franchise restaurant: why wait until lunchtime to begin to make money? More fundamentally, they underestimated the size of our planet and the receptivity of foreign countries to house an American tradition.

What the worrywarts should have said is this: "If McDonald's faces saturation fifty years from now, the stock will surely suffer. But just think of the ride we'll have until then!"

Lessons

Do your research . . . *Investors who understood how McDonald's franchises differed from those of its competitors were rewarded.*

If you can, get to a know a company or its products firsthand . . . *Be like Ray. When Ray Kroc first heard about McDonald's, he made a trip to visit one in person. At the time there were seven McDonald's, and he suspected that there was room for more.*

Know when to fold 'em . . . *Be realistic when the overall market gets ahead of itself (i.e., 1972), and don't overstay when it finally meets reality. When the stock market and the fast-food sector quieted down in the 1970s, the challenge to McDonald's investors was to stand by the company's good numbers: earnings that were increasing at an even greater rate than revenues. However, the stock price, laboring against a high p/e, was downtrodden for nine years. Investors eventually tired of being smarter than the market and having nothing to show for it.*

TIMELINE

1954 Ray Kroc becomes franchising agent for the McDonald brothers.

1955 Ray Kroc opens the first McDonald's franchise.

1961 Ray Kroc buys out McDonald brothers for $2.7 million.

1963 Advertising campaign featuring Ronald McDonald is launched.

1965 McDonald's celebrates its tenth anniversary with the first public offering at $22.50 a share.

1966 Listed on the NYSE.

1968 Big Mac added to the menu.

1973 Egg McMuffin and other breakfast items added to the menu.

1998 McDonald's added to the 30-company Dow Jones Industrial Average.

HARD DRIVE

Dell Computer

1990–1999

There was barely a bad day from 1990 to 1999 to buy stock in Dell Computer. During that time, its stock price increased from 19 cents, adjusted for the seven splits to come, to $108. This best-performing stock of the 1990s created thousands of millionaires, or "Dellionaires," as they are called. A person who invested $10,000 in the stock of the computer maker in 1990 had a holding worth more than $5.5 million ten years later. Not too shabby.

Innovation seems like a timeless concept, but timing can be the difference between an "innovative" business model and an outright failure. The expansion of the Sun Belt was a mere fantasy until air conditioning came along. The full-scale production of latex paint had to wait until after World War II. And could the Pet Rock have blossomed in any decade but the seventies?

When the personal computer came of age in 1981, consumers weren't immediately comfortable with these brand-new gadgets. The salesperson at the computer store played a critical role; in many cases, so did the IBM label on the machine itself. Within a few short years, however, the public became much better informed about computers, and became receptive to new methods of purchase. Selling directly to the consumer may not seem like a stunning breakthrough, but that was the niche exploited by Michael Dell.

Knowing When to Hold 'Em

If anyone ever deserved an award for patience, perhaps, say, an award of the 30,000 percent variety, it was the longtime holder of Dell. Year in and year out during the 1990s, these investors were prodded to sell by jittery analysts and reporters, who piped up regularly to wonder how much longer the Dell ascent could hold up. Even stockholders impervious to the push and pull of Wall Street had to overlook events that logically indicated trouble at Dell. For one thing, the business of making computers in the 1990s *was* trouble. Companies that stumbled sometimes never got up, or by the time they did right themselves again, the industry had passed them by.

At various points, Dell suffered the problems common to its computer-making brethren. These included a rash of quality complaints, a breakdown in service, the embarrassment of design flubs, failed ventures, and missed opportunities. The company nearly lost its balance. Whenever that happened, not surprisingly a battalion of stockholders made the perfectly rational decision to take profits and disappear. The person with that original 1990 investment of $10,000 might easily have been tempted to sell out for $173,000 in 1993—a year when Dell hit one of its banana peels.

Moreover, stories still circulate around north Texas about the people who bought Dell stock at $8.50 in the initial public offering in June of 1988 and jumped for joy when they sold it for twice that price just three years later. That resulted in a gain of $8.50 . . . and the loss of a potential $551.50.

Only one thing is more difficult than selecting a stock with a steadily rising price—knowing when to cash out, and why. It isn't enough to call oneself a "long-term" investor, only to grandly announce that stock will remain in the portfolio for an arbitrary length of time—ten years, twenty years, or forever and ever. Buying a stock and then forgetting about it is not the answer; nor does that approach constitute investing, which requires the application of intelligence at every step, or nonstep, along the way. The long-term investor has to know why he or she *isn't* selling. Dell Computer is an example of a stock that should have been held.

Dell Makes a Name

The early history of Dell Computer is every parent's nightmare. At the age of nineteen, Michael Dell quit college. However, he was different. He started a company to sell computers and became a millionaire within four years, a billionaire within thirteen. (Between Michael Dell, Bill Gates, and Larry Ellison—college dropouts, all of them—parents have surely had a hard time insisting that their children earn a college diploma in order to get ahead in the world!)

Michael Dell started in business in 1983 by purchasing IBM personal computers on the gray market. (That's where new products trade hands in violation of commercial contracts.) Dell found a ready supply from established dealers who were overstocked but forbidden by IBM from disposing of them on a wholesale basis. "It was IBM's sales policies that really set me up in business," he said a few years later. Dell then spruced up the PCs with features of interest to serious users and sold them nationally through magazine ads.

The next step was an obvious one for dozens of companies at the time: building IBM clone computers from scratch. New businesses flooded the market in the late 1980s with machines comparable in every way to the IBM standard, *except* in price. These clones shone on price, yet after the sale they often lagged badly. Either the PCs themselves proved faulty or the predictable need for service went ignored. Dell Computer established an early reputation for reliability in both respects. By the end of the 1980s, it had emerged from the anonymous soup of clone makers: Dell had a name.

Just as in the earliest days, Dell computers were not the least expensive on the market. This was a smart decision because the very lowest price segment in the market was also the most treacherous. The company steered clear of the bargain basement snake pit, offering mid- to high-level PCs instead. Within those niches, Dell computers represented an attractive value. Partly because the company sold its products directly to the customer, it was able to cut out the middleman's 20 to 45 percent markup. Customers shopped at Dell by telephone in a customized process that was more like ordering a sandwich than buying a computer from the typical computer store. As at the deli, the product wasn't made until the order was received. Dell computers were not only inexpensive—they were fresh.

In 1988, Michael Dell, at twenty-three, was CEO of a company with $159 million in sales and $9 million in profits. This had become an international company, too. The year before, while on vacation in London with his parents, Dell observed, as he later recalled, "the same high markup/lousy service phenomenon in the United Kingdom as in the United States." As a result, Dell UK opened in 1987 and was profitable almost immediately.

Michael Dell didn't wait for the company to outgrow his own business abilities, but boldly recruited men twice his age to help—and to teach. He depended on others and in the meantime learned how to run a $1 billion business—when he was still at the head of a $100 million one. In June 1988, Dell Computer issued a successful IPO that closed up $3 from $8.50 on the very first day, mostly because of an upswing in the overall market. That day the little company from Austin (or, to be more precise, Round Rock) arrived on Wall Street and Michael Dell began to learn his way around.

It's 1990: Who Should Invest?

By 1990, Dell Computer had a track record that it was glad to share with investment analysts: annual growth of 97 percent, without one quarterly loss. The formula behind the company's success could be explained in a simple sentence: Dell sold computers directly to customers. Not many companies in the high-tech sector could be called ancient in their missions, but Dell was. It knew its customers by name.

The key to trusting the company was trusting Michael Dell. The difference between Dell and most of the other computer whiz kids starting promising companies was that he was neither an inventor nor a techno-nerd. He was a seller. Inventions are supplanted; selling is not. Because of that, Michael Dell always had a wide perspective. Investors who were willing to let him grow with the business soon found what one early executive did: "Michael never makes the same mistake twice." Dell also surrounded himself with the most experienced executives he could hire: not his old friends, but a roster that gave the nascent company a think-big mentality. In terms of competition, Dell became the fourth-biggest computer producer, after IBM, Compaq, and Hewlett-Packard. None of them were direct-sellers, though. Dell's unique marketing strategy gave it a perennial 15 percent cost advantage over the others, each of which relied on retailers for distribution. That percentage translated into a margin for profit or, more important for a young company, a margin of error that let Dell forge forward even when it made mistakes. While the company had sharp competition in the PC industry, it was the lonely giant in direct selling during its first ten years.

Early along, Dell Computer developed a reputation on Wall Street for candid, reliable guidance on future earnings. An observation made by Janus Fund manager Scott Schoelze couldn't have been more on track: "Dell management really knows what the Street wants. They are great communicators."

One of the hidden strengths of Dell—and one not to be taken lightly—was that its clientele was eminently creditworthy. The company catered to large businesses, which generally paid on time, and to individuals or small businesses using credit cards. On the other hand, companies that sold to retailers might have to wait up to ninety days for payment. The difference showed up in the cash conversion cycle—that is, the difference between the date on which a company has to pay its suppliers and the date on which it receives payment from sales. Typically the cycle is seven to thirty days. At Dell, it was minus-eight days.

Companies that sell computers are known as "box makers" because, above all else, they have to push containers out the door. Some box makers, however, have found that it would be more profitable to actually make cardboard boxes than the machines inside. After computers became a mere commodity in the late 1980s profit margins in the business were sometimes shaved down to nothing, affected from time to time by the same factors as the bean market: oversupply of product, undersupply of customers. Dell logged above-average net margins of 5 to 6 percent, even in the midst of price competition. Influenced both by costs incurred and prices charged, the net margin is a closely followed figure in computer companies. Dell's stock generally followed its ability to keep its mark above 5 percent.

"Liquidity, Profitability, and Growth"

Dell Computer sales had been more than doubling every year when the company suffered what Michael Dell called "some growing pains," in 1993. Reports surfacing that the company was losing money in currency speculation did not go over well with investors. The mere mention of "derivatives" was enough to arouse suspicion. Although Dell's involvement with derivatives was relatively small, the implication that the company was trying to plump profits through a risky activity fell like lead on Wall Street. In addition, earnings declined by 48 percent in the first quarter, the first decline ever, and the stock fell over the course of the following year from 49 to 14. It was the big dip of the 1990s for Dell, as the bad news piled up. Net margins slid to about 4 percent, as the company absorbed a $90 million write-off on a new notebook computer that had to be abandoned. The notebook, one of Dell's first major forays into product development, simply wasn't good enough.

Worst of all for Dell's stock, other companies were copying the Dell model, as Compaq and IBM joined an ambitious newcomer called Gateway 2000 in direct sales. "It's not as easy as a couple of 1-800 lines and picnic tables," Michael Dell responded dourly. To bolster his own sales, meanwhile, Dell reversed his long-standing denigration of retail outlets, signing deals to distribute PCs through Staples, CompUSA, Sam's Club, and other stores. The result was a short-lived disaster that cost Dell more money than it made. And at the time, Dell didn't have much money to spare. The company was running short of cash and, with little hope of another stock offering in the near future, it was kept on track only through the intervention of several New York investment banks.

As of spring 1994, Dell stock was turning into one of Wall Street's whipping boys. Fully one-quarter of the shares that were not owned by Michael Dell had been sold. Long-term investors holding some part of the other 75 percent had a barrage of bad news to ignore in 1993–1994. Those who succeeded were rewarded, though, with a practically instantaneous turnaround in the stock's outlook and a five-year ride upward that was not only profitable but fun, as the share price increased by 211 percent in a bad year—and 550 percent in a good one. Dell short-sellers, so they were saying around Wall Street, "had to be carried out on stretchers."

The first step in assessing a good company in bad straits is to reassess the management. "Our people sleep aggressive," said Joel Kocher, who was the second in command in the mid-1990s. That is, when they slept at all: one manager claimed that he and others worked all night at least once a week. Michael Dell was fundamental in any assessment, of course, but so was the corps of new executives he hired as the company stepped up in 1993. On one side, Michael Dell encouraged the overachievers on the front line to "do whatever it takes," as Kocher once said. On the other side, Dell cultivated high-level executives and lofty advisors, who brought weight to the young company. "Instead of 'growth, growth, growth,'" wrote Michael Dell, "the new order of business at Dell would be 'liquidity, profitability, and growth'—in that order."

"Runaway Money Train"

One of the new recruits, chief information officer Thomas L. Thomas, implemented measures in 1994 that cut the standing inventory by 27 percent, even as sales increased by 43 percent. Sales continued upward, along with market share, and Dell tightened its grip on its core customer base, big business. In doing so, the company corrected an earlier problem: a product line too narrowly focused on PCs. By 1997, Dell had overcome its false start in notebook computers and was offering a line of well-received notebooks, along with workstations, servers, and an array of other products essential in information-based businesses. The same year, it started selling on the Internet.

Over the objections of other executives, Michael Dell insisted in 1996 that the company open an e-commerce site. Through the Internet, it could take care of customers just as easily and much more economically than through telephone calls, he argued. The website, combined with the bustling economy of the late 1990s, pushed Dell from a growth company into what *Fortune* magazine called a "runaway money train." Investors who were paying attention saw Dell earn $1 billion in sales during its first full year in cyberspace. It was recognized as the first company to make a successful, truly remunerative expansion to the Internet.

Epilogue

At this writing, Dell Computer has yet to fashion its epilogue, but it seems appropriate to close the story with a few words from the chairman himself, words that future Dell investors should keep in mind. When pessimistic analysts asked in wonderment why Dell Computer was the company with the stock best matched to the spinning 1990s, Michael Dell's response was, "We're constantly reinventing ourselves."

Lessons

Technophobes take heart . . . *Even if you feel uncomfortable with technology, it is possible to find low-tech winners within the high-tech world. Dell wasn't a computer company; it was a company that had discovered a superior method of marketing computers.*

Dell be nimble . . . *Dell recovered from its mistakes quickly, whether they were forays into retail stores or dabbling with financial derivatives. Missteps such as these can create panic on Wall Street, but if the company gets back on track, those panics are called buying opportunities.*

Too expensive? . . . *Just because a stock has a high value doesn't mean it should automatically be on your sell list. Companies with superior business models deserve their premium valuations.*

TIMELINE

1984 Michael Dell founds Dell Computer Corporation.

1985 Company introduces the first computer system of its own design: the Turbo.

1987 Becomes first computer systems company to offer next-day, on-site product service. International expansion begins with opening of subsidiary in United Kingdom.

1988 Initial public offering of 3.5 million shares at $8.50 each.

1991 Introduces its first notebook computer.

1993 Joins ranks of the top 5 computer system makers worldwide.

1996 Customers begin buying Dell computers via Internet at www.dell.com.

1996 Added to Standard & Poor's 500 stock index.

1997 Sales via Internet exceed $4 million per day, from $1 million at the start of the year.

2000 Sales via Internet reach $50 million per day.

FOUR
CREATING AND PRESERVING MARKET LEADERSHIP

HIGH ROAD TO RICHES: GENERAL MOTORS (1923–1929)

RECURRING PROFITS: GILLETTE (1958–1962)

We have already looked at the riches attained by consumer companies Polaroid and Xerox, each of which blazed entirely new trails en route to stock market history. But the products that created this history were by definition extraordinary. The vast majority of the time, companies aren't trying to revolutionize the world. They're simply trying to grow their market share.

It's nice to know, then, that new products can lead to extraordinary investments even if they look ordinary on the surface, as long as they do one of two things: 1) create market leadership; 2) preserve market leadership. Remember, market leadership is a uniquely desirable trait for a company to have. Leaders not only do more business than also-rans, they also tend to be far more profitable. The advantage of leadership is often self-perpetuating, but it cannot be taken for granted, as we will soon discover.

This chapter focuses on two stocks, GM and Gillette. The two companies appear unrelated except for the fact that either stock could have been held over the very long term to good effect. And there is another, less obvious connection. It turns out that the most exciting (and rewarding) time to own either stock was "launch time"—when new products were being introduced that would keep the companies ahead of their competitors.

In GM's case, we go back all the way to the 1920s, when the automotive market was still a relative newcomer. Ford's Model T was the undisputed king of its terrain, but GM managed to show just how wobbly that terrain actually was. Gillette's story is not quite that old, but still harks back to the 1950s and a long-forgotten duel in the razor blade market. The ultimate bond between the two stories is that they both led to great stocks. All an investor had to do was appreciate the power of being number one.

HIGH ROAD TO RICHES

General Motors

1923–1929

General Motors—more than any other stock—represents the transition of Wall Street in the 1920s from a circle of insiders to the very public domain of the individual investor. In 1917, two years after GM became the first automobile company listed on the New York Stock Exchange, 2,920 investors held its shares. By 1930, more than 300,000 did. Over the same span, GM went from being the second-biggest car company (trailing Ford Motor) to the biggest and grew from being the thirtieth-biggest industrial company of any type in the United States to third (behind only AT&T and U.S. Steel). Along the way, it passed the world's favorite car, the Ford Model T, using the fuel of automobile marketing.

The advantages of being number one in an industry—any industry—are extraordinary. Consumers get accustomed to the prevailing pecking order, and buying habits are hard to change. Often, companies are delighted to accept a number two position (Avis's "We're number two: We try harder" campaign was rooted in its slot behind Hertz).

Today's consumers identify General Motors as the biggest automobile manufacturer in the United States. But it wasn't always that way. Henry Ford's company sat atop the car market for more than a decade following the introduction of the Model T. Although Ford was the industry pioneer, GM inverted the pecking order via a trio of pivotal maneuvers. One was product introduction on a massive scale; two was changing the way customers bought the product; three was using its position as a public company to publicize numbers one and two.

Point of Admiration

The changes GM underwent between 1915 and 1930 were of a magnitude rarely seen before or since in any one company. The effects of the internal modifications—such as in the way the company organized its work, treated its employees, and kept track of its money—made GM the most influential company of its era, studied by academics, admired by journalists. Its methods were eventually examined by every other corporation in existence, and copied by more than a few. One point of admiration was in the way it regarded its stock *and* its stockholders. Even before the Securities and Exchange Commission (created in 1933) enforced standards of financial disclosure, GM conducted its market activities and investor relations "almost as a public trust," in the words of a financial reporter of the day.

A controlling stake in General Motors stock was effectively owned by one family, the du Ponts. The head of that family, Pierre S. du Pont, was an uncommonly straightforward businessman. At the time of his most direct involvement with GM in 1921, he had recently retired as the head of his family's chemical and explosives business. Considered the father of the modern corporation by business historians, du Pont displayed a sense of obligation to the shareholder that was refreshing, if not revolutionary, in the early 1920s. His long business experience had left him with an utterly objective view of corporate finance—it was his attitude that eventually became GM's.

GM's crisp reporting and prodigious stock offerings may have welcomed hundreds of thousands of new investors, but the fact that the company was the fastest-growing large company of its day did not hurt, either. From 1921, when GM began its makeover, to the end of the decade in 1929, GM stock grew in price from 3 1/8 to 91 1/4, while paying a total of.$49.80 in cash dividends. One of the most robust growth stocks of the decade, GM was typical in the way it minded its duty to the dividend. Today, growth stocks forgo dividends in favor of reinvesting profits in the business and, supposedly, enhancing share value. Expectations were different in the 1920s. Stock performance then was more likely to follow the size of the dividend than the earnings. During GM's breakout years of 1923 to 1925, for example, the dividend grew from $1.20 to $5 to $12. Investors caught on. GM was becoming a new force on Wall Street: one of the first companies to accommodate the individual investor by attempting to conduct its stock market activities out in the open. With accessible information and shares that were easy to purchase, GM's presence as the biggest auto stock gave it an edge that helped make it the biggest auto company.

Something from Nothing

There was no arguing that GM's founder, William "Billy" Durant, was one heck of a charmer. The grandson of a Michigan governor, he entered the automobile business by way of a successful wagon company. After he took control of Buick Motor Company in 1904, he helped to build it into the country's favorite family car. In the early 1900s the automobile business was composed of hundreds of small makes, cars that were themselves composed largely of components purchased off the shelf from other manufacturers. Billy Durant, displaying all the confidence of the visionary he was, decided that the industry should consolidate into a huge entity that could make cars and produce parts for a variety of makes, all under one umbrella. He started by organizing General Motors in 1908, which included the Buick Motor Company.

Bringing order to the chaos of the early auto industry was a tall order, but Durant was just the one to tackle it. Respected, popular, and cunning, he built Buick into General Motors by continually rolling out new stock to pay for acquisitions; he made twenty of them in the first two years alone. The plan went like this: new purchases had to make money to pay for subsequent purchases. Among his buys, Durant managed to snag gems like Cadillac and Oldsmobile for his automobile empire.

(Other acquisitions were not nearly as auspicious. One, an

utterly worthless headlight company called Heany Lamp, was especially mysterious. In 1910, Durant paid the owners about $6 million in GM stock and $112,000 in cash and received effectively nothing in return. It was a typical Durant deal, though, in that observers presumed it was part of a much more complicated and secretive exchange. For the record, however, the Heany stake in GM stock was worth $320 million in 1927, by which time it had yielded $50 million in GM dividends.)

Durant was a stock manipulator. He would explain deals such as Heany Lamp by saying that he couldn't be sure where the automobile industry was headed, and so he acquired a wide variety of companies. But there was more to it than that. Durant built his empire with paper: common stock or preferred. He showed where his priorities lay when he chose to build the factory for his new Chevrolet car in Tarrytown, New York, a Hudson River town barely an hour north of Wall Street. "The automobile business was foreign to these eastern bankers," one of Durant's colleagues explained. "They wouldn't come all the way out to Michigan to see what the industry was doing. With a factory at Tarrytown, we thought that they could run up and see it. . . . That was Durant's object in this Tarrytown factory—to get a few of them interested in his operations."

Month by month and year by year, Durant would issue stock, exchange it, or reissue it to fit the next deal and the next one after that. There was nothing illegal in Durant's manipulations and nothing untoward. In fact, Billy Durant was a prince among men, unfailingly honest and even unselfish. He had to be in order to be successful at what he did. In the Wall Street world of the 1910s, an investor did not so much buy stock in a company, as in the man behind it.

And Durant was unquestionably the man behind General Motors. He had a whole catalogue of investors, du Ponts among them, who were fiercely loyal.

The GM Crash

From January 1919 to March 1920, GM stock tripled, rising from 123 to 376. Booming along with the rest of the automobile industry, it was catering to pent-up demand left by World War I. GM not only expanded, adding a few new car companies, but placed large orders for parts and raw materials, even at inflated postwar prices. In the middle of 1920, though, the United States was hit by a sudden and treacherous economic depression. While car sales all but stopped, GM was laden with paid-for parts whose value it had no chance of recovering. By the end of the year, GM stock was down to $132 (split-adjusted). Though the company attempted to raise money with investors, its reputation for instability kept fresh money away.

Durant had tried to support the stock price on its way down, buying as many shares as he could afford, be it with cash or personal credit. But under those dreary market conditions the end was inevitable. By November, according to a Dow Jones estimate, Durant owed $27 million; with the GM stock price continuing to fall, his creditors closed in, demanding immediate payment. The "GM crash," as it was known, was no less steep than the fall of other stocks, but with the weakness of Durant's stake in the center, it threatened the future of the company. Had Durant been forced to flood the market with his shares, a panic could have easily ensued. Instead, the du Ponts led the way out by buying Durant's shares at a tense private meeting on the night of November 21, 1920.

Billy Durant may have been ousted but he was left with a comfortable cushion of shares—which he sold as soon as he could to start another car company. As for Pierre du Pont, he took over as president of General Motors and reorganized the company with the help of lieutenants including Alfred P. Sloan Jr., formerly the president of Hyatt Roller Bearing, one of the companies that Durant had acquired along the way. The days of GM's financial daring were over for good. Gone too were the days of its wild expansion through acquisition. General Motors had more than enough companies to work with. The question was whether or not it was too late to invest.

Back on the Road to Success

By 1922, the depression in automobile sales was over as quickly as it had arrived. Vehicle sales for GM doubled over the same period from the year before and continued to increase. Investors who kept abreast of GM's progress through industry journals and company reports soon began to see that it was a different company, ready for a changing automobile marketplace.

In 1923, Ford Motor commanded more than 60 percent of the automobile market, but it was a peculiar company in that it produced just one car, the Model T. While General Motors would soon pit its Chevrolet against the Model T, its competition on the corporate level was not Ford Motor in those days. Aggressively positioning itself to serve the entire auto market, the company was more keenly aware of three other growing conglomerates: Nash (later American Motors), Chrysler (see chapter 7), and Durant (started by Billy Durant, but failed in 1933). Alfred Sloan, president and chairman of the GM executive committee, took the lead in sorting out the lineup so that, as he wrote in the 1923 annual report, the corporation would have "a complete line of motor cars from the lowest to the highest price." No other car company could offer that in the 1920s.

Under plans designed by Alfred Sloan, GM organized its management to be decentralized, albeit coordinated. The divisions, including makes such as Cadillac, Buick, and Chevrolet, were to be autonomous, charged only with meeting goals set out by the corporate administration. What mattered to investors was that the true potential of the GM combination was being fully exploited. No mere gaggle of companies, the divisions themselves became parts in a meticulously calibrated moneymaking machine.

As of late 1920, General Motors was struggling with debt in the amount of $82 million—a substantial number in a year when net profits were down to $37 million. By mid-1922, the du Pont regime had repaid that debt entirely. Over the next four decades, the company would rely on earnings and new stock offerings for financing, thereby largely avoiding debt.

As for cash flow, GM had a novel and ultimately quite successful plan. The General Motors Acceptance Corporation (GMAC) had been launched in 1919 to extend credit for purchases of GM cars. The idea of selling cars on credit was entirely new at the time. Under the new management, GMAC became essential to fully serving the market, expanding until it accounted for one-third of GM vehicle sales by 1924. Through new car loans, GM not only expanded its profit on each vehicle, but it also extended payments over time, leading to increased cash flow with its particular advantage of projecting a base of revenue years into the future.

On Its Way

The efficiencies that General Motors instituted throughout its organization in 1921–1923 were fortunately timed to converge with a boom in auto sales in the mid-1920s. In fact, between 1924 and 1927, GM's production nearly tripled. Marketing savvy—that is, the understanding of exactly how customers perceived their own needs—allowed the dapper Chevrolet to surpass the dowdy Model T and force it out of production. Buick, Oldsmobile, and Cadillac were booming as well, while Pontiac was being groomed for success.

The increase in production was exciting, but investors were more interested in the numbers behind the hundreds of thousands of cars pouring out of GM factories. The most important factor was the comparative rate of the increase in sales and net profits. Though in many cases a company will "buy" market share by accepting a decreased level of earnings per dollar of sales, this wasn't GM's story. Between 1924 and 1927 sales increased by 123 percent, profits 428 percent.

General Motors returned some of the extraordinary earnings to investors through increased dividends, instituting a longtime policy of distributing two-thirds of earnings whenever conditions allowed. In 1927, the company paid out more than $134 million in dividends on GM common stock—a greater sum than any company had ever paid on common. Naturally, that brought attention and investors swirling around the stock. By the end of the 1920s, GM was by far the most actively traded issue on the New York Stock Exchange. In those days sharp-talking brokers were actively pressing shares on a vast number of new investors, encouraging them, among other things, to take shares on the credit system known as margin buying. As long as the share price kept rising, the margin was a winning proposition. GM's financial integrity and clear reporting gave it a trusted reputation among small investors, as did its brand recognition and, of course, soaring dividends. Brokers, good or bad, had little trouble selling GM stock in the 1920s.

Epilogue

When the crash arrived in October 1929, General Motors stock was relatively steady at first, though by the end of the month, it was down two-thirds from its high of the year (91 down to 33). The stock drifted lower during the next four years of the Great Depression, yet the company actually managed to keep its head above water, reporting profits in every year and making important gains in market share. At levels in the low teens, GM was a great buy for bargain hunters, but then again, investors with cash had their choice of stock market bargains in those days. General Motors, however, continued to be a positive investment for decades, hardly pausing again until it faced the new competition of the international automobile marketplace in the 1970s.

As competition became more targeted, the company's myriad divisions represented a hindrance rather than an asset. GM divisions such as Pontiac and Oldsmobile found it difficult to maintain their identity. The company never faced the financial peril of Ford and Chrysler in 1980, but its rebound in an improved economy was more muted. The stock offered little more than cyclical opportunities for the last two decades of the twentieth century. Ironically, individual investors during that same period benefited from a trend toward heightened shareholder awareness, improved communications, and share offerings that brought closely held companies and industries into the public domain. Who knew that the stodgy General Motors had pioneered all of these developments sixty years earlier?

Lessons

Innovate this . . . *The General Motors Acceptance Corporation* (GMAC) *was a great way to lure more customers. Leaders are tough to topple, but this time around, Ford didn't have a better idea.*

Nothing to hide . . . *Companies that are transparent are always the ones to look for, because you see everything that's there.*

Having a stake in things . . . *Smart activist shareholders can be a boon. It was true in the 1920s and remains true today.*

TIMELINE

1919 General Motors Acceptance Corporation (GMAC) launched to extend credit for purchases of GM cars.

1920 Durant resigns as president of General Motors and Pierre S. du Pont, then chairman of the board, is named president.

1921 Pierre du Pont issues GM's first "Message to Shareholders."

1923 Alfred P. Sloan is elected president and chairman of the executive committee.

1924 Executives become stockholders under a plan allowing them to acquire stock through the Managers Securities Company.

1926 The first Pontiac car is introduced.

1927 The milestone Cadillac La Salle, the first production car designed by a stylist, the legendary Harley Earl, is introduced.

RECURRING PROFITS

Gillette

1958–1962

In most countries of the world, men in the mid-twentieth century had little choice but to shave, a ritual requiring a new blade every two or three days. To the biggest provider of razor blades in the world, Gillette, that meant money in the bank. Lots of it. Investors who put $10,000 in Gillette in January 1958 could cash out in January 1962 for $57,000, and that didn't even include the typical 8 percent dividend per year.

Few companies have dominated their markets the way Gillette has dominated the shaving market. High market share, high profit margins, and a thriving international business have kept Gillette at the top for generations. But the single best time to own Gillette shares was arguably from 1958 to 1962, during which time the company took valuable steps toward cementing the leadership that it retained throughout the twentieth century.

An Understatement

In 1960 the Gillette Safety Razor Co. had everything going for it. Beards were out and sales were up. Profits had been rolling in year in and year out almost since the company began in 1903; they were on the way to a record in 1960. Worker productivity was up, costs were down, world revenues were whistling, and the competition seemed resigned to handing over some of their market share.

But there was a problem. The company had a terrific new product: Super Blue Blade, which joined the company's standard Blue Blade, was coated with a polymer to make it slide across a shaver's face easily. Indeed, it was Gillette's best blade ever and was like nothing else—and therein was the problem. Gillette had in essence been crying wolf for decades, using all the "best" adjectives about whatever product happened to be on hand. (To be fair, so had practically every other company with an advertising budget.) "Superlatives have lost their impact," fretted Vincent Ziegler, then a division president at Gillette. "We ourselves have not been overly modest in advertising our Blue Blades. Now we had a radical improvement. What do we do?"

The solution lay in advertising so understated that it might have been making a public service announcement. "Gillette Announces—A Remarkable New Razor Blade" was the headline on one text-heavy magazine ad. The quiet approach, combined with the extensive distribution of samples, inspired men to start talking about razor blades. In essence, by word of mouth, it made men sell one another on the new Super Blues.

"Volume has topped our most optimistic predictions by more than fifty percent," Ziegler said in the midst of the campaign. Even if the company's overall market share didn't rise—say, if new Super Blue customers were just old true Blue customers who graduated to the better product—it was fine; the profit margin on the more expensive blades was higher than that on the former standard. But the market share did rise, with a Gillette blade for every type of face and every type of wallet. Blades were the core of the Gillette Company, where all other products accounted for only 35 percent of sales and an even smaller percentage of profits.

In a way, some of the other blade makers were glad to see that Gillette was moving forward aggressively. For about a decade, the "wet shave" industry of razors, blades, and shaving cream had been crowded by a threat from electric shavers. "We're just on the verge of a much larger total market," concluded a spokesman for Schick. He was even more right than he thought. The boost from the Super Blue blade was nothing compared to what was coming next.

Flea-Bite Competition

"King C. Gillette," wrote Upton Sinclair, "a large, stout man, corresponded exactly to the cartoonist's idea of a plutocrat; but within that bulky body was the tenderness of a woman and the timidity of a child. He could not bear the thought of others' suffering, and he shrank from the clash of opinion and the anger of the world." Sinclair knew King Camp Gillette as a neighbor in the 1920s, when the Razor King, as he was known, was living in semiretirement in Southern California.

Always bright and full of ideas, Gillette had been an ace salesman for a bottle-top company in the 1890s. At that time, his abiding goal was to invent something like bottle caps, a product that people used every day and then threw away.

In the nineteenth century, men shaved with straight razors, devices that opened from a handle like a jackknife. Keeping the blade sharp was practically a profession in itself. A long leather belt called a strop was all right for daily tune-ups, and the kitchen flint was serviceable in an emergency, but professional grinding was required from time to time, too. A good shave depended on the beard, the blade, the humidity—too many things to master perfectly every day. When the strain was too much, a man could always repair to a barbershop: a sweet luxury, but expensive on a daily basis.

One day in 1895, when King Gillette realized that he'd let his straight razor get dull, he paused and imagined what was to become the Gillette razor blade: a disposable wafer of steel, honed to a sharp edge, and held in a handle. "I have got it," Gillette wrote to his wife. "Our fortune is made." Destiny wasn't exactly immediate, because Gillette wasted six years talking to consultants and machinists who told him he was bound to fail. He finally found the right people, who believed in the idea. The Gillette Safety Razor went into production and on the market in 1903. It was a success almost from the first. As president, Gillette advertised heavily and expanded as quickly as possible to overseas countries. In 1910, though, tired of fighting for control with his primary investor, King sold his interest in the company.

The company faltered badly in the early 1930s, not so much because of the Depression but because of the discovery that the management had been committing fraudulent accounting practices since the 1920s. In 1938, Joseph Sprang began an eighteen-year tenure as president and resuscitated Gillette. Sprang improved both quality and cost control, but his biggest decision, made in 1939 and considered daring for the time, was to sponsor radio coverage of major sporting events. It was a turning point for Gillette and for the sports world. From 1938 to 1939, the advertising budget grew from 18 percent of U.S. sales to 27 percent, as the company found its way to customers through the World Series, college bowl games, boxing, and horse racing. Under Sprang, salesmanship was also revolutionized as Gillette reps were coached to understand that they were selling not a razor blade but a profit margin—the biggest of practically any product in a store.

In 1952, the president of Pal Blade, a competitor making low-cost blades, gave an apt and battle-weary description of Gillette in the postwar years. "No one ever does more than flea-bite the Gillette market," he said. "They won't let us go beyond what they regard as our limit . . . nowhere in the world is there anyone able to give them real competition."

The Sharp Edge of Business

The dominant position of Gillette in and of itself during the late 1950s did not necessarily make it a growth stock. Its direction, however, did. For a company in a new industry, every step is a marker of growth. Likewise, for a fresh competitor in an established industry, the potential for market share is everywhere. Gillette was an old hand in a mature industry and so the growth in the stock followed signs that it was finding new sources of profit.

As of 1958, Gillette had reported profits every year for more than fifty, with strong increases in net income (also known as earnings) during the prewar period. The dollar figures were important, but so were the percentages on which they were based. That is, a growth company can grow in three ways: it can either get bigger in the basic sense of revenues or it can become more effective in extracting profits from its operations . . . or it can do both. The operating profit margin is often stagnant at an older company. In the late 1950s, Gillette was increasing sales as well as its operating profit margin (which describes earnings as a percentage of assets invested in the business). Gillette was also increasing its earnings return (the amount per dollar of sales), a sign that it was not "buying" an increased market share at the cost of profits.

Since Gillette was forbidden by antitrust laws from selling electric shavers—a niche that peaked at $138 million in 1956 anyway—the company set its sights on retrieving that "lost" revenue. To do so, it was especially aggressive in promoting its wet shave to teenagers. That made sense, since the potential, globally, was advancing the wet shave over the old straight razor. And no one had a better position than Gillette, since it was the leading name in every country.

Gillette's product line has long been a flashpoint for investors. For instance, the health of the core blade business seems to indicate the baseline of the stock pricing, while the results of its other product lines point out how high it can go.

The company began diversifying in 1948, with the acquisition of Toni, the home permanent company, and it added Paper Mate pens in 1955. Toni was successful at first, returning its cost within four years, while Paper Mate only held its own. Both acquisitions had management troubles by 1958, at which point Gillette moved to install its own executives.

It worked. That year each of those units became a turnaround. In different ways, the initial acquisitions actually represented two fundamental characteristics of the razor blade: first, a home grooming supply, and second, a disposal item. Nearly all future Gillette products would fit neatly into one of the two categories.

Growth companies normally reinvest a large share of their earnings in expansion. This is especially true today, when enhancing share price appears to be more important to most directors than returning dividends. However, even for the late 1950s, when the reverse was true, Gillette paid quite a large dividend—75 percent of earnings. To put that in perspective with two other growth stocks of the late 1950s: Polaroid returned 11 percent of earnings to shareholders in 1958 and IBM 25 percent. And even with all the largesse for the shareholders, Gillette had no debt and a sizable cash reserve of $56 million. As long as the company had more than enough money with which to pursue acquisitions, the assumption was that it was growing as fast as its management wanted.

Before the Storm

"There is nothing better than a friendly third party pushing your product for you," division president Vincent Ziegler had said of Gillette's clever campaign to instigate talk about blades in the Super Blue campaign. The trouble with Gillette in 1962, though, was that it was not listening very closely to what product all those third parties had started to talk about.

By 1962, Super Blue Blades had propelled Gillette's market share to 72 percent. The stock price had nearly doubled in 1961 and many investors looked forward to more of the same. In its slow and careful way, the company was introducing new products, winners such as Right Guard deodorant (as well as laggards such as Sun Up tonic), but fully 98 percent of revenues continued to come from blades—carbon steel blades that were cheap to produce and easy to sell.

Too bad Gillette wasn't the only one to pick up on those economics. In the summer of 1961, Wilkinson Sword Ltd. of Chiswick, England, introduced shaving blades made of stainless steel. Wilkinson, owned by the same family for 189 years, had made a business of manufactured swords and bulletproof vests. And not a very big business at that: in 1954, the first year it made its annual report public, sales were $56,000. That tiny revenue number was short-lived, however. Later that decade, Wilkinson came up with a new product line: premium garden tools. It intended stainless steel razors to be a sideline. No matter—it was the stainless steel razors that Britons immediately embraced. They thought stainless gave a better shave and knew it lasted at least twice as long as carbon steel. Wilkinson's share of the overall British blade market grew from zero to 15 percent in less than a year.

When Wilkinson blades went on sale in the New York area later in the year, they became a sensation. Was it because of a big advertising budget? Hardly. Wilkinson spent zero money—dollars or pounds—to promote the product. Deluged with orders, the U.S. distributor begged for more of the stainless steel blades. In response, the home office set up a rather strange business model: U.S. retailers would receive two cartons of blades for every set of garden tools ordered. The fascination continued unabated. Men found their way to hardware and garden stores; it seemed they'd do anything for the Wilkinson blades. Some Americans even ordered them from stores in England. Of course, Wilkinson production eventually increased and distribution in the United States was extended into traditional outlets.

Wilkinson Sword had opened a breach in the fortress around Gillette's market share. Schick was among the companies that rushed headlong into it, with stainless steel blades of its own. Meanwhile, inside the double-edge fortress, Gillette was strangely quiet: brooding, in fact. Company executives considered the Super Blue to be superior, but they had to admit that customers were drawn to stainless steel. And despite the fact that Gillette's marketing acumen reflected a detailed understanding of every nuance of the shaving experience, there was one thing the company's executives never bargained for: buying blades from a sword company had an extra appeal. Using Wilkinson products seemed to connect men at their most mundane to men at their most adventurous.

Still, Wilkinson's total U.S. sales in 1962 added up to one day's production at Gillette. At first, Gillette company executives conceded only that they were embarrassed, not worried. However, the 18.5 percent dip in profits in 1963–1964 was more than a matter of a red face. As was the stock price droop of 50 percent. In 1964, when Gillette finally introduced its "Silver" stainless steel blades with great fanfare, the launch was a success. The product was well received and Gillette regained its place among the top five most profitable U.S. companies. Nonetheless, lasting damage had been done. Gillette's share of the blade market had been trimmed by 10 percent, falling from about 72 percent to a level 62 percent at the end of the 1960s. The stock took five years to recover to its 1962 level.)

No one could have foreseen that an antiquated English sword company would arise to compete head-on with mighty Gillette. However, shareholders enjoying the halcyon days of 1958 to 1962 knew that, as in any war epic, things are most dangerous when they are too quiet.

Epilogue

The years immediately following 1962 would never be woven into the Gillette highlights film, but there was no need to feel sorry for the company. Along Gillette's multiyear journey, there have been numerous product introductions in the tradition of Super Blue, notably the Good News disposable razor and Trac II. Regarding the latter, comedians noted that you can't sell a company short when it doubles razor blade sales by getting people to shave with two blades at once—an appealing, if not completely accurate, tribute to Gillette's marketing prowess.

The company's fundamental strengths and modest valuation made it a takeover candidate for a while in the 1980s, although the buyout effort was eventually rebuffed in 1988. Just as well. Gillette continued to enjoy the fruits of market leadership, and flourished as a growth stock and a defensive stock: men keep shaving whether or not there's a recession. If that combination sounds a bit like a description of Coca-Cola, discussed in chapter 7, perhaps it should. Both Coca-Cola and Gillette are longtime core holdings in Warren Buffett's Berkshire Hathaway portfolio, known for favoring the safety razors of the stock world: sharp, but well-protected.

Lessons

*A **bigger slice** . . . In the late 1950s, Gillette was increasing its operating profit margin, not merely its overall sales. That's a key fringe benefit of being the industry leader.*

Being nimble . . . *When Gillette realized that customers weren't paying attention to its superlative marketing campaign, it was quickly able to change its strategy.*

Just one basket? . . . *Since Gillette was dependent on one product for the bulk of profits, it was pretty vulnerable to changes in the marketplace.*

Never underestimate the competition . . . *No matter how goofy they may seem. (An English sword company selling razors in gardening stores?!)*

TIMELINE

1903 Gillette Safety razor goes into production.

1910 Founder King Gillette sells out his interest in the company.

1960 Gillette announces Super Blue.

1938 Joseph Sprang takes post of president.

1948 Acquires Toni.

1955 Acquires Paper Mate pens.

1964 Introduces "Silver" stainless steel blades.

FIVE
BROADENING THE PRODUCT

GLEAMING PRODUCT DEVELOPMENT: REYNOLDS METALS (1950–1959)

SELLING BRAVADO: ORACLE CORPORATION (1992–2000)

Arm & Hammer didn't originally intend for its boxes of baking soda to be placed in people's refrigerators, but whoever came up with that idea surely got a big raise. Once a company has patented, produced, and distributed a particular product line, broadening the range of that product is surely a whole lot easier than starting another line from scratch.

Within this book we talk about companies such as Xerox and Polaroid, whose brilliant inventions created the new markets of photocopying and instant photography (see chapter 2). We also identify in our top 25 America Online and Home Depot, companies that were able to expand their underlying markets of the Internet and home improvement (chapter 9). We don't mean to split hairs, but broadening the product is a third category that deserves recognition. And we're not talking about razor blade companies persuading men to shave with two blades at once (as impressive as that was). We're talking about real innovation.

The reason this broadening category is so important relates to a theme we have seen before. It is all too easy for investors to place stocks in a mental box: fast-grower, slow-grower, and so forth. But what happens when a company finds new applications for something it already makes? If you've already put the company into your slow-growth box, you won't see the possibilities, and you'll miss out.

Two stocks made our top 25 list by broadening their products' reach, and they did it in very different ways. Reynolds Metals made market history by making aluminum foil part of the rush to suburbia of the 1950s. Many years later, Oracle did Reynolds several times better when its internal know-how found application in none other than the Internet. Along the way, both stocks even surpassed consumer company Church & Dwight, which once had an impressive market run of its own: it made Arm & Hammer baking soda!

GLEAMING PRODUCT DEVELOPMENT

Reynolds Metals

1950–1959

Before World War II, Reynolds Metals carved out a minor success for itself making the kind of product that people use every day yet never fully appreciate: foil wrappers for cigarettes, chocolate bars, and the like. Yet it was exactly these oft-overlooked products that offered Reynolds a practically perfect launch pad into the realm of very big business, one in which its stock made itself at home as one of the highfliers of the 1950s.

You live by the sword, you die by the sword. When a company piles on debt to take advantage of market opportunities, investors must decide whether the short-term benefits of the extra debt load are worth the longer-term burden. Sometimes the result is a split decision: a giddy stock market run when earnings gains mask the debt, and a hasty retreat when they don't.

Reynolds Metals was a great stock in its day because the company expanded its core franchise beyond its wildest expectations. The only wrinkle was the debt required to make these gains possible; slowly, insidiously, the heavy debt load sapped the company's strength. But the stock's "day" lasted longer than a decade, during which time its share price rose 2,000 percent.

Polishing Up for a Bright Future

In the decade after its official founding in 1928, Reynolds didn't actually produce any aluminum but just used aluminum in a variety of products. It relied on the Aluminum Company of America (Alcoa), which turned out all of the aluminum made in the United States, for the raw material. Alcoa set reasonable prices and normally made the job of procuring the metal as easy as turning a spigot. So at that time other companies in the aluminum business figured "Why bother?" since the process of refining the shiny metal was so demanding and, actually, unnecessary.

However, when the Great Depression lifted at the end of the 1930s, Reynolds was able to get only about half of the raw aluminum it needed to meet consumer demands. To a company like Reynolds, it didn't really matter that Alcoa was fair in its allocations—Reynolds needed metal. Period. Lest the United States find itself running short of candy wrappers, in 1938 the president, founder Richard S. Reynolds, went to Europe hunting around for new sources of aluminum.

What Richard Reynolds found out was nothing like what he expected. When he asked Germany for aluminum, the country could not spare even a pound because its capacity was turned over to military preparations, including aircraft production for the burgeoning Luftwaffe. France, interesting to note, had quite a different reaction to his inquiry. That country blithely contracted to ship Reynolds all the aluminum he wanted—15 million pounds' worth, in fact. That France, in such stark contrast to Germany, had no program for the production of war material set off alarm bells in Richard Reynolds's mind. If the other European nations were not ready, the United States would inevitably be drawn into the war.

As soon as he returned home, Reynolds paid a visit to the chairman of Alcoa. He implored him to increase production in the very likely event that the United States would need vast amounts of aluminum for warplanes of its own. However, neither Alcoa nor any of the government officials to whom Reynolds spoke shared his sense of imperative. Or, for that matter, his opinion that the capacity of Alcoa (and therefore that of the United States) should be increased by more than double. The aluminum establishment may have been correct that there was plenty of aluminum for civilian aviation and defense, but Reynolds wasn't just talking about defense. He all too correctly foresaw all-out war.

So, Reynolds took the bull by the horns and did something that no other American company, except Alcoa, had ever done. He set up refining facilities of his own, mortgaging all eighteen of his standing factories to pay for them, and competed with Alcoa head-on in the production of aluminum. After the attack on Pearl Harbor in December 1941, Reynolds's prediction that aluminum was indeed in dangerously short supply came all too true. And by that point aluminum was needed for more than just candy wrapping: it was called for in the manufacture of warplanes.

Richard Reynolds, however, didn't have much time to gloat. For one thing, he and his company were busy producing as much raw aluminum as possible, in addition to an array of aircraft parts. Nonetheless, the giant Alcoa's contribution was even more impressive: once the United States entered the war, it made a magnificent job of quickly building up new factories.

Opportunity Knocks

Alcoa's dominance was about to receive a shock. In 1945, just as the war was ending, the company received news that would change its course of business. Judge Learned Hand, of the U.S. Court of Appeals for the Second Circuit, acting in place of the Supreme Court, handed down a long-awaited decision about Alcoa. (The Supreme Court had failed to establish a quorum after four justices excused themselves on the basis of previous association with cases involving Alcoa; it had turned the case over to the Second Circuit Court.) According to the decision written by Judge Hand, Alcoa was guilty of violating the Sherman Antitrust Act, despite the fact that it had done nothing *overtly* wrong. The decision was the most influential of any affecting large-scale business in the postwar era, holding that bigness itself was enough to make a corporation anticompetitive.

With the antitrust law, Hand wrote, Congress "did not condone 'good trusts' and condemn 'bad' ones; it forbade all." Continued Judge Hand: "It is possible to prefer a system of small producers, each dependent for his success upon his own skill and character, to one in which the great mass of those engaged must accept the direction of the few."

One of the troubling aspects of dealing with the Alcoa monopoly was the fear of hobbling aluminum production—cracking that wonderful tap Alcoa had created. However, none of the government officials involved in the case really wanted to break up Alcoa. Instead of that dire alternative, Alcoa was simply to be held in check as others had the chance to grow. As part of that penalty, Alcoa would not be allowed to own any of the factories it had planned, built, and operated for the government during the war. It was a bitter hardship, since Alcoa had created the new plants to be the jewels of the industry.

One of the two companies that offered to take them off Alcoa's hands by leasing them was Reynolds Metals (the other was Kaiser Aluminum). Overnight the monopoly turned into an oligarchy—or a "tri-opoly," as one Wall Street wit put it. Not until more than a decade later, that is, the late 1950s, would any other companies join the ranks of fully integrated aluminum production in the United States.

The Very Good Years

"We never took a pound of business away from Alcoa," boasted one of Richard Reynolds's sons in 1956. "We've generated far more business for the entire aluminum industry than we ever got ourselves." Indeed, the company did more than any other to increase the use of aluminum in the postwar years, introducing aluminum to roofing and siding, small boats, furniture, architecture, toys, agriculture, and even sculpture. However, it never neglected its first love, sheet aluminum, becoming a household name when aluminum foil became a kitchen staple starting in the early 1950s. Reynolds Metals, which had precipitated the massive change in the aluminum industry, stood ready to benefit most from it.

With the company constantly interested in expanding the uses of aluminum, it was not enough just to lecture manufacturers that aluminum could improve on most other metals. Reynolds soon found that it had to show them.

The company developed a strategy—termed "opportunistic" by competitors—of creating the machinery to fabricate parts never previously made with aluminum and then lending it at no charge to potential customers. After the customer recognized the viability of aluminum firsthand, the machinery would be sold or leased at a nominal cost. In other cases, Reynolds took the initiative to make finished products of aluminum; however, it rarely remained in the business after other manufacturers took the bait and switched over to using aluminum for those products themselves. "Opportunistic" may have been intended as an insult in some circles, but for the shareholders, it was a sure compliment for a company trying to push out and grow.

On Wall Street, Reynolds Metals was soon seen as the fastest-growing company in an accelerating industry. Sales for 1948 were $114 million. By 1959, they were $489 million, reflecting a growth rate of just over 14 percent per year, on average. The stock price reflected the gleam on Reynolds aluminum, rising on a split-adjusted basis from 3.50 to 80 between 1950 and 1959. A $10,000 investment in 1948 would have been transformed into $228,571 in 1959, outpacing even the other aluminum stocks by a healthy 20 percent.

Shiny Past

When Richard Reynolds entered the business world in 1903, aluminum was little known, as it was just emerging from a long period when it was highly expensive to produce. Reynolds joined his famous uncle R. J. Reynolds in the tobacco business in Richmond, Virginia. A resourceful young man, Richard concocted a blend of Kentucky and Virginia tobaccos to come up with the "Camel" cigarette, a product that became the company's top seller. "Uncle Dick" was delighted with Richard, but the reverse did hold true after R. J. Reynolds, long a bachelor, took a wife and started having children. Not that Richard was against families. He and his wife, Julia, had already started their own brood, but he recognized that a mere nephew could not inherit a business as long as little sons and daughters were on the scene. So, instead of sitting around sulking, he decided in 1912 to start another business.

He began his new venture on familiar terms, starting with an offshoot of his old line of work, cigarettes. What he created was a business to sell tin and lead wrappers to cigarette companies. Called the U.S. Foil Company, it was a precursor to Reynolds Metals. In 1926, aluminum was substituted and Richard Reynolds could think of little else but the metal for the rest of his life.

In retrospect, it may be hard to discern the risk—aluminum has since become the most important of the nonferrous metals. However, at the time the prevailing wisdom in metals was that the peacetime aluminum industry would be quite weak because of the excess capacity created in wartime. Reynolds, in his single-minded way, rejuvenated the industry. After World War II, his company went on an expansion spree, projecting itself into a limitless future for aluminum.

In 1948, Richard Reynolds did exactly what he was once afraid his uncle would do: turn his business over to his children. Reynolds Metals may have been a publicly held company, but the family held a majority stake and so, as chairman, Richard was at liberty to name his successor. In 1948, he named Richard Reynolds Jr. The oldest, at forty, of the four Reynolds sons, he was well educated and experienced in Wall Street ways, having operated a brokerage before joining the metals company. "We set ourselves to grow twice as fast as the economy," Richard Jr. said later, looking back on his first dozen years as president.

The Wrap

Now for the pièce de résistance. As the 1950s began, Reynolds Metals was just becoming well known thanks to its Reynolds Wrap foil for the home market. Some even felt that in marketing the foil the company had an ulterior motive: trying to up the visibility of aluminum as a metal. Many investors already knew of the company, either because they followed aluminum as a commodity or as a result of the famous 1945 verdict against Alcoa. But now the company was in the public eye, with a brand-new audience. What this audience found was a company intent on growth, and supremely optimistic about the future.

Unlike many family-controlled companies, which shear off big dividends in order to support private ventures (not to mention the occasional French château), Reynolds Metals reinvested 85 percent of its profits. In the 1950s, dividends at other companies more typically ran to half of earnings. Investors could look to the low dividend of Reynolds as one indication of the priority of the management: no shareholder was more aggressive than the Reynolds family in their expectation of appreciating a share price.

In addition to the new president, Richard Jr., three other Reynolds sons held executive posts. In the case of Reynolds, the four sons were well matched to their various duties and utterly committed to the overall goal. Louis was the executive vice president in charge of operations, including overseas business. William developed new products in the company's fabricating plant in Louisville, Kentucky. The youngest and most outgoing, David, was the merchandising and sales vice president. The brothers formed a flying wedge that made things happen just a bit more quickly at Reynolds than at other companies. "It can be described," a 1953 *Forbes* article suggested, "simply as a hereditary reluctance to stop growing."

One worrisome by-product of this growth was the debt. In 1950, Reynolds carried a large debt load because of its purchase of the former government/Alcoa facilities the year before. The liability concerned some investors, who called for the company to issue more stock in order to reduce its dependence on the banks. Others, though, were delighted with the way that Reynolds protected the value of its stock by refusing to flood the market with more shares. Hefty debt, however, would be a characteristic of Reynolds for decades as the company expanded its facilities around the world.

In terms of competition, Alcoa was still the behemoth of the industry, but in the aftermath of the 1945 Hand decision, the company was closely supervised by the government. Alcoa executives reported that the surveillance was hardly necessary. Alcoa company management was stilted and almost tremulous, backing away from any activity that might be deemed aggressive, let alone monopolistic. Though Kaiser Aluminum, the only other U.S. producer, was growing fast, it was no real competition for Reynolds. Kaiser's growth was in a more predictable way, certainly missing the marketing moxie of Reynolds.

The Age of Aluminum

Who would have thought that one farmer on the island of Jamaica could change the course of a company based in Virginia? One day, this farmer in question, frustrated that his land would not support grasses very well, sent a soil sample to England for analysis. The response was: "Forget grass, grow aluminum." Turns out that his farm was lying on the largest deposit then known of bauxite, the claylike soil that contains aluminum. So, in 1950, Reynolds Metals snatched up the tract for $11 million.

Until then, Reynolds owned only one source for bauxite, depending on Alcoa for the rest of its raw materials. By becoming a fully integrated producer, Reynolds was moving toward lowering costs. In a commodity market in which it had no choice but to meet the industry-wide price, Reynolds was constantly chasing Alcoa, which had by far the lowest costs of any of America's aluminum producers.

For those who bought stock in Reynolds Metals in 1950, the first concern was the market disruption caused by the Korean War. Reynolds navigated the potential pitfalls deftly and emerged in 1953 stronger than ever. Even as the expansion of production facilities had led to a 25 percent increase in capacity at the company each year in the early 1950s, demand in the civilian market surged after the hostilities. Reynolds Metals' hell-bent rush for greater sales translated into increased profits, which jumped by 77 percent in 1955. The whole industry was booming, with 1955 production double that of 1950.

Reynolds Metals stock outpaced that of the rest of the industry, tripling in 1955, a year that included a five-for-one split. With investors continually nervous about oversupply—despite Reynolds's assurances that it would always find a way to sell all the aluminum it could produce—the stock price closely followed earnings reports. When they dimmed a bit in 1957, the stock did, too, but it spiked up again on rebounding earnings in 1959. The high for that year, just over 80, turned out to be its all-time high.

Epilogue

Earnings after 1960 were unpredictable, as overcapacity finally caught the Reynolds tiger by the tail. An unyielding level of debt ultimately reduced Reynolds's flexibility and so, too, its control over its own destiny. When that occurred, investors lost interest in the stock. Through the 1960s, demand increased, but the industry-wide price remained low. By the 1980s the Reynolds brothers were mostly retired and the company drifted.

In the year 2000, Alcoa shocked the business world, suddenly announcing a deal to buy Reynolds Metals. Like the patient gray-beard that it was, Alcoa had in the end outlasted the bursting energy of the gadfly. By the time the sale was completed in 2001, global competition had long since eroded old fears of domestic monopolies. Even if future history books treat Reynolds as a footnote to the Alcoa dynasty, in its own Aluminum Age of the 1950s Reynolds recast the industry itself and gave it a shine in which investors could see the future.

Lessons

Spread the word . . . *Reynolds would stop at nothing to evangelize about aluminum. This cheerleading upped revenues and helped this growth stock to keep growing.*

Lots of products . . . *Reynolds was inventive. This company proved that there was more to aluminum than just foil.*

Just say N.O. to the I.O.U. . . . *Eventually all of Reynolds debt caught up with it and hurt the company. Watch out for companies with too much debt.*

TIMELINE

1928 Reynolds Metals founded.

1945 U.S. Court of Appeals decision in *United States v. Aluminum Co. of America* boosts competition in aluminum industry.

1948 Sales of $114 million. Richard Reynolds Jr. becomes president.

1950 Purchases bauxite deposit in Jamaica, assuming full-scale production of aluminum.

1955 Profits increase by 70 percent.

1959 Sales of $489 million.

SELLING BRAVADO

Oracle Corporation

1992–2000

For individuals or corporations, early success holds unexpected dangers. For one, it can hide serious flaws. In the case of Oracle Corporation, galloping growth in the 1980s was wasted because the company didn't seem to understand that sales had to result in revenues, and revenues had to result in profits. At Oracle that equation (commonly known as corporate accounting) had to be created practically from scratch fully five years after the company went public. Investors who studied the company in transition, however, and gave it another chance were rewarded with a ride on one of the top 5 stock picks of the 1990s.

The Internet boom of the 1990s made market stars out of stocks such as Amazon.com, Priceline.com, AskJeeves.com, and dozens more. Market capitalizations of tens of billions of dollars became routine for companies that by definition hadn't even existed just a few years before. But some of the biggest winners were companies that had already made their imprint. As with the Alaska Gold Rush a century before, the suppliers of the Internet's picks and shovels made out better than anyone.

Microsoft and Cisco were among the most prominent pick and shovel makers, of course. But a less-told tale is that of Larry Ellison and Oracle, a company that starred in the 1980s, foundered, regrouped, and emerged as the leader in the red-hot client-server market. Here are both halves of the Oracle story.

Does "Excitement" Have a Ticker?

With perfect timing, Oracle Corporation made its initial public offering of stock in 1986, a vintage year that also welcomed Sun Microsystems and Microsoft on Wall Street. Investors had forgotten the pounding of 1982–1983, when a flood of computer-related IPOs rushed to the market, most representing companies that had yet to make their first profit. Fortunes made overnight on many of those flimsy IPOs were lost at the end of 1983 as reality knocked down prices on all computer stocks—especially those companies that were better at selling stock than computer components. By the time Oracle arrived with the class of 1986, though, nearly all of the stock market chaos of 1983 was a faint memory. High-tech IPOs were back in favor, but they came in on a different horse. "In general," wrote a computer-industry analyst at *PC Week,* "the initial public offerings this year have been from companies that are more mature, financially stable, and predictable."

Sales at Oracle, which produced business software, were certainly predictable—doubling every year but one since the software company started in 1978. That pace naturally caught the attention of Wall Street, and Oracle stock became a favorite, consistently rising from its IPO price of $15. In October 1987, the company brashly announced the second stock split in its one-and-a-half-year history. The split wasn't exactly necessary. The stock was only trading at about $28 per share, but Oracle was sending a signal to the market. "We are anticipating a very significant reaction to our upcoming product releases," a spokesman explained, adding that Oracle wanted "to make sure the company and its financial supporters" had the preparation and ability to benefit.

The move was typical of Oracle at the time—if excitement itself was a type of stock, Oracle found ways to split it, too. And in 1987 investors bought anything Oracle was selling. One analyst explained that although the premature stock split might be unusual for a typical company, it wasn't for Oracle. As William Shattuck of Montgomery Securities in San Francisco keenly observed in 1987, Oracle had a proven ability to "perform beyond expectations."

The reasons behind Oracle's overachievement began to become obvious to investors in 1988. Three questions commonly cropped up in the wild dash of the software industry in the late 1980s: could the company supply the product, would the product work, and would the customer pay? And all three were happening at Oracle, but were hidden behind its dazzling sales figures.

By 1990, Oracle was closing in on sales of $1 billion, up from $2.5 million in only eight years. Value Line, the investor's research service, predicted that earnings would increase that year by 39 percent. But alas, Value Line was wrong. Earnings climbed, sure, but by all of 1 percent.

If a drop in sales had caused the drop in earnings, investors might have understood. However, Oracle reported record sales. Something basic in the company was wrong. Oracle, which made its reputation helping other companies run their businesses, couldn't run its own.

House of Cards, Er, Disks

Trading at about $28 in March 1990, the stock was at $6.25 in November. According to rumors said to come from the boardroom, bankruptcy was a close possibility. To add fuel to the fire sale, word spread that the chief financial officer had sold half of his Oracle holdings just before the drop, when the company was still stoking grandiose forecasts. Stockholder lawsuits were filed. A cartoon in *Business Week* at the end of the year portrayed Oracle as a toppling house of cards made out of floppy disks.

Oracle was undoubtedly weak in parts, but it was still a strong company, positioned at the front of the growing industry. Investors who watched it revamp over the following two years and were savvy enough to purchase the stock in 1992 were rewarded with a fairly nice return. Over the following eight years, $10,000 in Oracle stock increased to a holding worth $900,000.

All About Larry

A trio of California programmers, émigrés from early high-tech leaders Ampex and Memorex, started Oracle Corporation in 1977. The new partners were smart and well connected, but they didn't really have any core concept to harness their talent. Fortunately, they were also well read and became familiar with a concept known as the relational database, first suggested in 1970 and developed at IBM. The relational database would be their workhorse.

While American business was already using computers in the 1970s to store copious records, information could only be retrieved in a rudimentary way. The new concept assigned characteristics to each piece of information and divined relationships between them. The relational database, as it was called, allowed users to ask pertinent, even complex questions and receive quick answers from among millions of pieces of information. The concept was promising, but IBM did not pursue it immediately; as in many such cases, the company was fearful of legal action if it seemed to dominate too much of the computer industry. And so the relational database was left out in the open. The new team at Oracle was one of several new firms to pick it up and run with it— Oracle being even faster than others. It made a working version within a year. And not surprisingly, it had presold a couple of copies long before that.

Two of the three original partners remained through Oracle's first twenty years. Bob Miner was the production man, overseeing the programmers who actually created software, the company's only product. Larry Ellison was the president, driving the company into the business marketplace just the way he drove his beloved sports cars: as fast as possible. Miner and Ellison didn't have much in common except the company they built, but they got along and both became billionaires many times over. Miner became a billionaire because he didn't care about money and quietly held on to his original stake while living the same middle-class lifestyle he'd always known; Ellison became one because he cared very much about being rich, richer, richest. In business matters, Miner deferred to Larry Ellison.

Ellison's was the personality behind Oracle. Like the company he helmed, he was hard to ignore, with his entertaining way of exaggerating the truth, his adventurous lifestyle, and his showman's mixture of humor and cynicism. Under Ellison, Oracle was anything but a boring company. He created the wind-whipped sense of velocity that became a part of its aura. Within the business, Ellison's guiding goal was increasing market share, an effort that succeeded in making Oracle the top-ranking name in relational database software.

Sometimes Shimmering, Sometimes Shoddy

Larry Ellison, the dominant force in the company, was essentially interested in biting off market share. George Schussel, an industry insider, watched as Oracle took the lead over others—including IBM, which eventually brought out its own version of the database software. "Oracle was in the right place at the right time, with a person, Larry, who put marketing first and everything else second. Average technology and good marketing beat good technology and average marketing every day."

Oracle set and attained an annual growth rate goal of 50 percent in the late 1980s, but lost control of itself in the process. Products were often "sold," in Oracle's loose definition of the term, even before they were finished. Worse, they were sometimes shipped even before they were ready, giving Oracle's software an uneven reputation: sometimes shimmering, sometimes shoddy.

The push for sales dominated the corporate ethic at Oracle, then located in a modern office park in Redwood City, south of San Francisco. Sales *was* the ethic. Some reps took advantage of the frenzy, doing anything to get a signature on a sales contract, even to the point of writing a "side letter" to the customer, unbeknownst to the company, altering the terms of the contract. Unscrupulous sales reps were even known to create false companies, which duly placed orders that went on the company books. Why not?—commissions were paid on orders, often long before products were shipped or money changed hands. With drastic quotas and rich incentives, the reps had every reason to be frantically greedy. They were not only pushed from behind by drastic quotas, but also pulled from the front with the promise of riches. For a while in 1989, Oracle paid its sales staff in real gold coins, a move that only accentuated the fever in the air.

When the company did establish new controls in 1988, it was still acting in the delirium of its fever, mistakenly shifting responsibility for financial accountability and auditing to the sales department. The tigers were given the keys to their own cages.

The company kept racking up sales, but customers, analysts, and even employees were wondering what was really going on inside the Oracle juggernaut. A fall was inevitable, and in 1990 it occurred. In March of that year, the company reported a 54 percent quarterly increase in sales—and a 1 percent rise in earnings. The stock dropped by almost a third in price on the day of the announcement and continued to slide all year. "We had to get hit upside the head with a two-by-four," said Larry Ellison at the time.

In Control

Oracle had to go back to basics. Without putting fundamental corporate systems in place, Oracle remained tainted, and many investors in 1990 steered clear of it. By 1992, however, there were signs that Oracle had transformed itself without losing any of its remarkable momentum, like an executive changing from sweats to business clothes at a dead run.

Larry Ellison himself survived the crisis of 1990 with the usual excuse: he hadn't really known what was going on. Since he owned about one-quarter of Oracle's stock, no one called—very loudly, that is—for his head. However, in 1992, having accomplished as much of a reorganization as he could in-house, Ellison recruited a team of executives unlike any ever seen at Oracle before: people with firm experience in business. Grown-ups, not wunderkinds. Raymond Lane, a consultant with a Texas consulting firm, took over as president; James Abrahamson, who formerly supervised the Space Shuttle program at NASA, became chairman of the board; and Jeffrey Henley, a CFO with a highly regarded investment group in California, became Oracle's CFO. Bob Miner continued in his capacity as the head of programming. Although Ellison had long professed disdain for the bean-counting mentality, he recognized that until accounting expertise imbued the company, Oracle would never be anything but an overgrown start-up.

In April of 1992, Oracle announced that it was taking a charge—a special adjustment to its books—subtracting $50 million in sales. A special charge is nearly always worth examining, as it usually indicates some shift in company outlook. For Oracle, the charge reflected new accounting standards, which would not allow sales to enter the books until the product had been shipped to the customer. Most of the $50 million would show up again eventually, but the special charge heralded a significant refinement in Oracle's financial reporting.

In the early 1990s, Oracle's products were part of a general trend toward increased worker productivity. If it seems as though the company had already been through a lot, that's exactly right. But the most important chapter was only beginning.

By 1992, Oracle was ready to enter the client-server market, which would be the basis of the "information superhighway," although that term was still unfamiliar. An investor who bought one hundred shares of Oracle at the time said, "It may be my chance to get in on the ground floor of what could be the hottest information services stock of the 1990s." Since the Internet was nothing but one enormous, gaping database, Oracle software became essential as it developed, creating search engines, online catalogues, and streaming media, among other popular features. Oracle wasn't founded on these hopes, but it was perfectly positioned to broaden its own market.

Riding the Internet Up (and Down)

Oracle Corporation stock had a buoyant ride through the rest of the 1990s, rising from a split-adjusted 45 cents to $50 in March of 2000. By then the company was ensconced as the second-biggest software company in the world. The biggest, of course, was Microsoft, on which Larry Ellison had pinned his sights for years. In April 2000, Ellison had the distinct satisfaction of becoming, at least temporarily, the richest man in the country, as his $52.1 billion stake in Oracle passed the $51.5 billion in Microsoft stock held by his rival Bill Gates. "People keep saying IBM is the present and Microsoft is the future," Ellison complained in 1993. "That's wrong. IBM is the past and Microsoft is the present." (One guess as to which company Mr. Ellison thought owned the future. . . .)

In the late 1990s, Ellison made good on his bravado, using the new potential of the Internet to realign his company as a full-service business provider. Oracle didn't just run a database; it could run a whole company. The company was uniquely positioned to cater to the bumper crop of dot-com companies that emerged in 1997–1999, as well as internal or business-to-business uses of the Internet. While the Internet surged, so did Oracle, rising from a split-adjusted 10 to 50 in only five months over the winter of 1999–2000.

Epilogue

By 2000 then, a very good decade was over for Oracle. In general terms, the company's stake in the Internet became a liability, as Internet euphoria passed and a stern reassessment of the profitability of the Web began. Industry momentum was in reverse during late 2000 and Oracle couldn't fight it. The stock dropped to $14 in early 2001. More specifically, investors worried as Larry Ellison pushed Ray Lane out of the presidency in February 2000, without an immediate replacement. With no transition plan in place, Oracle's management reverted to an old reality in early 2000; as a longtime observer said, "Oracle and Ellison are essentially the same." Investors could take heart, though, in that both were proven survivors.

Lessons

Here's a clue . . . *Oracle's 1990 accounting disaster made it a good bargain for investors. "A special charge" is a little tip-off about big trouble.*

Lots of momentum . . . *Oracle was a company with the excitement (and market potential) of the Internet trend behind it. When the bubble burst, Oracle sank, but as a pick and shovel provider, its decline was less than that of the dot-coms.*

With a larger-than-life CEO . . . *You better really like him. As with Oracle, he often is the company.*

TIMELINE

1977 Oracle Corporation founded.

1982 Sales of $2.5 million.

1986 IPO at $15 a share.

1990 Sales of $1 billion.

1990 54 percent quarterly increase in sales with 1 percent rise in earnings.

1992 New team of executives in place.

1992 $50 million adjustment in the books.

1997 Moves client-server applications to the Web.

1998 Launches Business Online, the first hosting service for enterprise applications designed to be run over the Web.

2000 Launches e-Business Network and Oracle Mobile, a wireless applications service provider.

SIX
ACQUIRING NEW TASTES: THE URGE TO MERGE

THE GUIDED MISSILE: LING-TEMCO-VOUGHT (1966–1967)

WARREN BUFFETT'S INSPIRATION: TELEDYNE (1975–1986)

THE LOVE INTEREST: PARAMOUNT COMMUNICATIONS (1991–1994)

The mergers and acquisitions game has been around for as long as there have been markets. It is axiomatic that acquisitions create wealth, but how do you make sure that you're the one who's getting wealthy?

We'll soon find out that the answer to that question depends on when it is being asked. The last half of the twentieth century treated investors to an accordion file of corporate whims, where one decade's acquisition sprees led to the next decade's yard sales. Throughout this time, the key to investment success was to remain flexible. Those who understood the cyclicality of the mergers and acquisitions game stood to reap enormous profits.

The 1980s will go down in history as the decade of the corporate takeover. Stock prices began the decade at depressed levels. New methods of financing became available, and so-called leveraged buyouts enabled acquisitions to be paid for after the fact. Individuals, whether in the form of activist shareholders or corporate raiders, had influence like never before. Companies were left with the choice of creating shareholder value or having someone else do it for them. Identifying takeover candidates became almost a parlor game for investors.

That era is history. The takeover wave of the 1980s eventually crashed in a sea of debt, perhaps never to return. Nowadays, takeover candidates are identified by their strategic value to a potential acquirer, not by their financial vulnerability alone. But knowing how acquisitions work remains an important part of an investor's arsenal.

In this chapter we'll encounter three conglomerates: L-T-V, Teledyne, and Paramount Communications. Each of these companies was deeply involved in acquisitions, but at different times and in completely different ways. Together they show that an investor can make money by backing either the suitor or the target; you just have to know when. This piece of condensed market history should provide some important tips.

THE GUIDED MISSILE

Ling-Temco-Vought

1966–1967

L-T-V was a swinging stock in 1967, when earnings grew by a whopping 68 percent. An early conglomerate, it grew by acquisition, leveraging a mixture of debt and stock into a formula for buying companies much bigger than itself. Investors may not have completely understood L-T-V's business strategy, but they certainly gave its stock one heck of a memorable season.

Ever since there have been markets, there have been manias. Tulip bulbs in Holland, gold nuggets in Alaska, land in the South Seas: the names may change, but the pattern of boom and bust remains the same. History ends up laughing at such faddish excesses, but when you're in the middle of the action, it's tough to separate hype from reality.

In the late 1960s, the stock market experienced a brand-new type of mania in the form of corporate acquisitions. Companies discovered they could grow their earnings by acquiring companies with lower price-to-earnings ratios, even if there was no business fit. L-T-V, whose very name combined three disparate companies, was at the epicenter of the conglomerate push. The stock is an exception within our list, because its meteoric rise presaged an equally spectacular fall. But even though its fame was fleeting, L-T-V was emblematic of the go-go markets of the late 1960s, a unique era that deserves recognition.

An Unusual Company

Anyone wandering around the Texas State Fair in 1955 could have come away with all the usual souvenirs—Kewpie doll, bad case of indigestion, pocketful of ride stubs—*and* a prospectus for a new stock issue from Ling Electric of Dallas. It was an unusual offering, although IPOs in electronics companies were all the rage in the mid-1950s. As one observer put it, "A pig farmer could rename his farm Hogotronics, Inc., and have a public offering." However, at first no one in the local investment community showed this Dallas electrical contracting company much interest. Perhaps it was the firm's relatively low revenue of $1.5 million. Perhaps it was that, among new offerings, electronics was in, but electricity was not. For one reason or another, Ling Electric had to launch its offering without an underwriter.

Jimmy Ling came up with the idea to sell shares directly to the people. A great gathering place to do this? The state fair. Ling took a booth there and sold shares his own way. Not content with merely selling them over-the-counter, he sold them—at $2.25 apiece—over a folding table.

A decade later, Jimmy Ling was widely hailed as a genius. He was presiding over Ling-Temco-Vought, the $1.3 billion electronics giant he'd created out of his old electrical contracting firm. Ling's complex methodologies stretched the bounds of equity finance, but at the core they were dependent on the value of L-T-V stock. For other companies, a healthy share price is a boon; for Ling, it was an essential part of his formula. Fortunately, a chart of L-T-V's stock price looked like the trajectory of one of the missiles the company's aerospace subsidiary was building. In the ten months starting in December 1966, the celebrated stock soared from a split-adjusted $25 all the way to $169, turning $10,000 into $67,000. It's not surprising, then, that as far as some investors were concerned, stock was L-T-V's only real product.

Wall Street Alchemy

L-T-V did not grow because of any inventions on Ling's part. He was not involved with the production side of his company, where, among other things, engineers created electronics systems for NASA. Rather, Jimmy Ling created L-T-V through acquisitions, masterminded through the new techniques derived from some of Wall Street's oldest tools of finance. His philosophies were sometimes easy to explain, but they were invariably complicated to implement. Perhaps he had learned the essence of high finance by laying out wiring diagrams. In both practices, after all, the job is to route a flow, whatever the obstacles, and make it continuous, no matter what.

L-T-V jumped in status from a local firm to a company headed toward $2 billion in sales and became synonymous with the go-go climate of the 1960s. The company's fame grew along with everything else about it, not least of which was its stock price. Investors were hearing that L-T-V had found the recipe for a kind of Wall Street alchemy: a small company that found the way to acquire much bigger ones. The term *leverage* came into vogue with Jimmy Ling's short but dazzling reign. Another word on everybody's lips was *conglomerate*.

By 1967, L-T-V controlled thirty-three subsidiaries involved with eighty different lines of business. Among other things, L-T-V Aerospace was responsible for creating one of the U.S. Navy's most ingenious aircraft, the A-7A attack plane, used on aircraft carriers in Vietnam. What mattered to Ling, however, was not what the potential acquisition produced, but just that it was well managed, had a bright future, and, most important, was available.

After great financial fisticuffs ensued when Ling-Temco acquired a defense company called Chance Vought, Jimmy Ling never again attempted a hostile takeover. If the executives of a company refused L-T-V's advances, the deal was dropped without another word. The result was a remarkably amicable sort of a conglomerate, in which the component companies were accorded, in most cases, even more autonomy than they'd had before being acquired. Indeed, once Ling added the firms to his roster, he oversaw them from his small headquarters in Dallas, leaving specific management decisions to those on the scene.

Under Suspicion

The word *conglomerate* was coined in the waning days of the New Deal as government regulators began to address the possibility that a corporation could develop almost invisible power by spreading itself among many different industries. While the nation was used to combating monopolies in single industries, officials were aware that a monopoly wasn't the only form of "bigness" that could disturb fair trade. Moving money and influence between industries, a conglomerate could also undermine competition. At the very least, it could alter the accepted processes of business and its priorities.

THE FEAR OF CONGLOMERATES

Through the years, the idea of the conglomerate has elicited suspicion from Americans, an instinctive response growing out of the opinion of dominating businesses found in various foreign countries. Since the end of World War II, the most sophisticated of all conglomerates have been the zaibatsu *found in Japan and other Asian countries. Typically engaged in everything from manufacturing to shipping to banking, they have traded individualism for the ability to bring a huge scale of investment to new industries. The thought of a handful of massive American businesses deciding on which people, products, and industries to promote was anathema to the guiding American spirit of entrepreneurism.*

Up until the 1960s, there was little to fear in conglomerates. There were a few early examples, such as Textron and Merritt-Chapman & Scott, which had moved the concept onto the pages of the business publications, but a few didn't make for a trend. Come the 1960s, however, conglomerates became rampant, hungry to gobble up independent companies. By 1967, two thousand firms had indeed been gobbled, absorbed by companies that seemed to do nothing else but grow.

The usefulness of conglomerates in the market became a divisive issue (not that it was so hard to divide people into two camps in the mid-1960s, mind you). For those against, conglomerates were just a new trick to concentrate power in the hands of the few, to the detriment of the individual. Those who were in favor of conglomerates considered themselves more realistic. After all, they pointed out, companies such as General Electric and General Motors were not only more diversified but also more powerful in each of their individual businesses than almost anyone realized. In this raging debate over conglomerates, both sides were right.

Ling's Story

James J. Ling was born in Oklahoma on December 31, 1922. After his mother died, he was sent to live with an aunt in Louisiana. However, money was tight—something that Ling was all too aware of. Though he was bright academically, Ling dropped out of school at fourteen. He made his own way in the world, serving later with the navy during World War II. With $3,000 in savings and navy training as an electrician, he founded Ling Electric in 1946 and nurtured it into a successful contracting company. Grossing over $1 million per year, Ling was earning a good living—actually, a very good living for a man without any formal education. A voracious reader, Ling educated himself and was notably articulate. One interviewer later observed that Ling's words were so well chosen, it was as though he were reading a cue card just over the listener's shoulder. A strategist at heart, Ling wasn't content with the comfortable life ahead for him in small business. The realm he sought was high finance.

Once Ling Electric went public through its highly unusual offering at the Texas State Fair, its first acquisition was vital to its future direction. That move was buying a California company that made vibration-testing equipment. Not only did the acquisition give Jimmy Ling a company on the verge of major success in aerospace, it allowed him to change the name of his company. As Ling *Electronics,* the company meandered through other deals, including an amiable merger with a neighbor in Dallas, Temco Electronics and Missiles, and its only truly unfriendly acquisition, of Denver's Chance Vought Corp. Both new partners made major defense-related material. When the company came together as a military contractor, it adopted the name Ling-Temco-Vought. The nation's general prosperity, combined with the escalation of the Vietnam War, increased business for L-T-V. By 1967, Ling was the owner of 16 percent of L-T-V and worth $39 million. "It was a thrill to watch him do business," said a fellow investor of Jimmy Ling. "You could see the excitement coursing in his veins."

Public Value vs. Accountant Value

Wishing to diversify, and motivated by sheer opportunity, Ling wanted to make more deals. In 1964, he found a way; an unlimited way, it seemed.

Ling's technique was called Project Redeployment, a military-style term, well suited to the Vietnam War era. He explained it as both a financial and a management strategy. The ultimate in decentralization, redeployment made its debut when Ling broke up L-T-V into three stand-alone parts. Stock was sold in each, L-T-V keeping a majority, of course. In essence, the plan gave the parent L-T-V new buying power in two ways: 1) it brought in cash on the shares sold in the companies; 2) the stock price could increase the perceived value of the company. Ling perceived that assets as valued by an accountant are rarely worth as much as those on which the public has placed a value through stock pricing. That's because the public adds a premium for the future potential of the company. Accountants do not.

When Ling went to the banks and asked for a loan (which he was wont to do) against the book value of his component companies, he would be allowed a certain amount. But when he visited the banks after Project Redeployment and they examined the *market value* of the components, he received in most cases something like six times as much credit. He would use it to go out and buy companies—which then underwent redeployment. Jimmy Ling had more money at his disposal, and L-T-V shareholders watched earnings soar.

In late 1967, the company completed a terrifically successful redeployment of Wilson & Co., which produced a hodgepodge of meats, pharmaceuticals, and sporting goods—"meatballs, goofballs, and golfballs," in the wit of Wall Street. Jimmy Ling was launched as a celebrity and L-T-V, likewise, as a glamour stock. Neither was anywhere near its peak, however.

The L-T-V Decision

Few people outside of the Pentagon knew Ling-Temco-Vought before the end of 1965, when it began its shopping spree. The next year, it was highlighted as the fastest-growing company in the Fortune 500, ranking fourth for profitability (based on return on shareholders' equity).

The company's earnings per share were certainly going in the right direction, increasing by 64 percent in 1964 and a lower but still outstanding 32 percent in 1965. Those years, of course, coincided with the first years of Ling's Project Redeployment.

L-T-V may have grown through leveraging, but at the base of any financial lever there's always some kind of a loan, and the company's level of debt tended to be high in the face of its acquisitions. Investors were able to note that because of high earnings, the debt load was falling in 1964–1965. However, as at any company, that particular trend depended vitally on earnings growth outpacing the interest rate. The figure that really showed L-T-V's strength was not its own price-to-earnings ratio, which remained around 10 in 1966, but that of the underlying companies. When they were in the teens or higher, it indicated a heightened market value for the parent's assets. In addition, when the components showed a higher p/e ratio than the parent company, the feeling was that markets undervalued L-T-V.

Debt: The Most Desirable Thing?

In 1968, Ling accelerated the pace of acquisition, in part to extend his string of successes, and in part to outrun the rumble of coming action from the Justice Department. In one week during August, he announced plans to acquire both Greatamerica, another Dallas conglomerate, which owned a plum in Braniff Airlines, and Allis-Chalmers, the Wisconsin equipment maker. The latter deal fell through, but no matter. It was soon replaced by the purchase of Jones & Laughlin, the nation's sixth-largest steel manufacturer. The debt accrued from the two acquisitions, however, was bending the back of L-T-V.

Ling wasn't worried. He studied the stock market going all the way back to 1923, finding solace in the fact that over any reasonable length of time, interest rates lagged behind profit rates. "Hence," he concluded, "the most desirable thing to issue when you buy a company, if you can buy good, solid operating assets and recurring earnings, is debt."

If recurring earnings were the key to staying ahead of even the most odious debt, then L-T-V seemed to be all set in 1968, a year in which recent acquisitions had expanded sales by 50 percent. Nonetheless, the earnings per share dipped, to the consternation of many investors.

Just as L-T-V hit its stride, making headlines during the big week in August 1967 with its twin acquisition plans (Allis-Chalmers and Greatamerica), the American Institute of Certified Public Accountants announced a subtle but terribly important rule change. In direct response to fast-growing conglomerates like L-T-V, the professional board deemed that any debt that could be converted into shares of stock had to be included in the calculation of earnings per share. The increased number of shares in the calculation was bound to lower the all-important earnings number. "This is a time bomb with a five-month fuse on it," said a convertible bond specialist at Salomon. And, sure enough, in 1968, when the time bomb exploded, L-T-V's earnings per share were substantially lower—and so was its stock price.

Even worse, by the end of the decade those same serpentine financial rules that Ling had used to create L-T-V were tightening around his neck. Later, in 1968–1969, bad news came to L-T-V from three new directions. One, the Justice Department filed a complaint attacking L-T-V's absorption of Jones & Laughlin, which led to an expensive legal battle. Two, the economy slowed, affecting the earnings at the conglomerate's biggest components. And three, at the same time, money tightened, making creditors impatient and inflexible.

The least desirable thing—to paraphrase Jimmy Ling himself—was debt without recurring earnings. That, however, would be exactly L-T-V's situation. Forced to sell what Ling considered good, solid operating assets to fulfill a painful agreement with the Justice Department, L-T-V managed to stave off its debtors through early 1969. It unfortunately couldn't stave off a falling stock price, however. Shares were plunging almost as quickly as they had risen in 1967. Ling desperately reworked Project Redeployment and attempted new stock issues, but Wall Street wasn't buying it—literally.

"It looks like more paper shuffling to me," said one analyst. By the end of 1969, L-T-V stock was down to $25 per share—and sinking. The following year, Jimmy Ling was deposed, blamed for allowing the company's interest payments to more than wipe out its humble profits. To his creditors went his château in Texas right along with the rest of his company.

L-T-V eventually divested itself of everything except its steel operations. No longer a conglomerate, and enduring not one but two bankruptcy filings, L-T-V was considered a penny stock in 2000. And, no longer an emperor, Jimmy Ling rounded out his career at a small energy company in Texas.

Epilogue

Growth stocks often spring from new industries, yet the conglomerate constituted something just as bold in the 1960s: an emerging corporate structure. In its pioneering way, L-T-V took advantage of Wall Street finance, but also proved why a company cannot *live* on Wall Street. Growth, which should be a priority anywhere, was instead practically all that mattered there. While Wall Street richly rewarded "Jimmy Ling's Wonderful Growth Machine," as a 1967 *Fortune* article called L-T-V, it also propelled Ling to rev it up and up and up until it exploded.

The next time you find yourself in a boom-bust sequence, well, you might not know it; that's what makes manias so difficult to analyze. But the takeaway from the go-go markets is that while you can't predict how long a mania will last or how much excess will finally be realized, what you can do is understand that the downside will be every bit as painful as the upside was giddy. Fad stocks that have passed their prime are not rebound candidates. "Catch a falling star and put it in your pocket"? Only if you haven't learned your lesson from L-T-V.

Lessons

Time to buy . . . *An investor's interest in a stock should be piqued when earnings are growing by more than about 15 percent annually and are keeping well ahead of any increase in long-term debt.*

One product Charlie . . . *It may have looked as though L-T-V had a million different products generating all that growth. In reality the market believed it had just one: the stock itself.*

Beware of I.O.U.s . . . *If earnings don't outpace debt payments, they had better at least outpace the interest rate. When they don't, the stock price will likely fall, at least in the short term.*

Momentum must be respected . . . *Keep an eye on your holdings that need to buy earnings growth to keep up the momentum. But even if your analysis proves that a company cannot sustain its level of earnings growth, don't leap to sell the stock short. The more path breaking your analysis, the longer you'll have to wait for others to see the light.*

TIMELINE

1946 Ling Electric is founded.

1955 IPO.

1960 LTV acquires Temco Electronics and Missiles.

1961 LTV acquires Chance Vought.

1964 Hits upon the idea of Project Redeployment to acquire more companies through a combination of stock sales and long-term debt.

1965 Acquires Okonite Co.

1967 Wilson and Co., with nearly $1 billion in sales, acquired with only $80 million in new debt.

1967 American Institute of Certified Public Accountants changes accounting rules, deeming that any debt that can be converted into shares of stock has to be included in the calculation of earnings per share.

1967 LTV controls 33 subsidiaries engaged in 80 different lines of business.

1967 Announcement of intended acquisitions of Greatamerica and Jones & Laughlin Steel.

1968 Greatamerica and J&L Steel formally acquired.

1968 Justice Department files a complaint attacking L-T-V's absorption of J&L.

1969 Earnings fall.

1970 Jimmy Ling is deposed and L-T-V begins a long process to reduce its size.

WARREN BUFFETT'S INSPIRATION

Teledyne

1975–1986

*When Warren Buffett was just a budding guru, he was a con-
fessed disciple of Henry Singleton's Teledyne Corporation.
"I've never been a person who vacillates back and forth with
the ups and downs of the economic cycle," Singleton once
said, perhaps explaining how his company remained one of
the greatest stock picks over three decades of changing environments. Teledyne stayed on course and even charted new
ground by remaining true to one concept: shareholder value.*

If you've just read the previous section on L-T-V, the word *conglomerate* might have left a bad taste in your mouth. If so, you
know exactly how investors felt in the mid-1970s. By 1976, conglomerates were strictly out of favor, a fact that Henry Singleton,
founder of Teledyne, shook off: "We don't refer to ourselves as
a conglomerate," he said, "but we don't care what other people
call us."

When a group falls into disfavor, it carries a shroud that can
last several years. When the quiz show scandal hit the United
States in the late 1950s, the development of new show concepts
came to a screeching halt. But rebounds can and do occur. NBC
bided its time and introduced a show called *Jeopardy!* in 1964; the
timing was right, and the rest is history. Wall Street works in a similar way. When sweeping characterizations bring a sector to its
knees, smart investors look for the exceptions. Those who looked
at Teledyne in 1976 were in for the rebound of their lives.

BY ANY OTHER NAME

Teledyne was certainly a conglomerate. It was made up of
145 acquisitions, the vast majority of which had been purchased

at the height of the market using its own high-priced stock. There were differences, however, between Teledyne and the typical, tattered conglomerate of the early 1970s. It wasn't burdened with sour deals, having stopped its buying spree in the nick of time. It was laden with both cash and good managers. It was still turning profits nearly every year. Most of all, investors who took the time to study Teledyne on its own merits realized that the head of the company, Dr. Henry Singleton, was quietly making a fundamental change in the way the company hitched itself to growth segments of the economy.

After 1969 Teledyne rarely acquired whole companies. Instead, Singleton used the portfolios of two insurance subsidiaries to collect stock in companies with potential for growth. Before long Teledyne was making good money in its manufacturing businesses and great money through its insurance portfolios. If that sounds like the general arrangement of Berkshire Hathaway under Warren Buffett, it is probably because Buffett made no secret of his admiration for Teledyne and its highly independent founder.

General investors in the mid-1970s might have been aware of Teledyne, but common knowledge was not as positive as one might think:

- It was wildly out of favor, with a price-to-earnings ratio of 4, down from 60 eight years before.
- It didn't pay a dividend. Up until the high-tech surge of the 1990s, established, profitable companies were expected to pay a dividend.
- When the company, which was sick and tired of hearing complaints about the low stock price and the lack of dividends, made an offer to buy back shares at a slight premium over the market price, it was hit with a riot of shareholders happy to bail out. That led to the perception that Teledyne was not even popular with its own shareholders.

Those who took the company up on its offer to buy shares priced in the market at $14 for all of $20 did not rejoice for very long. Teledyne stock topped $150 by the end of the decade and in another ten years was up to the equivalent of $750.

Actions Speaking Loudly

With a general emphasis on metals, defense, and high tech, Teledyne Corporation's subsidiaries reflected a wide range of businesses. For all of its heavy industry and high finance, it was probably best known for one of its few consumer products, the Teledyne Water-Pik, a dental care system. Although many of its subsidiaries were given Teledyne as a first name, the company maintained a low profile, even for a conglomerate.

It was founded in Los Angeles in 1960 by Singleton, an M.I.T.-trained scientist with executive experience at Litton Industries; Arthur Rock, the legendary venture capitalist from San Francisco; and George Kozmetsky, another Litton alumnus (who would later help Dell Computers through its 1990s growing pains). The dour Dr. Singleton was the guiding spirit, and even he was surprised at how quickly Teledyne grew, with earnings soaring from all of 3 cents in 1961 to $1.91 in 1970—an annual rate of 70 percent, compounded. Most of the company's growth in those early days derived from acquisitions. Investors didn't care, as long as it just kept coming.

Singleton suddenly became conservative during 1967 to 1969. Instead of gobbling up semiconductor companies or the most advanced heavy military contractors, Teledyne started buying insurance companies. For the growth investor, it was anathema. Insurance companies were, at best, predictably dull in terms of growth. Teledyne had veered off the usual course for conglomerates, but as it turned out the timing was perfect. Falling stock prices starting in 1969 left its overdiluted brethren among conglomerates with a double death blow: crashing stock prices with surging debt levels. Teledyne's price sagged with the rest of the market, but its little cash machines in the form of its insurance companies kept its bottom line from sagging as well. This kept everyone at the company employed, but failed to thrill investors; the stock languished at about $6 per share, as it was punished along with the rest of the conglomerates.

"When the acquisition race was on," said one analyst in 1972, "Teledyne was a very glamorous company. But now that it is over, I'm inclined to think it is just another pretty face. I can't regard it as much more than a run-of-the-mill company." Henry Singleton, inscrutable as ever, professed not to care what such people thought. He used the early 1970s to pay down debt.

When the hue and cry about the company's refusal to pay a dividend reached a crescendo in 1972, Teledyne snapped to. The company surprised Wall Street by offering to buy $1 million of its own shares at a handsome premium over the market price. To the surprise and chagrin of company officials, 8.9 million shares were offered—over a quarter of the outstanding stock. With stubborn fury, Teledyne borrowed the money with which to buy out every last infidel. Dr. Singleton was a firm believer that the only smart investing was long-term investing. Anyone who could be happy with a quick profit, as in the buyback, didn't mesh with the philosophy behind the company and probably shouldn't have owned shares in the first place. In fact, even as the stock price decreased over the next several years, Teledyne continued its buybacks. Within four years, the company had purchased more than two-thirds of its own outstanding shares. "I used to joke that Teledyne was the only conglomerate to go private. Now I'm not so sure it's a joke," said analyst Robert Hanisee.

In the mid-1970s, Teledyne's stock dislodged itself from its lows and was rising handsomely. Those who had sold out during the buybacks had the nerve to sue, charging Singleton with something like *insider buying,* by arguing that he knew something good was about to happen to Teledyne when he made his tender offer.

Of course, Henry Singleton knew something. He realized that a CEO should always be willing to bet on the future of his own company. The case was dropped.

To Buy or Not to Buy?

Teledyne was notoriously tight-lipped about what it was going to do or why. That was especially true in the mid-1970s, when the company was changing its priorities. One business magazine summed up the attitude abroad in Wall Street: "Investors seem to feel: Why bother? There are plenty of less secretive dividend-paying bargains around." As the following fifteen years would show, there weren't many bargains like Teledyne around. Investors who understood Teledyne knew that it wasn't really secretive; its company reports detailed its prospects and performance. Expending little effort on investor relations, it was focused on business—and, more than any other company of its time, on shareholder value.

Those stock buybacks were not fits of pique at Teledyne; they were signs of management's strong belief in the company. At the same time that the corporation was starting to make large-scale investments in other downtrodden stocks, it only made sense that it put most of the money where it counted most, taking in more than two-thirds of its outstanding shares. A stock buyback is the sincerest form of conceit on Wall Street.

Henry Singleton once pointed out that between 1965 and 1975 earnings per share at Teledyne grew by an annual compounded rate of 32 percent—a record, as he said, "not matched by any sizable company in the United States today." A hefty proportion of that growth took place over the two years, 1973 and 1975, when earnings per share leaped from $1.01 to $4.79. Teledyne subsidiaries were largely responsible, since underperformers were lopped off or reshaped. The rap on Teledyne was that it was so tight with a buck it didn't expend enough money on research or plant investment. In the short and medium term, at least, erring to the side of thrift helped its earnings soar.

Teledyne and its 120-odd businesses were so complicated an octopus that few analysts even tried to cover it. Those who did were not fed much information from the company; neither were financial reporters. The result was that Teledyne was regarded as mysterious, if only because it refused to pander to the day-to-day hand-wringing of Wall Street. One result may have been the low representation of institutions among stockholders, at about 20 percent. However, what Teledyne's low rates of analyst coverage

and institutional investment reflected most was that conglomerates as a whole were out of favor. Whether that was deserved in
Teledyne's case, isolation from the attention of market watchers
and movers does constitute a strike against a growth stock.

Singleton often described the company attitude as "conservative," which was certainly unusual in a conglomerate. One sure
sign was that no one business accounted for more than 3 percent
of the company's sales. Another was that the company made a
transition from buying companies to buying their stock, holding it
within the portfolios overstuffed with equities. Teledyne was, in
part, a grand mutual fund, run by a deft manager. The best place
to chart the transition and its effect on the bottom line at Teledyne
was in the company reports, which listed holdings.

Upward Mobility

Teledyne's gaggle of subsidiaries was only connected through the
financial controls put in place by the parent. In fact, the primary
source of Teledyne's control was the oldest one: cash. Only headquarters could authorize expenditures, with the result that
Teledyne and its subsidiaries were nothing if not efficient. The
profit margin on sales hovered at around 7 percent, compared with
5.4 percent on manufacturing businesses nationally. "They are a
major cash generator," analyst Jon Gruber said of Teledyne, "and
they don't spend a lot in facilities." Cost control was a major facet
of Teledyne's success.

While the management continued to reduce risk in every way
possible at the subsidiaries, Singleton began his ultimate diversification: buying stock in other companies. The takeover game had
become too expensive, he concluded, with companies demanding
and receiving premiums for cooperation. Teledyne decided it didn't
need whole companies, not when pieces of them would do just as
well and came without any of the added expense. Those pieces
were nonetheless substantial; for example, Teledyne amassed one-
quarter of Litton's shares and more than half of Curtis-Wright's. It

was taking over 50 percent of the shares in other well-run conglomerates, including TRW and GAF.

As Teledyne earnings grew, the share price rocketed forward,
from a dip to 7 1/2 in 1975 to more than 100 in 1978. Of course,
that is the usual scenario, but in Teledyne's case, the effect was
even more exaggerated because relatively few shares were still left
after repeated buybacks. The key to understanding Teledyne was
that everything Henry Singleton did was intended to increase book
value: culling subsidiaries and improving their profitability; buying
back shares; investing cash in growing companies; and reinvesting
the profits. It was a monument to the art of building as much value
as possible into each share of stock.

BOOK VALUE

Book value is defined as the assets behind each share, as recognized in standard accounting practice.

However, stockholders—those few who were left—continued
to offer pockets of protest. On the face of it, though, there doesn't
seem to have been much to protest; mostly they resented the fact
that Teledyne was by far the largest company on the market not to
offer a dividend. The company held firm. "Our people," Singleton
said, referring to shareholders, "don't want any more income. They
want to see increases in book value and ultimately in the price of
the stock when the underlying buildup in values is reflected." In
other words, Teledyne could do a better job of investing the money
than shareholders could, with its 33 percent return on equity and
a stock price growing at 50 percent a year. The people who could
not see that was true were not only looking a gift horse in the
mouth, they were wasting their time trying to change Henry
Singleton's mind. He was a businessman, not a man of the people,
and he did what was best for shareholders even when a vocal group
of them disagreed.

Singleton was ahead of his time with his plan. More recently, stockholders have come to accept the difference between a "growth stock" and an "income stock." Teledyne was one of the first companies that didn't try to provide both. The result? Book value, lots of it. Teledyne's book value rose dramatically, from $6.50 in 1971 to $131 in 1984. Over the same span, the price of the stock rose from about $5.50 to $350 in 1986. The following year, Teledyne changed direction for the third time.

Epilogue

The signal of the final turn would have been innocent enough at any other company. All of a sudden, Teledyne declared a dividend of $1 per share, payable quarterly. With only 11.7 million shares outstanding by that point, the dividend was not likely to deplete Teledyne's huge cash reserves. It was a thunderbolt, nonetheless. Robert Hanisee, the Los Angeles analyst who followed Teledyne closely, called it "the beginning of the endgame at Teledyne." He was right. Teledyne management was passive for about five more years, spending as little money as possible and allowing earnings to plateau as management grew dull. Singleton began to devote more of his time to environmental interests on his large landholdings in New Mexico and California. He retired from active management in 1989. Oddly enough, a company with estimable executives in place at the subsidiaries had no obvious choices to take over at the top. Teledyne was slowing down, and it might have been time to sell, except that rumors of a breakup value far in excess of the $360 trading price kept investors' attention.

Teledyne was preparing for its own demise. But as with its first two phases, the buildup of the businesses in the 1960s and of the portfolio from 1975 to 1985, the end of the company would be entirely profitable for shareholders. After spinning off several major subsidiaries, what was left of Teledyne was folded into Allegheny Ludlum in 1996, forming Allegheny Teledyne. It was a friendly buyout, beneficial to Teledyne shareholders. Henry Singleton came out of retirement to make sure of that.

Lessons

Avoid naysayers with long memories . . . *When investors start criticizing an entire category of stocks because of some bad experiences in the past, that category is almost certain to contain rebound candidates—solid companies that have been tarred with the same proverbial brush. Just remember that rebound investing calls for unusual patience.*

Read a good book . . . *Book value may be irrelevant for fast-growing technology companies, but not so for companies with hard assets and low p/e ratios. When these companies succeed at upping book value, they're keepers.*

Believe in a company that truly believes in itself . . . *Teledyne kept buying back shares. When done sincerely—not just to pump up the stock price in the short term—there is no better vote of confidence. But when Singleton started coasting, doing a complete 180 by issuing dividends, investors should have sensed the huge change in philosophy.*

TIMELINE

1960 Founded by Henry Singleton, Arthur Rock, and George Kozmetsky.

1969 Ceases acquiring entire companies and focuses on acquiring stock.

1973 Offers to buy back its own shares, acquiring 8.9 million of them.

1986 Dividend offered for the first time—$1 per share.

1996 Folded into Allegheny Ludlum in a friendly buyout.

THE LOVE INTEREST

Paramount Communications

1991–1994

> *If it were a movie, the fortunes of Paramount Communications, circa 1990, would seem to be less about a corporate takeover than a frothy romantic comedy. Sure, there were more lawyers than laughs, but the theme of the story was always one of unrequited desire. On Wall Street, it was a season of hotly contested takeovers, when jealousy, desperation, and stubborn pride translated into fast gains for stockholders.*

The conclusion to our trilogy on conglomerates is also a conclusion to an unforgettable era on Wall Street—the era of the corporate takeover. The bull market of the 1980s was built on the theme of creating shareholder value. If a company didn't find a way to turn its hidden assets into shareholder wealth, someone else would.

This trend sounded the final death knell for the run-amok conglomerate, whose stock market valuations were often held back by the performance of its weakest link. Analysts tired of trying to figure out hodgepodge companies, favoring instead the "pure plays" in any given industry. Within this environment, the entertainment industry found itself ripe for consolidation. But even if you missed the entire 1980s, you could have applied the methods of a decade to find Paramount Communications in 1991.

"More Interested in Profits Than Awards"

Paramount Pictures in the mid-1980s was one of the more dependable movie studios in Hollywood. It was the most visible part of an entertainment and publishing powerhouse named Gulf & Western, which in 1989 was renamed Paramount Communications, Inc. This multinational conglomerate also owned publishers Simon & Schuster and Prentice-Hall, the New York Knicks basketball team, the New York Rangers hockey team, the Madison Square Garden cable sports channel, a half share in the USA Network, and a handful of independent television stations. The core, though, was Paramount Pictures, which turned out television comedies and movies such as *The Untouchables* and *Friday the 13th,* all while keeping an eye on the bottom line. "Here, we're more interested in profits than awards," said Marvin Davis, the chairman.

Movie reviewers may not have always been enthusiastic, but business analysts—critics of another stripe—certainly recognized that Paramount was an underrated star of Wall Street. The entertainment industry was rapidly changing, with the development of new means of distribution that included video, cable television, and an array of new networks.

Distribution has always been the driving force in the entertainment industry. It's no coincidence that theater chains predated the rise of the major movie studios in the early days of the industry. In the new Hollywood heyday, however, distribution through cable television created the need for a steady stream of "product," in the form of movies, TV shows, and other forms of programming.

New media giants not only created programming for TV shows and movies—and sometimes both, as in the case of Paramount's *Star Trek* series—they also went on to do a lot more. They licensed them for theaters, exploited them in toys, books, or ancillary products, and then, most important of all, they held on to the copyrights and piled up programming for broadcast in perpetuity on cable. As Marvin Davis put it: "We like anything that feeds screens."

Always a Bridesmaid

To a conglomerate, the programming derived from studios was a renewable resource. So, as this started to become more apparent, it made a lot of sense that during a short span at the end of the 1980s, movie studios suddenly came into vogue on Wall Street. They were looked on as jewels that could complete a crown in the form of vertically integrated entertainment. Companies in cable or electronics led the hunt for studios like Paramount, MCA, Warner Brothers, and Columbia. In 1988, Time Inc., a cable provider and publisher, made one of the first moves, arranging a friendly merger with Warner. It was considered a good marriage, but for his part, Marvin Davis didn't take well to Paramount's role as a bridesmaid.

So, on the eve of the merger, Davis shocked both Time and Warner by launching an aggressive, last-minute campaign to take over Time. He planned to construct his own media giant. The Time board of directors fought hard against Paramount, finally changing the deal with Warner from a merger to a buyout, elegantly terming it a "strategic alliance." Even after being challenged in court, Time managed to repulse the unwanted Paramount offer, although it was more immediately remunerative to stockholders. Time's strategy was simply to reserve its board's prerogative to do what was best for the company in the long run.

Davis and Paramount had no choice but to accept a bitter loss. For several years thereafter, while other media companies paired off and followed the trend toward mega-conglomerates, Paramount stood as a wallflower. As the most important of the remaining studios, it drew attention from analysts and institutional investors. Yet the longer it lagged in the entertainment industry's race to bigness, the more rumors there were that the best opportunities had passed Paramount by.

Unlike many of our greatest stock picks of all time, the Paramount play was a question not of start-up but rather of end-up. Investors who were paying attention to the situation behind the flat stock price knew that something had to happen to Paramount. The question that kept some people waiting on the sidelines was whether a three-year string of dalliances made the company enticingly hard-to-get or just shopworn.

A Star Is Born

Paramount Pictures began in 1914, formed from a combination of companies born with the movie industry. In the 1930s, Paramount earned its reputation for turning out refined movies, showcasing such stars as Maurice Chevalier, Claudette Colbert, and Bing Crosby. In the television era, though, when theaters closed by the thousands every year, movie production was drastically reduced. Paramount eventually learned to adjust, instead turning out hit TV shows such as *Mission Impossible* and *The Odd Couple*. The pride of its movie side was 1973's *The Godfather*. Ten years later, Marvin Davis, a veteran of movie publicity and marketing, took charge of Gulf & Western, which included Paramount.

By the 1980s Paramount's chairman, Barry Diller, its president, Michael Eisner, and Davis were turning out hit movies with new stars such as Eddie Murphy, while at the same time developing promising talent in pictures such as *Pretty in Pink*. The television side was even better, with production of two of television's top shows, *Cheers* and *Family Ties*. However, Diller, a square-set man with a reputation for blunt talk, couldn't work under the demanding, bottom line–oriented Davis. Years of arguments ended in late 1984, when both Diller and Eisner quit in a twenty-four-hour span. Eisner started a successful run as head of Disney, while Barry Diller helped to start the Fox Network for News Corporation. For his next move, he surprised everyone in Hollywood by leaving for Philadelphia and—of all things—something called QVC, a cable television channel that turned the process of selling trinkets into something like entertainment.

As Davis replaced his departed executives he began to depend more heavily on sequels—*Beverly Hills Cop III,* for example, and *Friday the 13th* renditions. Paramount may not have been a model of creative daring, but it was piling up cash. And Davis was piling up control: with takeover frenzy breaking out all around Hollywood, his company bought back more than 25 percent of the outstanding shares in ten years following 1983.

While Davis armed his fortress against a hostile takeover, speculation continued as to why his company remained independent. General Electric was named among the companies that might have been interested in acquiring it, as were Turner Broadcasting, Bertelsmann A.G., a major German music company, and the electronics company Hitachi of Japan. Davis dallied with about thirty potential alliances, but none suited his future or that of Paramount. In fact, some stockholders felt that he was being too picky, looking for a deal that benefited him first and Paramount second. In the midst of a growing tangle of rumors, Davis may have been best actor on the whole Paramount lot. No one knew what he was thinking. "We have many visions," he said when asked about the future, "but times keep changing so quickly, so does our vision."

Lights, Camera . . . Action?

As far as the investors of early 1993 were concerned, Paramount's future didn't depend on little things like the annual results and whether the company had succeeded in entertaining more people than last year. The big stock price rise would depend on a deal. Nonetheless, a great strategic stock is nothing but a bet if the company can't make money under actual conditions.

The entertainment industry was growing into the information age, with outlets in new technologies, such as the Internet, and across international borders. "No media company can be sure of how entertainment programming will be distributed in the future," ran a report in the New York Times in 1993, "but all are aware of their need to have films and television series, like those that Paramount owns and produces, to attract viewers." The industry was closely followed as an adjunct to the high-tech sector, but with a certain defensive aspect, too: in good times or bad, people must be entertained and the conglomerates were turning entertainment into a commodity more effectively than ever before.

The most important customers in the Paramount situation were not the book readers and moviegoers who put cash in the drawer, but media conglomerates hunting for studios. In 1989, one year after Warner was purchased by Time, Columbia Pictures was snapped up by Sony. Another cash-rich Japanese electronics company, Matsushita Electric, bought MCA in 1990. By then, companies on the creative side of the entertainment business were becoming scarce. Paramount was the strongest of the creative companies still available, both to the conglomerate looking for a takeover candidate and to the investor looking for a play in the entertainment sector.

Paramount's management controls would have been tight for a gravel company or a knitting mill, let alone for an entertainment giant. Cash on hand remained well above long-term debt, giving it a wide scope of options in outside financing—as when it tried to take over Time and needed to borrow $11 billion. The strong balance sheet was also a bulwark against an unwanted takeover. A company with a high level of debt couldn't be sure who would gain control of that debt.

To acquire Columbia, Sony paid three times the book value: the assets "on the books" divided evenly among the outstanding shares. Yet throughout most of 1991, when Paramount Communications was trading at about 40, it was trading for only about 23 percent over its book value. Even as it drifted toward 60 over the next two years, Paramount's stock was anything but overpriced.

Enemy at the Gates

Paramount stock was held by about 100,000 investors. Individuals undoubtedly had many reasons for owning the shares, including in some cases a sentimental attachment to one of the great names in Hollywood history. Sentiment had nothing to do with it for those with the largest holdings, a corps of about one hundred individuals and institutions. Most were takeover specialists, who made a point of identifying companies that would be attractive targets—and who had acquired Paramount shares waiting for a juicy buyout or even a bidding war. They were rewarded with the latter.

In April 1993, Marvin Davis accepted an invitation to dine with Sumner Redstone, the chairman of Viacom, an aggressive entertainment company that syndicated shows such as *Roseanne* and *The Cosby Show*. Viacom also provided cable to 1.1 million homes and operated cable channels including MTV. The negotiations to merge Paramount and Viacom were unproductive, until Davis got a tip from John Malone of Tele-Communications, Inc., that someone was preparing a hostile takeover of Paramount. The name of the raider was none other than former employee Barry Diller, now of QVC. Few pieces of news could have spooked Davis more. On September 12, 1993, Paramount announced plans to merge with Viacom.

Redstone, who had started in the movie business by helping to run his father's two drive-ins, was born and raised a distribution man. He wanted Paramount Communications in order to help fill in programming on Viacom's cable. As friendly as the merger was, it called for Viacom to survive as the dominating entity. For each share of Paramount, investors were to receive $9.10 in cash and Viacom stock worth $60.04. Paramount's stock rose 5 percent on the news, to $68.50. For Paramount stockholders, it was a nice reward, if not exactly a bonanza. All that was left, it seemed, were the technicalities.

On September 20, Paramount stock unexpectedly jumped to nearly 80. Barry Diller had just announced that he wanted to buy it, and he was prepared to pay $80 in cash for the first 51 percent of Paramount stock tendered. Diller's company, QVC, was on a roll of its own, with the stock price jumping by a factor of 5 over the previous year.

In early October, Viacom and QVC took turns topping the bidding for Paramount. At that time it was not only profitable to hold Paramount shares, but it was starting to be fun. In mid-November, QVC topped the bidding once more. By then institutional holders of the stock, led by such well-regarded veteran investors as the Gabelli Group, the Capital Group, and State Street Research, were wondering why on earth Paramount wasn't taking the fat QVC offer more seriously.

Davis, meanwhile, had a plan of his own. He was practicing exactly what he learned through the court ruling that went against

Paramount in the Time takeover—that is, aligning corporate governance to the interests of the company's future, rather than the immediate return for shareholders. To Davis, Viacom, with its array of distribution channels, was a better long-term fit than a twenty-four-hour selling show like QVC, no matter how rich and ambitious. The fact that Davis and Diller were old adversaries may have also affected Paramount's preference for Viacom. It was that very possibility that enraged certain shareholders, who didn't want their gains trimmed by old squabbles.

Whether or not you think the shareholders were worthy of much sympathy from the public, they certainly got a real boost from a court ruling on November 24, 1993. The judge insisted that Paramount had to recognize the QVC bid. The Paramount board of directors found this galling. Why did they have to do exactly what Time had not had to do four years before?

Siege of Paramount

The court's ruling has been studied by legal students ever since. The verdict held that the difference between the two similar cases (Paramount's attempted takeover of Time in 1989 and QVC's of Paramount in 1993) was that in entering a "strategic alliance" with Warner to evade takeover, Time had left a majority of shares in public hands. Paramount couldn't call its own situation with Viacom a strategic alliance, because Sumner Redstone was to emerge from the deal controlling a majority of the voting stock in the combined entity. That made it a sale and opened the way for QVC to join the bidding, fair and square.

In the decision, the judge actually chastised Paramount for taking faulty advice from its team of high-priced lawyers and consultants. That was surely one part of the decision with which Paramount must have concurred completely!

Both QVC's bids and those of Viacom came as a combination of cash and stock, but with caveats attached. The latest bids came in like this: QVC's was worth an estimated $86 and Viacom's was worth approximately $78. In December, the Paramount board had little choice but to duly recommend the merger with the hated QVC; nonetheless, Viacom was accorded two weeks to top the bidding.

The grand old dame of Hollywood was certainly in a spot. "Its fate is being chosen by people whose idea of long term is noon the next day," wryly noted Larry Haverty, an analyst with State Street.

As the so-called Siege of Paramount was drawing to a close, Barry Diller was being congratulated on his victory. Observing what looked like Sumner Redstone's loss of momentum in the pursuit of Paramount, a trader on Wall Street said, "It's like a dog chasing a car down the street." Not for long, however. Redstone was back on a roll again soon enough, when he announced that his company would be merging with Blockbuster Video, one of the brightest companies of the day. The sudden deal added yet another layer to Viacom's distribution strata. More than that, with the injection of five-day rental fees from Blockbuster's 3,593 stores, the final bid was worth $82.06 per share. Significantly, more of it was in cash than QVC was offering. And shrewdly, Redstone also included a guarantee against a decrease in its share price, a second factor that won over short-term investors.

Sumner Redstone was having dinner at New York's old speakeasy, the "21" Club, on February 14, 1994, when he got some great news. Word came that Paramount's shareholders had tendered enough shares to give Viacom its sweetheart. Redstone raised a glass of champagne with a simple toast that might have well included all the Paramount shareholders: "Here's to us who won."

Epilogue

The Paramount takeover, though hardly the biggest of its kind, exemplified a changing era in the mergers and acquisitions game. Whereas takeovers in the 1980s were often conducted to make a quick buck, leveraged buyouts were now passé, and piling on the debt was unthinkable. Takeovers of the 1990s were more strategic in nature, no more so than in the entertainment business. In 1995,

Disney bought ABC/Cap Cities, bringing a major studio together with a major network for the first time. And as the decade came to an end, AOL was poised to swallow Time Warner, itself a product of the takeover era.

With Sumner Redstone's toast, the "deal from hell" was finally over. Viacom won the hearts and minds—and wallets—of Paramount's shareholders. Those of at least five months' standing realized a 50 percent gain and Paramount was folded into the empire that was Viacom.

Lessons

Patience will be rewarded . . . *Takeovers occurred every day in the 1980s, but no more. Paramount investors knew that there was a pot of gold at the end of the battle—they just had to hang on.*

A good company with good products . . . *Usually a safe bet. No exception here. If you like the company's portfolio, an acquirer just might share your opinion.*

The sum of the parts . . . *The stock market often undervalues companies with disparate divisions, especially if a "weakest link" division brings earnings down. An outside buyer interested in the company's crown jewels may be willing to pay up.*

Look for a fit . . . *A company cannot be a takeover candidate on its own. For shareholders to be rewarded, the company must be a good business fit with a potential buyer.*

TIMELINE OF A TAKEOVER

Sept. 12, 1993 Viacom launches the battle with an agreement to acquire Paramount in an $8.2 billion cash-and-stock deal. The agreement, worth $69.14 a share, included $9.10 a share in cash.

Sept. 20 QVC announces an $80 a share bid for Paramount. The deal includes $30 a share in cash and 0.893 of a QVC share for each Paramount share. The proposal includes $1 billion in backing from cable television companies Comcast Corp. and Liberty Media Corp.

Sept. 29 Florida-based video rental firm Blockbuster Entertainment Corp. agrees to invest $600 million in Viacom, strengthening the company's bid for Paramount.

Oct. 4 Viacom lines up another investor, telephone company Nynex Corp., which agrees to invest $1.2 billion in Viacom to support its bid.

Oct. 21 QVC announces a hostile tender offer of $80 a share for 51 percent of Paramount and 1.43 QVC shares for each remaining share of Paramount.

Oct. 24 Viacom counters with a $80 a share cash bid for 51 percent of Paramount and offers stock for the remainder.

Nov. 6 Viacom raises its offer by $5 a share to $85 for 51 percent of Paramount, with the rest in stock.

Nov. 12 QVC ups its offer for Paramount to $90 a share for 51 percent of the company and the rest in stock.

Dec. 22 Paramount agrees to a merger deal with QVC, under which QVC will pay $92 a share in cash for Paramount and the rest in stock. But the company reserves the right to consider new bids from other suitors.

Jan. 7, 1994 Viacom says it will merge with Blockbuster in an $8.4 billion deal, and Viacom-Blockbuster offers $105 a share for 50.1 percent of Paramount. Viacom values the total deal at $79.25 a share.

Jan. 18 Viacom raises the cash portion of its bid to $107 a share and adds a financial instrument to protect the value of the securities portion of its offer.

Feb. 15 Viacom claims victory, saying Paramount stockholders had at midnight EST, Monday, Feb. 14, tendered 74.6 percent of Paramount shares at the expiration of its bid.

July 7 Viacom buys Paramount Communications, Inc., for $10 billion.

SEVEN
INVESTING DURING BAD TIMES

KEEPS ON BUBBLING UP: COCA-COLA CORPORATION (1929–1940)

IT'S A GUSHER: SCHLUMBERGER LTD. (1970–1980)

RETURN FROM THE DEAD: CHRYSLER CORPORATION (1981–1987)

Once upon a time, a finance professor recommended to his classes (and to thousands of young professionals preparing for their Chartered Financial Analyst exam), "Before you invest in a stock, make sure that the conditions are favorable for equities in general."

Balderdash. You don't have to flee the market even when the macroeconomic picture is bleak, nor should you even try. Stockpicking is a diverse craft, one that can pay off in bad times as well as good. But you have to start by knowing the possibilities. It turns out that there are three fundamentally different strategies for coping in difficult times. Wouldn't you know that each of these three approaches is represented among the twenty-five greatest stock picks of all time.

The first strategy is to seek out companies whose businesses can thrive independent of the national economy—in other words, companies for whom "bad times" means "someone else's bad times." Stocks that fit this description are called defensive stocks, and this category is proudly represented by Coca-Cola, a defensive star as far back as the Great Depression.

The second strategy for difficult times is to recognize that some economic downturns are quite specifically to the advantage of certain market sectors. The sun is always shining somewhere, and the headline stock in this category is Schlumberger, which was a shining light during the dreary and inflationary decade of the 1970s, a time most stocks were struggling just to break even.

The third, and riskiest, "bad-time" strategy is to head straight for the companies who are faring the worst, once you are convinced that brighter times lie ahead. Hope alone won't do the trick; the process requires both analysis and patience. But the rewards are great enough to make the effort worthwhile. Our model for this strategy is Chrysler, perhaps the greatest rebound stock in Wall Street history.

KEEPS ON BUBBLING UP

Coca-Cola Corporation

1929–1940

No crisis seemed to set Coca-Cola back. It thrived during Prohibition in the 1920s. It swelled during the Great Depression of the 1930s and expanded even more during World War II. The sturdiest of defensive stocks, Coca-Cola's success was based on sales of the fizz that somehow became a daily necessity, one cheap enough to withstand the hard times that toppled other business empires.

It's no secret that stocks tend to move together; that's why the nightly news gives you the Dow, S&P, and Nasdaq indexes and calls it a day. What the news doesn't have time to tell you is that certain groups of stocks are perfectly capable of handling market downturns. When the economy hits a roadblock, an investor's best offense just may be a good defense.

For another definition of a defensive stock, just say "Coca-Cola." Its investment performance made it "the real thing" long before the advertising copywriters chimed in. Whatever was in its secret formula, Coke had the right stuff.

Unstoppable Growth

"P.S.—" wrote the baseball great Ty Cobb in a personal letter to a friend at *The Sporting News* in 1953, "if you ever buy any stocks, just remember I have written you to buy Coca-Cola now, around 108, pays regular $4.00, has always paid and will always increase their earnings each year. . . . I am buying more now, have advised my daughters, also daughter-in-law, a *widow*."

Cobb, a native of Georgia, had the good fortune to be game bird hunting pals with Robert Woodruff in the early 1920s. Woodruff and his father had taken large holdings in Atlanta's Coca-Cola Co. in 1919, when the family led an effort to take the company public. Woodruff was so intent that his friend Ty Cobb buy Coca-Cola stock, he even loaned him the money to do it. The investment eventually made Cobb millions. But then again, Coca-Cola stock made a great many people rich.

While the public paid $40 per share for Coca-Cola in 1919, insiders like Woodruff and Cobb got it for a mere $5. Through splits, that one share would have turned into 4,608 shares by 1999, when the stock hit a high that made the $5 investment worth $387,072—and more than $4 million, if all dividends were reinvested. But Coke's reign as a growth stock didn't start with the Woodruffs; Mark Pendergrast, author of the company history, *For God, Country and Coca-Cola*, calculated that $100 invested in a share of the original corporation in 1892 was worth more than $2.5 billion one hundred years later.

Coca-Cola has been reckoned as one of the best stock picks of the whole twentieth century, high on a list with General Electric and IBM for long-term, practically unstoppable growth. What the three have in common is that each combines the strength of a battleship with the nimbleness of a kayak. A long-term stock must have both. If change is the only certainty in business, then Coca-Cola's record of turning outside pressures into opportunities for growth proved that the company was not merely protecting shareholder value, but rather continually enhancing it.

A steady, long-term stock should present only one problem for an investor: avoiding the assumption that it is too late to invest, that the easy money has been made and the growth days are through. For at least seventy-five years, the negative comments heard on Coca-Cola stock were nearly always the same—although past growth was impressive, the market for soft drinks was finally becoming saturated and, anyway, the competition was closing in.

WRONG TRAIN

In the late 1930s, a story went around Wall Street about an investor who chose to invest in Southern Railway rather than Coca-Cola in 1928. You could say he chose the wrong train. Over the

*next ten years, Southern Railway was a victim of the Depression—
its stock falling by 90 percent. Coca-Cola, on the other hand, met
the Depression with ease, improving its sales throughout, while its
stock rose by 350 percent. Many an investor heard that story and
smiled, only to go away thinking that that was fine for 1928, "back
when Coca-Cola was still growing." But then—guess what?—
Coca-Cola grew some more.*

A Soda's Tale

Many soft drinks originated at drugstore fountains in the nineteenth century because customers drank them in search of quasi-
medical relief from daily complaints such as fatigue, indigestion,
or stress. At a time when many people were either adamantly
opposed to alcohol or else reeling with a hangover from it, fountain drinks offered an answer for everyone. An Atlanta pharmacist
with just that in mind devised Coca-Cola in 1886; it was a drink
that was supposed to cure headaches and, anyway, tasted good.
One reason that the green drink—in those days that was the
color—might have had some effect on headaches was that it contained a minute amount of cocaine. That sort of narcotic additive
was hardly unusual for drugstore sodas in the nineteenth century,
but in any case, it was removed from the Coca-Cola recipe in
1903. Otherwise, the original formula has never changed (except
during the "New Coke" debacle of 1985).

The pharmacist never earned much of a fortune serving
Coca-Cola to locals in Atlanta, and a businessman named Asa
Candler eventually purchased his business. With wider distribution, Coke's momentum grew. It was the first soft drink to cross a
crucial barrier: it was sold in bottles, starting in 1899. Candler's
success with Coke soon brought the first generation of what would
lead to thousands of imitators over the years: from the early King
Kola and Koka-Nova to the more recent Virgin Atlantic Cola.
Candler fought copycats in the courts and at the fountains, but by

1919, he was tired. He was also fearful that his soda, already the national leader, had no further room for expansion. So, Candler sold out to the group headed by the Woodruffs. Robert Woodruff, at thirty-four, was named president of Coca-Cola in 1923 and would remain with the company until his death sixty-two years later.

Sales of Coca-Cola skyrocketed during the 1920s under Woodruff's imaginative administration. For one thing, the company introduced the six-pack, known then as the "six-box." It was a simple marketing strategy that increased sales in grocery stores and, as a Coca-Cola executive expressed it, "put Coca-Cola within an arm's length of desire." Second, the company had the good fortune to be selling a legal beverage during a fourteen-year span when liquor was prohibited. Starting from a split-adjusted $20 per share in 1919, the company's stock rose to $137 in 1929.

The increase, huge for the time, should have made Coke's biggest investors happy. However, many of them were haunted by the belief that their stock's price was filled with the same hot air that had inflated prices all over Wall Street. Even Robert Woodruff, Coca-Cola's most loyal supporter, was nervous, since there wasn't any firm reason for the stock to increase by nearly 20 percent per year. In 1928, Woodruff sold all of his shares short. In those pre-S.E.C. days, such activity was neither illegal nor especially unusual. Woodruff's move didn't reflect any lack of confidence in his company, only the intuition that the whole market was ready for a fall. And fall it did, on October 29, 1929.

In the mess that followed, one of the few stocks to remain firm was Coca-Cola. The price dipped from $137 to $128, but no farther. And it soon recovered. Coke's 6.5 percent hit was hardly a nick compared to the stocks decimated by half, two-thirds, or even more. Woodruff had the foresight to sell short before the crash, and had he done so with almost any other stock, he'd have made a fortune. As it was, he was rewarded for his feat of acumen with a loss of $400,000. That was what it cost him to replace his shorted shares. For Woodruff, the president, it was marvelous that Coca-Cola stock held up. For Woodruff, the investor, it was a disaster.

Time to Drink Up?

The desire to shift money into defensive stocks is nothing unusual during market turndowns. On the assumption that in any economy, however woeful, someone is going to make money, investors huddle close to those companies producing the absolute necessities: food, energy, pharmaceuticals, etc. That was the sentiment right after the crash of 1929, except that the economy was so sickened that no company seemed absolutely sure to make money. Investors had to look hard to find a winner.

In terms of a potential market it was not hard to see Coca-Cola. In 1929, Coca-Cola syrup was doing phenomenally well; sales were at record levels. Although the soda was sold at 110,000 fountains and in 800,000 stores in the United States, it was decidedly more popular in the South than in the North or West. A question for investors was whether millions of people in the country's largest markets would be willing to swill Coke at the same rate as those in the South. Investors also had to assess Coca-Cola's international business, which had been started in 1927, in order to decide whether or not "America's favorite drink" could actually prosper in foreign lands.

Coca-Cola's price was nearly as well known as the product itself. A standard 12-ounce soda fountain serving cost a nickel. At that, the company made an average profit of 38 percent on revenues. The profit was susceptible to only one major factor: the price of sugar. After the crash, commodity prices were also depressed. Translation: Coca-Cola paid less for its main ingredient and reaped more out every nickel. Smart investors knew that the equation was tipping in Coca-Cola's favor, even in the onset of a Depression.

Many investors look for two things in a company's management: first, competence, and second, a financial stake in the business. With so much of the Woodruff fortune tied up in Coca-Cola stock, company president Robert Woodruff could be counted on to serve the stockholders sympathetically. After his adventure with selling short on Coke, he settled into the more conservative investment climate established in Roosevelt's New Deal years. "Things you worry about don't happen if you worry enough" was one of his expressions. As to Woodruff's abilities, the company had set new records in sales every year since he'd taken office. Another reason that Coca-Cola was peculiarly immune to the overall business reversal was its lean corporate structure. From the very beginning, the company kept its administration small. It bottled only a small fraction of its own soda, leaving that end of the business to over a thousand independent franchisees: the bulk of the investment in Coca-Cola was theirs. In fact, Coca-Cola was anything but top-heavy or laden down with liability in the form of equipment or employees.

The company was certainly growing. From 1923 to 1929, Coke sales increased by 50 percent. Moreover, profits increased by 160 percent, as the company raised the productivity of its franchisees. Woodruff's business philosophy was that everyone associated with his product, from bottlers to shopkeepers, should make a juicy profit. Their hard work was essential to greater profits for the parent, a fact that Coca-Cola recognized in the late 1920s when it organized a team of field representatives to teach effective selling methods throughout the loose-knit organization. Among other innovations, the company taught bottlers to install coolers in grocery stores, stocked with Coca-Cola products.

No Retreat

Coca-Cola stock not only rose during the Depression, it proliferated, splitting four-for-one in 1935. The company never missed a beat, as sales doubled between 1929 and 1937. By then, the company had a market capitalization of $500 million—yet it claimed hard assets of about $9 million—making it far from the fourth-biggest company in America. Throw in goodwill and Coca-Cola was working hard to become the biggest company in the world.

Coke's advertising had been untiring since the 1890s, but even in the face of the 1930s business downturn, the company didn't retreat. That year, the advertising budget was $6 million, a huge outlay on sales of $34 million and profits of $13 million. The budget was liberal, either by itself or as a percentage of sales, but Coca-Cola had no reason to slow down. In an era of nickel luxuries, of movies and candy bars, Coca-Cola pushed hard to become something more than a drink. It was promoted as a momentary indulgence: "the pause that refreshes." Nickel by nickel, the company was rewarded with half of the country's fast-growing market for soda.

The advent of World War II, which changed nearly every American business somehow, was as much a boon to Coca-Cola as to any aircraft manufacturer. The company worked closely with the military in order to provide Coke as near to the front lines as possible. It was regarded as a tremendous boost to soldier morale. No sooner was a country liberated from Axis control than a Coca-Coca bottling plant started turning out cases. The availability of their hometown pop not only reinforced the popularity of Coke with Americans (General Dwight Eisenhower was an aficionado) but also introduced it to populations around the world. For investors, Coca-Cola's activities in the war may have been of long-term interest, providing a base for the company's vast international expansion to come after the war. However, during the hostilities, investors were only too aware that sugar was among the most heavily rationed of all commodities. Coca-Cola struggled to find supplies; sometimes falling short in production or selling nickel bottles at a loss. Other soda makers used substitutes for cane sugar. Not Coca-Cola. It preferred to lose money or sales rather than compromise the recipe.

Epilogue

After the war, Coca-Cola stock stalled in the face of serious competition. Pepsi-Cola had surged from nowhere to third place in the industry during the 1930s by selling bigger bottles of soda for the same five-cent price as Coke. Emerging from World War II, Pepsi had aggressive managers determined to turn the cola industry into a *cola war* for the first time in a half-century. Coca-Cola's share price stalled, as investors worried anew whether the stock's glory days were over. In the 1950s, Coke executives wouldn't refer to Pepsi by name, calling it only "our chief imitator." But they knew Pepsi's blue signs were out there. For the third time in as many decades, Coca-Cola faced a crisis; having survived the Depression and the stresses of World War II, it had to face a worthy adversary for the first time. And for the third time, too, the sow's ear turned into a silk purse.

While the cola war put pressure on Coke's market share, the overall market expanded enormously. The promotional efforts of two ingenious companies were trained on turning more and more people into soft-drink customers. The real loser, in truth, was tap water; it gave up market share to the two beverage sellers.

The company continued its march in the 1980s under legendary leader Roberto Goizueta. Portfolio managers flocked to the stock first because of its low valuation, then because of its impressive international growth, and later, when the U.S. economy faltered at the end of the decade, as a defensive stock. The realization that food and beverage companies had recession-proof characteristics may have been news to the latest generation of money managers, but those who knew their history weren't surprised.

Coca-Cola stock reflected the growth of net profits from $38 million to over $3 billion between 1950 and 2000. Although there were plateaus and a few dips during that half-century, there was not one single decade during that span when Coca-Cola did not register a strong upswing in its stock price.

Lessons

A *generally adverse situation* . . . *Doesn't mean adversity for your investment. When the nation experiences a crisis, economic downturn, or even both, the resulting concerns often take their toll on the broader market averages. But look at one company at a time. Coca-Cola thrived first in the Great Depression and then again during World War II, proving that winners can be found even in the darkest times.*

***Speaking of adverse situations* . . .** *If you want really long-term growth, look for those few gems of steady defensive stocks that have a product that everyone not only needs but can't get enough of.*

***The two phantoms* . . .** *Competition and market saturation: as a general rule, investors have to make sure they really exist before deciding against a stock.*

TIMELINE

1919 Prohibition becomes law in United States.

1923 Robert Woodruff becomes president of Coca-Cola.

1927 Coca-Cola expands internationally.

1929 The bell-shaped fountain glass is adopted as the standard for fountain Cokes.

1929 Onset of the Great Depression.

1930 Women are sent door-to-door to install openers to make drinking Cokes at home easier.

1931 Haddon Sunblom's Santa drinking a Coke first appears in Coca-Cola advertising.

1933 Prohibition is repealed.

1935 First standardized coin-operated vending machines are used.

IT'S A GUSHER

Schlumberger Ltd.

1970–1980

Even before investors figured out how to pronounce the company's name, they were aware that the more the world needed oil, the more drillers needed Schlumberger. Tightly managed and innovative, the company saw its stock rise 2,100 percent during the 1970s.

The 1970s were a time that investors would love to forget. Never mind bell-bottoms, lava lamps, and disco. Once the oil embargo struck in 1973, Wall Street faced the ugly combination of soaring energy prices, runaway inflation, and lofty interest rates. The Dow Jones Industrial Average, which first cracked the 1,000 barrier in 1972, remained trapped below that level ten years later. These were the worst of times.

As we saw with Coca-Cola and the Great Depression, even a dire economic backdrop will have winners as well as losers. What made the 1970s different is that the obvious beneficiaries of inflation—Big Oil—were the companies that many held responsible for the troubled times. (Rightly, wrongly, it didn't really matter.) The first challenge for an individual investor was to put personal feelings aside and go where the profits were. But put everything into Exxon and Texaco? Not so fast. As the old chess maxim goes, when you see a good move, wait, don't play it: there might be an even better move around the corner. It turned out that oil service companies were making even bigger strides than the big oil companies, and no one played the game better than industry leader Schlumberger.

Bubbling Up

The energy crisis of the 1970s was a turning point for the oil industry. During that decade the price of wholesale crude rose by more than ten times. Though unquestionably irritating to most people, the crisis rejuvenated the industry of oil exploration.

French-American conglomerate Schlumberger (pronounced *Shloom-bear-zhay*) couldn't have been more ready for its moment. Since the mid-1960s its earnings had been fattening up, thanks to a solid 49 percent profit margin in oil services. The oil industry was so healthy in the late 1960s that Schlumberger's earnings per share practically doubled in six years, from 71 cents in 1964 to $1.41 in 1970, and stock and revenues followed in kind. The company was growing faster than the general economy *and* both the oil or electronics industries. Though at the beginning of the 1970s Schlumberger may have been little known outside oil engineering circles, by the 1980s it was credited with helping to find more oil than any other single entity. A legend in business circles, it was referred to as "the best company in the world" by business publications and stock analysts alike.

Wild Card

When the first oil strikes were made in the rolling hills of western Pennsylvania in the 1850s, the liquid stood in puddles on the surface. All fortune hunters had to do to harvest the black gold was scoop it up in cans. From that point on, unfortunately, the search process was never as simple or in any place quite as pleasant. Modern-day engineers, hovering over a well miles deep in a jungle, desert, snowdrift, or ocean, are loath to make a mistake. It may be a poker game against the unknown, but there is a wild card: a green-and-white Schlumberger truck, loaded with electronic equipment.

Whenever engineers wonder what kind of earth the drill is going through, or right past, they can use the truck's equipment to make a "wireline" analysis, using data from probes to describe the geology around the well. The more urgent the need for oil, the more frequent the calls to Schlumberger. The demand for the service became so popular that folks even termed it "running a slumberjay." Mispronunciation or not, they were paying Schlumberger the ultimate compliment of calling the generic product by the company name.

Sonde's Good

Schlumberger incorporated in the United States in 1934 and has been officially headquartered here since the aftermath of World War II. Its stock hit the market a little later, in 1956. Its roots, however, are European.

WHAT'S IN A NAME?

The Schlumberger family was French, though with a German surname—not unusual, since they were from Alsace, a region that has shifted back and forth between France and Germany many times during the past five hundred years.

In the mid-1800s, the Schlumberger family made a fortune in the engineering and selling of textile equipment in Alsace's prosperous cotton industry. This was to be the first of many fortunes to come. The family's symbiotic business approach would be repeated by two brothers from a later generation, Marcel and Conrad Schlumberger, trained physicists who invented a way to describe the underground formations surrounding oil wells. Starting in 1927, they started a company that didn't drill for oil, but helped people who did.

One key component of Schlumberger's wireline service was a missile-shaped device called a sonde, which was lowered into the well. This sonde contained delicate equipment that had to withstand subterranean temperatures of more than 400 degrees. As the sonde was steadily raised, it logged the characteristics of the surrounding earth foot by foot, using electric (later electronic) and ultrasonic detectors. Oil company geologists received a log full of numbers and other readings that gave them a picture of the well, top to bottom.

The Works

Texas-based competitors Halliburton and Dresser Industries may have offered wireline services, too, but it was Schlumberger that still claimed more than 50 percent of the U.S. market. More important, it served 80 percent of the overseas business. This meant that its technical advantage could pay off in remote or even hostile environments, including offshore wells, where profit margins ran higher than the average.

One key advantage for Schlumberger was that it invested so much in research: approximately 3.7 percent of its gross revenues, which was twice the average for the oil services industry. An expanding technological base kept the company—and the industry—at the forefront of oil exploration. While it can be hard for an individual investor to gauge the effectiveness of research on a stock, the company was so aggressive that, typically, one-quarter of sales derived from services and techniques that did not exist five years before. This made an enormous difference in the company's ability to sustain growth, rather than merely react to it in the industry. In 1976 one analyst, Peter Vig of Oppenheimer & Co., pointed out that although oil-drilling activity had fluctuated widely during the first part of the decade, Schlumberger's earnings continued to grow at a gallop. "It has done this," Vig said, "through research and development. It has introduced new services and it has benefited from the trend toward drilling more wells offshore in remote areas."

The undisputed leader in technological innovation, Schlumberger even benefited from the prosperity of its competitors. Since it owned most of the important patents in wireline services, it was able to make money from licenses.

Luckily for Schlumberger, services like wireline were not price sensitive. Since Schlumberger's customers tended to be much more concerned with a complete, accurate report than with saving a few dollars on the cost, the company didn't have to worry about cutting the standards of the wireline services. Competition was centered not around price but around quality of service. Quality competition may be no less challenging, but it allows companies to plan their own pricing and gives successful ones an extra margin.

Schlumberger's reputation for excellence in the field—for example, it hired only college-educated engineers to operate its wireline trucks—allowed it to charge high prices. But consider this: even $50,000 for an accurate wireline was peanuts to an oil company risking $1 million per day on a speculative well. Or on the flip side, the wireline can discover untapped oil in seemingly dry wells. One favorite story has it that thanks to a wireline a client turned up just a few more barrels of oil than expected—one billion more.

To Schlumberger's credit, it carried one of the lowest levels of long-term debt of any company in the Fortune 500; debt ran at about 6 percent of equity when the average for American businesses was 38 percent. While debt is certainly not a bad thing if its purpose is to stimulate growth, a company that can expand without piling up debt is an even stronger investment.

During the 1970s, Schlumberger was a spotlight stock on Wall Street. It was the investors' favorite combination: a big company with big growth. One analyst referred to it as "near-monopoly," and a magazine called it "the second coming of Xerox or Polaroid." Magazines covered the story heavily, with at least a couple of major articles appearing about it each year.

Even a couple of years into the energy crisis, it still wasn't too late to invest in the company, because economic conditions were playing right into Schlumberger's strength. Boosted by increased oil drilling and enhanced profits from technological introductions, Schlumberger delivered spectacular growth between 1972 and 1978. The stock was flourishing, rising from about 5 to 45 over the 1972–1978 span. Revenues shot up from $792 million to $2.619 billion. At the same time, the company reported return on stockholders' equity of 33 percent.

RETURN ON EQUITY

Return on equity is the statistic that purists use to analyze profitability, since it answers the question of how efficiently the man-

*agement is utilizing the cash paid in by investors. It is unrelated to
the stock price, but treats a company, however large or complex,
as a basic business—that is, how much in the way of nice, plump
profit is being generated by the cash put into it? Schlumberger was
sustaining a rate of return on equity of more than 30 percent, a rare
feat for an established company.*

"Schlumberger hasn't had a down quarter in over fourteen
years," said John B. Walker, an analyst for Paine Webber, in 1978,
referring to overall revenues. "Its growth has been phenomenal—
25 percent a year the past ten years, 35 percent a year the past six,
and I'm predicting 20 to 30 percent a year the next five."

Schlumberger was also rich in cash: it had more than $2 bil-
lion in undistributed profits—usable capital. In the short term, its
stock was as good a pick as there was in the market in 1978, still
pumping along; it doubled in price by the end of 1979. Investors
who bought it in 1970, when its record was stabilized and its future
becoming clear, got great deal. They enjoyed an appreciation of
2,100 percent, as the stock rose (split-adjusted) from $5.90 to $130.

Too Much of a Good Thing

There was only one weak spot, however, and it was easily con-
cealed under the profits rolling in from the oil fields.
Schlumberger's conceit was its insistence that it was not an oil
services company—it was an electronics company that happened
to specialize in analyzing oil wells. That attitude led the company
to the conclusion that it should expand into electronics and, more
specifically, into computers: a reasonable inclination in the late
1960s and 1970s. For Schlumberger, though, making money in
electronics was, shall we say, harder than striking oil on the moon.
Tactics that were prudent and effective in its own circle of businesses proved to be clumsy in the fast center lane of the computer
industry. The harder the company tried to grow in that direction,

the more money it wasted. Whenever a company is in the midst of an identity crisis, especially one that is leaking money fast, investors lose faith.

In 1970, Schlumberger Ltd. made the first of a series of bad purchases. It acquired a flagging French electronics firm, Compagnie de Compteurs—a money loser despite all of the management expertise that Schlumberger lavished upon it. "It's fine to say you have a high p/e ratio," said Schlumberger's chairman, Jean Riboud, "and therefore you can buy cheap. The point is, no matter what price you pay for a company, you have made a bad buy if its contribution to earnings cannot increase at your overall rate of earnings growth. We've learned that diversification through acquisition is a very difficult, hard, time-consuming, tough problem." Unfortunately, neither he nor the company would remember that excellent advice.

(In fact, Riboud succinctly described Schlumberger's sadly unnecessary problem through the years: its tendency to acquire troubled companies that did little but drain profits from the company's oil services business.)

Investors who owned the stock were patient with the company's checkered record in acquisitions, because the corporate profits—perhaps even with a hole or two at the bottom of the bucket—were still excellent. However, one statistic in particular showed how unbalanced those balance sheets really were. Although wireline and other oil field services accounted for only one-third of Schlumberger's sales in 1973, they brought in two-thirds of the profits. That, if nothing else, showed how crippling the lagging acquisitions really were.

In 1979, Schlumberger went ahead and did it again. It purchased another electronics firm, Fairchild Camera and Instrument Corporation. Right idea. Wrong company. As one of the firms that established the Silicon Valley, Fairchild was an evocative name in the short history of electronics. During the 1960s, it was a high-flying maker of semiconductors, the Intel of its day. By the 1970s, the computer revolution was leaving it behind and so were many of its brightest employees. Fairchild was just one of a handful of acquisitions that Schlumberger made in 1979–1981. While adoring analysts praised the initiative of the company to grow beyond mere oil services, others worried that Schlumberger knew electronics but not the electronics *business*.

CAPITALIZATION

The capitalization is the worth of a company as perceived by investors, and is equal to the number of outstanding shares multiplied by the stock price.

Even if an investor wasn't aware of the internal struggles at Schlumberger, the stock itself was sending a worrisome signal. At the end of 1980, Schlumberger's stock price hit highs that gave it the fifth-largest market capitalization on the New York Stock Exchange. Today it seems difficult to believe that Schlumberger, a company known to practically no one outside the investment or oil businesses, had a larger capitalization than General Electric, General Motors, or nearly all of the oil giants it served. It was behind only IBM, Exxon, AT&T, and Standard Oil of Indiana. With revenues of just under $6 billion for the year, Schlumberger was in fact much smaller than those other companies, each of whose revenues exceeded $40 billion. This was strong evidence that Schlumberger had outgrown itself in the eyes of investors, but in this case some institutions were caught napping. Paine Webber placed Schlumberger second on its list of undervalued large companies, setting a value about triple its going price.

The 1980s were not as kind to Schlumberger as the 1970s had been. As the oil industry slowed, the company was burdened by massive losses at Fairchild. In 1983, it reported its first decrease in earnings per share in twenty years. That, unfortunately, was only the beginning. Two years later, the company reported its first quarterly loss ever and then a loss of $2 billion for 1986.

With the stock sliding by more than 50 percent, the decision points that may have once turned investors toward the obscure company were reversed:

1. The oil industry was contracting, with operating oil wells in the United States down from nearly 4,000 to 800.
2. The company's long-term profitability was in question, due to ill-advised acquisitions.
3. Worst of all, perhaps, expenditures on research and development were shrinking noticeably. Instead, the company was spending its cash on stock buybacks, which succeeded in supporting the price, but did not mean as much as new technology would have to customers.

When industry momentum accelerated toward increased oil drilling in the 1970s, investors sifted through the companies positioned to benefit and discovered Schlumberger. With its enviable profit picture and emphasis on innovation, it grew even faster than anyone would have predicted. However, it was these very same aggressive managers and investors who allowed a magnificent flow of profits from wirelining to cover up Schlumberger's disastrous efforts to expand into the electronics field.

Epilogue

Granted, it's tough to sell a winning stock such as Schlumberger, but it's easier when you look past the halo. Remember, the company soared to greatness not because management was infallible (in which case you'd want to hold it forever), but because the oil services business meshed perfectly with the unique economic circumstances of the 1970s. As if to confirm that point, around the same time, Wang Labs was earning its halo with dedicated word processors, a field whose days in the sun would soon be setting. Investors place sell orders because change is a part of life, whether we like it or not. If we were willing to bid disco adieu, we should have had the perspective to do the same with Schlumberger.

Lessons

The hair of the dog that bit you . . . Sometimes individual investors must mimic institutional money managers, who are paid to look at an industry's profitability, not its popularity. In unusual circumstances such as the oil stock, good companies in out-of-favor sectors can make for great stock picks.

No price is too high . . . *If a company can make products that its customers will pay for, that's good news. Schlumberger's hidden edge was that the price of its services was high enough to create impressive profit margins, but still easily justified by an oil company on the exploration trail.*

The halo effect . . . *When a company has enjoyed a period of success, investors sometimes make the mistake of attaching that success to a magical corporate ethos rather than to the specific (and maybe unusual) economic circumstances that made the company successful in the first place. If you wait for the halo to disappear before you sell, a lot of your profits will disappear as well.*

TIMELINE

1927 Schlumberger Ltd. is formed in France.

1934 Incorporated in the United States.

1956 Listed on the NYSE.

1964 Earnings per share 71 cents.

1970 Earnings per share $1.41.

1970 Acquires Compagnie de Compteurs.

1972 Revenues $792 million.

1978 Revenues $2.619 billion; holds 72 percent of wireline services market.

1979 Acquires Fairchild Camera and Instrument Corporation.

1980 Revenues $5.1 billion; fifth-largest capitalization of companies listed on NYSE.

1981 Oil rigs reach a high of 3,970 worldwide.

1983 First decrease in earnings per share in twenty years.

RETURN FROM THE DEAD

Chrysler Corporation

1981–1987

The Chrysler Corporation certainly proved that being down is not the same as being out. From 1979 to 1981, this was a company commonly given up for dead.

The category of "investing in bad times" has one more dimension. Whereas Coca-Cola and Schlumberger were good choices because they flourished despite challenging times, there is also money to be made from stocks that get beaten down to the ground, because they can be the biggest winners once the economy turns around. This investment strategy is inherently risky, because no one said that a recovery was assured, but the gains from the winners can more than make up for a choice gone awry.

To paraphrase Lee Iacocca, if there's a better turnaround story than Chrysler, we'd like to see it. As the 1980s rolled in, institutions had forsworn its shares. The dividend was long gone, and bankruptcy loomed. Of course, even a $2 stock isn't a bargain if zero is the final stop, because you can't do worse than lose all your money. In this case, Chrysler shareholders had the last laugh.

A Sick Company

For the year 1978, the Chrysler Corporation lost $204 million. Not a pretty figure, but the company had lost money before without worrying anyone. Automaking is, after all, the classic cyclical industry, in which demand naturally surges some years and then trails off in others. A car company could lose money without decimating its stock price, as long as the indications for the future remained secure: market share, new product development, dealer loyalty, and profit per vehicle among them. Unfortunately, Chrysler was also failing conspicuously in each of those areas.

By the end of 1979, Chrysler's market share was half what it had been three years before. Its products were outdated and there wasn't enough capital available for new designs. A hundred dealers per month were folding or jumping ship. The profits on Chrysler vehicles were a mess. Full-size cars, which delivered good returns, weren't selling; profits may have been negligible on compacts but those cars couldn't be produced quickly enough. As a result, the company's sales were off 18.8 percent from the year before.

A sick company had collided head-on with a dampened market, and the result was worse than anyone might have guessed. Chrysler, the nation's tenth-largest industrial company, was on the verge of bankruptcy. The stock that had been going for $70 per share a decade before, sank to less than $5 at the end of 1979.

In December, Chrysler was in crisis. Its losses during the first three quarters were $53 million, $207 million, and a whopping $460 million, respectively. The company's creditors—a network of more than four dozen banks—flatly refused to extend new loans. Even Chrysler's outside accountants, Touche Ross & Company, doubted the automaker would survive. Their report was branded with the qualification that if the company did fail, its losses would be even greater than those stated. The talk in the business world was that Chrysler's only hope was absorption by another automaker, but it was even too late for that. The only taker was the federal government.

New Chrysler

Chrysler's management, led by Lee Iacocca, offered the administration of President Jimmy Carter a choice: either save Chrysler or say good-bye to 250,000 jobs in the nation's anchor industry. The "bailout," as it was known, was a radical idea. Even if President Carter could work out a deal, it would still have to be authorized by Congress. Lawmakers divided across party lines on the prudence of government intervention in private business. Common opinion was that if U.S. automakers were in trouble, it was their own fault for growing lazy and complacent. On top of that folks couldn't help noticing that the Japanese competition was constantly improving. All but the most laissez-faire business observers wanted to save those quarter-million jobs, even if they didn't care about saving Chrysler per se. So, just before the end of the year, Congress passed the Chrysler Corporation Loan Guarantee Act of 1979, giving Iacocca a chance, in the form of $1.5 billion, to do just that.

At the time, Chrysler was not merely out of favor on Wall Street, it was looked upon as a symbol of everything that was wrong with a woeful economy. To buy Chrysler was to invest in the Rust Belt, the industrial North, which was then dismissed as the relic of prosperity long since passed by. However, those few who believed in Lee Iacocca and the "New Chrysler," which he espoused, would see the stock become one of the steadiest investments on Wall Street, rising from $2.25 (split-adjusted) in 1980 to $48 seven years later.

"Voting for Our Survival"

As of 1980, the Chrysler Corporation had been America's third-biggest automaker for fifty years, perennially trailing General Motors and Ford. However, its average 12 percent market share put it ahead of American Motors and a gaggle of companies that had tried and failed to survive in the brutal and demanding automaking industry.

Walter Chrysler founded the company in 1924 and guided it until his death in 1940. After World War II, Chrysler, encompassing Dodge and Plymouth, produced a full line of cars, but made its money and its reputation on fairly large cars at a medium price. Those were the cars that boosted Chrysler shares throughout the 1960s—and those were the cars that were piling up in inventory during the gas crunch of the mid-1970s. Chrysler did offer two viable compact cars, the Plymouth Horizon and Dodge Omni, although even that class carried bad tidings for the company. It had neither the capacity to fully exploit the opportunity, nor the capital with which to expand in order to meet demand. Most of Chrysler's factories were still devoted to full-sized gas guzzlers. Americans wanted reliable and fuel-efficient cars, but domestic companies couldn't provide them. Instead, it was the Japanese who made gains in the automobile industry and seemed to dominate its future.

Overstocked with big cars and tottering against Japanese competition, Chrysler was helpless against the third calamity to hit U.S. automakers in the 1970s: soaring interest rates. The whole industry, including the nimble Japanese automakers, struggled against rates that discouraged customers from borrowing money.

Chrysler left Washington with its loan guarantees in the nick of time. Two months after receiving the backing of the government, the company reported a fourth-quarter loss of $375 million, bringing its red ink for 1979 to a staggering $1.1 billion, the largest operating loss ever reported in American business history. The loss for 1980 was predicted to be $750 million. Even with the government-backed loan, Chrysler still had to arrange for more than $3 billion in unguaranteed credit in separate arrangements with four hundred banks.

"Little by little, all you have to do is watch and you'll see the banks voting for our survival," said Gerald Greenwald, Chrysler's vice president for finance and one of the firebrands working directly with Lee Iacocca to save the company. In a sense, Chrysler was on a campaign throughout 1980, asking banks, customers, and investors to "vote" for its survival, by continuing to do business with a company that was struggling, day by day.

By the Book

Lee Iacocca took pride that on the same day he was announced as the new president of Chrysler in November 1978, as the company reported the first in its disastrous string of quarterly losses, shares went up three-eighths of a point. Obviously Chrysler stockholders, a generally loyal lot comprised overwhelmingly of small investors, put great faith in Iacocca and his potential to perform a miracle. This was surprising since in 1978 Lee Iacocca was not the celebrity he would later become. The former president of Ford Motor, he came to Chrysler with a somewhat checkered record in the automobile business. By 1980, though, he had started to shine. He was spearheading the drive to secure government backing and union concessions, all the while undertaking a reorganization at Chrysler that would replace thirty-three of the firm's thirty-five vice presidents. Anytime there is strong new management in place, one thing is for sure: a company won't remain the same for very long. In the case of Chrysler in 1979, that was good news.

Even as Chrysler's stock crashed through the five-dollar level, its book value kept it above the ranks of a penny stock. At the beginning of 1979, the company had assets with a value of $42 per share. The massive $1.2 billion loss in 1979 reduced the book value by an incredible $16 per share, but $26 was still an encouraging amount of hard, material backing for a $5 stock. Investors who looked at Chrysler not as a company but as a future tag sale regarded that book value in terms of breakup value. The logic was that if everything was sold off, the beaten-down shares could still be a bargain.

The U.S. automobile business was in the midst of its second consecutive year of depressed sales in 1980 and, according to the buying cycle for passenger vehicles, a rebound was overdue. When it arrived it would be bound to help domestic automakers since their Japanese counterparts had already agreed to voluntary quotas on their imports. While many investors realized that U.S. manufacturers had that window of opportunity coming, they wondered if Chrysler could take advantage of it. The company certainly didn't have much in its petered-out pipelines, but it did have the vaunted K-car: a reasonably priced mid-size vehicle that offered good gas mileage. Best of all, the K-car was destined for a niche that met with no competition from the Japanese.

Investors looking at Chrysler as a potential turnaround knew that the one thing—perhaps the only thing—a company can control is its own costs. No doubt that Chrysler had undoubtedly run amok in that respect, but even it couldn't say to what extent. Iacocca claimed that his greatest frustration on taking over the presidency was that no one could supply the answers to even the simplest financial questions. That changed pretty quickly. Within two years, he cut the payroll by half, dropping the number of workers from 133,811 to 87,825; even so, they were able to build the same number of cars. Over the course of 1980, with union cooperation, updated operations, and necessary layoffs, Chrysler's cost per car was reduced by $600. Moreover, its break-even point, the number of cars that it had to sell in order to start accumulating profits, dropped by half.

Uphill Battle

Even with the burst of energy from Iacocca's management team and the flood of cash from the government-backed loans, Chrysler faced quite a steep climb in 1980. In a nutshell, customers were wary of buying Chrysler products. No one wanted to own a car (much less a warranty) that could be orphaned by the sudden demise of its parent company. Customers were staying clear until they were absolutely sure that it wouldn't go out of business.

The overall automobile industry had stagnated, with 1980 its worst year ever. GM lost money for the first time since its own 1921 reorganization, and Ford reported a whopping $1.5 billion loss. Chrysler did worse, however, losing $1.7 billion and breaking its own record from the year before. As the stock price dipped to its all-time low of $3\frac{1}{2}$, the question of survival continued to swirl around the beleaguered automaker. The decision point that was becoming very troubling was book value, which dipped again even as debt rose, prompting the *New York Times* to make the truthful remark that "companies with more debts than assets are not considered very viable."

Opinion began to turn around when Iacocca launched an influential television campaign in 1981. The slogan "If you can find a better car, buy it" increased showroom traffic, as did the

company's offer to pay $50 to any car buyer willing to test-drive a
Chrysler.

Meeting in a Phone Booth

In early 1981, Chrysler had to return to Washington, hands out-
stretched for a second dip into its $1.5 billion well of government-
backed loan guarantees. To raise the cash, the government backed
a series of bonds with a unique feature: they paid a premium in
interest if the company defaulted within ninety days of issue.
Investors who thought that Chrysler was doomed to fail bought the
bonds. (Other naysayers shorted the stock.) In fact, Chrysler's
uncertain fate earned it the dubious honor of being the most commonly shorted stock of 1981. However, those who believed in the
company's future stayed with it. One of those believers? Peter
Lynch. His Fidelity Magellan mutual fund filled 5 percent of its
portfolio with 1.2 million shares of Chrysler stock.

Loyalists were rewarded. In 1981 Chrysler blossomed, selling
more cars at a far greater profit than in the previous half-dozen
years. Part of those profits were rolled back to the customer as
rebates and other sales incentives. No matter, the company was
regaining its lost market share, not to mention some of the customer confidence that had long since departed.

"If you go back two years," said Greenwald in 1982, "all
those who thought Chrysler could be turned around could have
had a meeting in a phone booth." By that year, the company's
market share had rebounded to more than 12 percent. The company had sold one of its most valuable assets, Chrysler Defense,
but it was in the automobile business to stay. The company's
return to profitability at the end of 1982 received as much publicity as its brush with bankruptcy had two years before. Profits
rolled in, more than $700 million strong, and the stock was the
best performer of the large caps that year, increasing 419 percent.
With the stock price in the high teens, Chrysler issued 26 million
new shares of common stock in order to refinance its debt.
"Chrysler has made the most remarkable recovery ever from a

financial point of view," noted Roger Altman of Lehman Brothers Kuhn, Loeb.

Epilogue

Far from being a symbol of what was wrong with American business, Chrysler became a symbol of what was right. "In the summer of 1983," wrote Robert B. Reich and John D. Donahue in *New Deals: The Chrysler Revival and the American System,* "Chrysler did something nobody could have anticipated two years earlier: it paid back all $1.2 billion in federally guaranteed loans." Iacocca cemented Chrysler's place in the annals of the greatest corporate turnarounds of all time by proudly and very publicly announcing his company's triumph. With the introduction of the first minivans in 1984, the company hit a grand slam; for that year it reported earnings of $2.3 billion. It was indeed a "new" Chrysler, and the difference lay in costs. In 1979, the company had produced 10.2 vehicles per employee. In 1984, that was nearly doubled, at 19.9 vehicles per Chrysler worker. The market pushed the stock price up to a peak near 50 in 1987, when the company used some of the market value to go shopping, purchasing American Motors for its valuable Jeep brand.

The acquisition made investors nervous, as expenditures often do; the stock price had trouble recovering after the October 1987 stock market crash. Clearly the rebound phase was over, and turnaround investors had to move on. What they discovered was that the "next Chrysler" was a snare and a delusion, because the blueprint of the Chrysler rebound was tough to replicate. Not until USAir in 1994 did such a prominent company stare bankruptcy in the face before recovering, and the rewards were again extraordinary: USAir shares climbed from 4 in 1994 to over 80 in 1998. Unfortunately, that particular ticket was round-trip, as the stock gave back all its gains in the four years that followed. As for Chrysler, it was finally snatched up by Germany's Daimler Benz in 1996. But it had already cemented its place in the folklore of American business by showing that a company flirting with bankruptcy may just be ready for a new start.

Lessons

Gotta believe . . . *Trust in Lee Iacocca certainly paid off, didn't it?*

Good book . . . *Companies with good book values will be more likely to hold up during difficult times. Just make sure that the book value isn't overwhelmed by the company's losses.*

Springing back . . . *Rebound stocks operate like tightly coiled springs; they have potential energy just waiting to be unleashed. When profitability returns, the spring lets go, and the extent of the rebound can be surprising. You can still make money, even if you weren't there on day one of the turn-around.*

TIMELINE

1978 The Chrysler Corporation loses $204 million.

1978 Lee Iacocca is named president.

1979 Congress passes Chrysler Corporation Loan Guarantee Act of 1979 in the form of $1.5 billion loan. The company produces 10.2 vehicles per employee.

1980 Chrysler loses $1.7 billion.

1981 Returns to Washington for a second dip into its $1.5 billion well of government-backed loan guarantees.

1981 K-cars debut as the Dodge Aries and Plymouth Reliant.

1982 Sells one of its most valuable assets, Chrysler Defense.

1984 Introduces first minivans.

1984 Reported earnings of $2.3 billion.

1984 Produces 19.9 vehicles per employee.

EIGHT
FORGING A NEW IDENTITY AND CHANGING FOR THE BETTER

MAKEOVER FOR A WASHINGTON BELLE: FANNIE MAE (1982–2000)

HIGH-TECH HIGHS: INTEL CORPORATION (1990–2000)

With thousands of issues on the New York Stock Exchange alone, investors don't have the time to investigate each and every possible equity investment. The result, all too often, is that companies get stereotyped rather than studied.

"A little knowledge is a dangerous thing"—whoever said that must have had the stock market in mind. Anyone who invests on the basis of outdated stereotypes is looking for trouble, because even some of the great growth stocks discussed in this book did not stay great forever. The great Polaroid went from stardom to bankruptcy in a generation and a half.

More optimistically, other companies get wrongly pigeonholed as losers, only to forge a new, winning identity. The investor who can identify companies that are changing their stripes has a big edge on the field. This edge requires both a sharp pen and a firm constitution, because you must keep an open mind to companies whose very future is in question. Turnaround stocks are inherently risky, but they are considerably less risky when companies are committed to change and have the means to make it happen. The beauty of corporate change is that it can take years for the word to get out; one by one, investors recognize the new and improved entity; and all the while the stock gets pushed up and up.

In this chapter we look at two success stories of the modern age: Fannie Mae and Intel. It may seem hard to believe, but if you turned the clock back to the 1980s, you'd find each company surrounded by a crowd of naysayers and a flood of red ink. Their problems were more than just some bad public relations, and their solutions went to the very nature of how they did business. In both cases, the companies reinvented themselves in order to survive—and kept on going!

MAKEOVER FOR A WASHINGTON BELLE

Fannie Mae

1982–2000

Rarely has a stock been as misunderstood as Fannie Mae was in the mid-1980s. On every level, the common perception was either sorely outdated or just plain wrong. Apparently individual investors didn't know what to think; more than 90 percent of the stock was owned by institutions. Had individuals looked twice at Fannie Mae, they would have seen that it was not only poised to grow but was practically bound to grow—with less risk than ever before. This was a stock safe enough for widows and orphans, yet it belonged in the high-growth category. A rarity indeed.

Sometimes a stock is misunderstood because the company's underlying business is considered too complicated to get a handle on. If so, the investor's challenge is to crystallize the reasons to buy in terms that don't require an accounting degree.

With Fannie Mae in the early 1980s, the thought that its future was dependent on something called "duration matching" might have seemed daunting to the layman. But the basic thrust behind duration matching—to insulate the company from swings in interest rates—was a move that anyone could appreciate. Even as investors lazily accorded Fannie Mae the same risk status as failed savings and loans, the company was applying the lessons from the S&L crisis and creating an unstoppable cash machine.

Fannie's Back Story

During the Great Depression (and prior) one of the biggest problems for this country was that home mortgages were typically written for only four or five years. When that period elapsed, the mortgages could be refinanced at prevailing rates, if both the bank and home buyer were willing and able. The short-term mortgage may sound like a form of variable-rate financing, whereby interest is periodically adjusted to keep up with prevailing conditions. In practice, though, the short-term mortgage fell heavily on the home buyers, who lost their houses if they couldn't adjust to changing rates. This, in turn, was also hard on banks—which lost steady loan business—adding to the general instability of the era.

The underlying problem with long-term mortgages was the lack of liquidity in the secondary mortgage market (the system by which lending institutions could raise money by selling loans outright to other firms). Why would banks want to tie up their cash assets for twenty years or even more? To encourage longer-term lending, Franklin D. Roosevelt's New Deal created the Federal National Mortgage Association, or Fannie Mae (adopted many years later as the official corporate name) in order to free up money so that banks could make more long-term loans. Starting in 1938, Fannie Mae began to buy out mortgages—good, 20-year mortgages on lower- and middle-price homes—so that banks would have the money to go out and write more home loans. (This practice gave rise to a common misperception that Fannie Mae lent money. In reality, it only purchased loans secondhand from lending institutions, such as banks.)

Fannie Mae is one of a handful of entities created by the government with the expectation of someday turning a profit. (Other examples include Amtrak, the passenger train system, and Comsat, the satellite service.) In the financial arena, Fannie Mae's closest relative would be the Federal Home Loan Mortgage Corporation (Freddie Mac), created in 1970. Like Fannie Mae, Freddie Mac bought mortgages, but it paid for them by issuing securities based on packages of the loan debt. Freddie Mac was a middleman, in effect matching pools of mortgages to bond market investors.

In 1954, as the federal government recognized that Fannie Mae was turning a nice profit, the agency was granted a charter as a corporation, with stock issued to participating lending institutions. But by then some people in the financial community felt threatened by Fannie Mae. Those with a conservative outlook on economics felt that government should not be involved in a competitive financial market. This was not exactly a widespread opinion, but it did encourage lawmakers to increase the agency's independence. The government soon developed reasons of its own to give Fannie Mae even more independence: Fannie Mae had become the second-leading borrower in the country, behind only the U.S. Treasury itself, and the government was tired of recognizing Fannie Mae's debt from mortgages in its own strained budget. In 1968, Fannie Mae was cast out into the world as a publicly held company, just like any other—but with two exceptions. The government retained "general regulatory power" over it. In exchange, Fannie Mae received the tacit backing of the federal government and markedly better interest rates on its own debt because of it.

Works Like This

Fannie Mae didn't actually grant loans, but operated as a wholesaler, buying packages of mortgages from banks and holding them until they were retired. And until the early 1980s, Fannie Mae paid for these mortgages by borrowing money. While interest rates were stable, the formula generated a nice return: the difference in, say, the loan Fannie Mae took out at 7 percent to pay for mortgages paying 9 percent.

Interest rates didn't remain stable, though, and starting in late 1979, they rumbled upward in response to inflation. Two years later, rates had more than doubled. Fannie Mae was as adversely affected by the rates as other financial institutions, from banks to life insurance companies. Unlike the others, it had no other business to help carry it through the crisis. Forced to take on new debt at upward of a staggering 17 percent to fund long-standing mortgages paying about 9 percent, Fannie Mae was losing money at the rate of $1 million per day in 1981–1982.

If people knew anything about Fannie Mae, they knew its fate was strictly tied to interest rates. That had always been the case, since Fannie Mae paid for 20-year mortgages by borrowing money on notes lasting on average two years. The lag, known in banking as "borrowing short, lending long," meant that when interest rates changed direction, so did the flow of money at Fannie Mae. If interest rates sagged, it earned more money because it could, on average, pull in money on, say, 9 percent homeowner loans, paid for with money it was borrowing at 7 percent. However, when they rose, it lost. And when they rose sharply, as they did in the early 1980s, the company was in serious trouble.

New Management Shakes Things Up

The situation at Fannie Mae was changing, even in the midst of the crisis. A new CEO, David Maxwell, arrived on the scene in 1981, determined to change the formula specifically so that the company would no longer be at the mercy of interest rates. When Maxwell, a lawyer and former mortgage banker, was named president, the institution was best known for years of noisy squabbling between the previous regime and the overseeing Department of Housing and Urban Development. The company returned healthy dividends to shareholders, but the stock had stagnated throughout the 1970s. In addition to the tepid earnings outlook, potential investors were overly sensitive to the government connection and nervous that it somehow put a restraint on Fannie Mae's prospects. The truth was that Fannie Mae was entitled to make all the money it could within the bounds of its charter, which restricted it only to activities related to the home mortgage market and reasonably priced housing within that realm.

MISCONCEPTIONS

The misconception that Fannie Mae was a nonprofit government agency was best put to rest by a HUD official who complained, "It's tending to be a company run for its shareholders." In a publicly held company that was precisely the point. But Fannie Mae's special purpose, too, was expressed best by one of its own officials: "Anybody remotely connected with the real estate

*finance industry understands Fannie Mae and what its potential
for good is."*

Losing money and utterly out of favor in 1981–1982, Fannie
Mae underwent a transformation. Maxwell and his team treated
Fannie Mae exactly like the private company it was, moving it
around in the marketplace to give it an advantage. Magazines such
as *Barron's, Forbes,* and *Business Week* closely followed the list of
changes that Maxwell was making: exerting greater control over
dealings with lending institutions, developing new fee-based businesses, and accepting variable-rate mortgages for the first time. To
lay off some of the risk associated with holding long-term loans,
Fannie Mae also began to package mortgages as the basis of a new
series of securities, intended as a vehicle for long-term savings.
Based on Freddie Mac's original mortgage-backed securities, they
were known humorously on Wall Street as "Fannie Savers."

According to David Maxwell, in the early 1980s there were
two Fannie Maes. The old Fannie Mae had been a pure interest
rate play, its return tied to the general trend in rates. The new company, however, was broad based and far more independent, an
earnings play that could generate strong profits as long as
Americans yearned for homes of their own.

Noteworthy

For any company leading its industry, the momentum of that particular industry is especially crucial. Fannie Mae was at the center
of the secondary market for mortgages, which was projected to grow
from about $40 billion in 1981 to at least $225 billion by 1990.

In an industrial company, too much liability—that is, debt—
is dangerous. For Fannie Mae, though, debt *was* the business. For
a company in the shadow of the U.S. government it was allowed
to develop a surprisingly high debt-to-equity ratio. This meant that
when interest rates eased the company would enjoy a return as

steep as its fall had been in 1981. Or at least that was the thinking in 1982.

Indeed, as interest rates eased off in the mid-1980s Fannie Mae's stock rose from its 1982 low of about 7 to 48 in 1987. As impressive as this rise was, it was still based on the erroneous investor perception that Fannie Mae required falling interest rates in order to thrive.

In the first quarter of 1987, however, something peculiar happened. Interest rates were falling gently, precisely the environment that Fannie Mae investors had longed for in the old days. So most investors counted on predictably higher earnings, but surprisingly they didn't find them when Fannie Mae reported. While the company did make more money by trading its retiring debt for new notes with lower rates, homeowners were doing roughly the same thing. The fad to "re-fi," or refinance, swept the country, as people calculated that it was well worth the trouble to replace a standing mortgage at a lower rate. This was bad for Fannie Mae, as it found the average interest rate on its huge mortgage pool sliding downward.

"Liquidations of mortgages have exceeded expectations," admitted Maxwell, "and the spread hasn't been as good as expected. That's something that happens. But it's only now that we've gotten the company on a sound financial basis, where we've got the assets and liabilities reasonably matched and the mortgage-backed securities product producing earnings." Investors who were perplexed by Fannie Mae's new means of making money finally saw the light in the second quarter of that year. Interest rates rose sharply all of a sudden—and yet Fannie Mae reported an increase in earnings of 32 percent. A new Fannie Mae had emerged, with more sophisticated moneymaking techniques. An earnings increase in a climate of surging interest rates was something that couldn't have happened in the old company. Fannie Mae was emerging as a more complicated company than ever before, but one that could produce earnings in practically any environment—and stellar earnings when there was increased activity in the mortgage market.

The savings and loan crisis of 1988 to 1991, in which scores of institutions went belly-up by making bad loans at low rates, bypassed Fannie Mae, in part because the crisis had its roots in commercial loans, not in Fannie Mae's area of residential mortgages. To its benefit, Fannie Mae had taken its medicine at the beginning of the decade and its financial guidelines were more sophisticated than ever in weeding out poor risks among lending institutions and mortgage-holders. While Fannie Mae was reporting its eleventh (!) consecutive quarter of record earnings at the beginning of 1991, the confusion surrounding the crisis depressed its stock, along with that of most other financial institutions. That presented yet another misunderstanding (*and* another buying opportunity for investors considering Fannie Mae).

Many analysts concurred that unless the housing market shattered, as in the Great Depression, Fannie Mae's success would continue. Morgan Stanley analyst Nancy Spady looked at the probable fate of Fannie Mae under a doomsday model that expanded on the conditions of an actual scenario, the drastic reversal of the Texas housing market in the mid-1980s. The Texas situation, involving both banks and real estate, was one of the worst crises in postwar America, and so it made an apt model by which to judge an institution like Fannie Mae. Spady found that even if the whole country found itself operating under the default rates and other conditions that dealt such a hard blow in Texas, Fannie Mae would still return 10 percent on shareholders' equity. That scenario never came to pass, thank goodness, and in the 1990s Fannie Mae continued its string of record earnings.

Because Fannie Mae was so successful, resentment of its "most favored" status with the government grew in the late 1980s, along with pressure in Washington to make it entirely independent. This meant specifically that it would no longer receive preferred rates of interest. Such rumblings had been heard in Washington before, but nothing ever came of them. A Fannie Mae that was more successful than ever in making profits was also more effective than ever in helping maintain a liquid mortgage market, one in which people of moderate means could buy a house because banks had the cash on hand to loan. So, essentially what Fannie Mae had provided through the years was a means by which every bank could broaden its lending strength. While Fannie Mae had new competition from a private program called the Federal Home Loan Banks System in 1997, the prevailing fear in Washington was that tampering with Fannie Mae would stagnate the housing market.

A Bona Fide Growth Stock

Fannie Mae, the queen of the home mortgage market, grew in assets from $62 billion in 1982 to $641 billion for 2000. Fannie Mae was at the center of the secondary market for mortgages, which was projected to grow from about $40 billion in 1981 to at least $225 billion by 1990. With a portfolio worth $85 billion, the company held over 7 percent of the home mortgages in the country. Quite an achievement, especially considering that the company was reporting a loss in 1982.

Once on track, Fannie Mae reported earnings increases of 33 percent per year from 1986 to 1999—one of only seven stocks with a record that good. Shares followed suit, appreciating by a whopping seventy times from 1982 to 1998, with an extra push late in the decade. By the end of the '90s the price-to-earnings ratio, which had long perplexed fans of the stock by hovering around 10, finally bounded to just over 20 in 1998. According to believers, even that reflected a bargain, since the average p/e on the Standard & Poor's index at the same time was 27.

For all of its new glitz and glamour, Fannie Mae stock was still laboring under some of the old perceptions. Every time interest rates jumped, Fannie Mae stock jiggled lower. After a discernible pause, investors would remember that things had changed and then the stock would right itself again. Just as a company that doesn't change with the times is headed for oblivion, investors who don't keep up with changes, large and small, in a wide range of companies—even government-related ones—miss the best picks.

Epilogue

In theory, investors looking for meaningful change could have bought Fannie Mae in 1982 and not done another thing. But if the success of that investment created an appetite for more, the 1980s were a fertile playing ground. Financial services companies such as Merrill Lynch, which a decade before had feasted on fat commissions, found new profit centers in underwriting and other services, and found new life in the resurgent stock market. Tobacco companies, finding themselves in an uncertain, litigious world, used their enormous cash flow to acquire food companies and secure their future. Walt Disney & Company, led by its new CEO Michael Eisner, found new profits from theme parks and moved aggressively into animated features.

When 1990 came around, investors might have thought that the new decade couldn't possibly live up to its predecessor. But they'd have been wrong, which leads us to our next selection.

Lessons

Misunderstand this . . . *Any "misunderstood" stock should be a magnet, another way of saying* opportunity *to a diligent investor.*

What price debt? . . . *For most companies, having a pile of debt is a terrible thing. But when a company's business is debt, its balance sheet can be in great shape even if it doesn't meet conventional standards. Fannie Mae's debt was linked to its mortgage assets so as to produce a positive "spread" with every new loan, ensuring profitability even as interest rates fluctuated.*

Industry momentum . . . *For any company leading its industry, the momentum of that industry is especially crucial. And the mortgage market was moving.*

Institutional interest . . . *Practically all of this stock was owned by professional money managers. Did they know something we didn't?*

TIMELINE

1938 Federal National Mortgage Association formed by Franklin D. Roosevelt.

1954 Granted charter as corporation.

1968 Becomes a publicly held company.

1981 David Maxwell becomes CEO; Fannie Mae posts loss of $190 million.

1982 Assets of $62 billion.

1984 Holds more than 7 percent of home mortgages in the country.

1988 Earnings of $507 million.

1993 Earnings of $2 billion.

1998 Assets of $485 billion.

2000 Earnings of $4.8 billion.

HIGH-TECH HIGHS

Intel Corporation

1990–2000

For years, Intel dominated its competitors but was held in check by the capricious market for personal computers. Selling the "brains" of the computer—tiny microprocessors— earned billions of dollars for Intel but failed to ignite skittish investors. Consequently, Intel's share price languished during the 1980s. When personal computers turned into household necessities in the last decade of the twentieth century, the stock broke free of its former image, rising 8,564 percent from 1990 to 2000.

Being a commodity producer is a difficult business. As long as customers don't accord your products extra value, customers are won or lost on price, and profit margins go from thin to thinner.

Once upon a time in the PC business, customers were familiar with the brand name on the outside of the computer but largely ignorant about the workings within. For a while, investors gave Intel the unwanted label of "commodity chip producer." But it wasn't long before a new, real-life label—"Intel Inside"—became a computer's biggest claim to fame.

Like Oxygen

There were two "best" times to own Intel stock. The first was from the mid-1970s to 1983, when the company was responsible for the most exciting breakthrough in electronics since the transistor. Intel's microprocessor was equivalent to thousands of transistors on a silicon chip smaller than a penny. The potential of the microprocessor sent Intel stock up 2,540 percent from 1975 to 1983, this in a period not known for the buoyancy of most stock prices.

But in the mid-1980s, Intel stock hit a wall. Competitors closed in, lawsuits mounted, and the market for Intel's primary product—the memory chip—was hit by a tsunami. Japanese manufacturers overtook Intel in that market and left it gasping. The company survived by relegating memory chips to its memories as it turned to focus on microprocessors. The market for microprocessors, the little brains used in watches, appliances, and personal computers, was regarded as cyclical. Translation: unpredictable. Even while the demand rose and fell with the fortunes of client businesses, the supply was not *enough* of a problem, from Intel's point of view. Other companies crowded into the nascent industry. Microprocessors, known colloquially as chips, were in constant danger of becoming commodities: objects as common as kernels of corn and difficult to differentiate on the basis of quality. Though still the industry leader, Intel's shares fell 15 percent from 1983 to the end of the decade. Investors were attracted to the stock, but they may have been the wrong kind of investors, jumping in and out so often that Intel gained a reputation as the most volatile stock on the market—moving 1.7 percent for every 1 percent that the overall S&P 500 index moved.

In 1990, Intel's outlook changed. The company was nothing if not fast moving, and the year before it had introduced an impressive new chip, the 486, that lent fresh powers to personal computers. Most pointedly, the 486 could accommodate the new Windows operating system that Microsoft introduced in 1990. Windows, the point-and-click exercise that depended on icons (and made spelling out commands obsolete), was easy to use and even pretty in comparison to previous computer graphics displays. The reason for both characteristics was that most of the work was being done not by the computer user but by the computer. And more specifically, by the microprocessor.

Without Intel's 486, very few PCs could run Windows. But hey, without Windows, very few PC users really needed an Intel 486 processor. The marriage of two very aggressive companies that had made sure they were in the right place at the right time was a phenomenon known in investing circles as "Wintel." While

Microsoft depended on aggressive marketing to stay in that lucrative place, Intel had to depend on aggressive technology—new chips so fast they gave the competition no time to catch up.

First Windows and then the Internet made Intel's potent microprocessors commodities, all right, but commodities as necessary as oxygen to the 1990s economy.

Going Forward

Before Gordon Moore and Robert Noyce founded Intel, the most talked about electronics company of the 1970s, they helped start Fairchild Semiconductor, the glamour stock of the industry in the 1960s.

In 1958, Moore and Noyce were members of a whole team of prodigies working under Dr. William Shockley, who shared credit for the development of the transistor, which conducted impulses through a silicon semiconductor, replacing vacuum tubes in electronics. Shockley was certainly a difficult man, later denounced for his opinions on the intellectual capacity of the races, and in business, he alienated many of the people who worked for him. It was no surprise then that Moore and Noyce were at the forefront of the so-called Traitorous 8, a group of engineers who left Shockley to start a more progressive company of their own. To fund the company, they turned to Arthur Rock, a San Francisco–based investment banker.

Rock put the group in touch with a backer, Fairchild Camera and Instrument Corporation, which had launched a pioneer company in the production of semiconductors. For his part, Arthur Rock also became a Silicon Valley pioneer, but on the financial end, as a venture capitalist. He often said that when evaluating a potential business, he was concerned more with the people behind it than with the idea. To that end, during the 1960s he occupied himself with helping Henry Singleton start Teledyne (see chapter 6), but was on hand, too, in 1968 when Moore and Noyce staged their second mutiny, bolting from Fairchild. It had become, in their eyes, a clumsy giant (Fairchild was later sold to Schlumberger). With Rock's help, Noyce and Moore started the Intel Corporation in Santa Clara, California. The name Intel may seem like an abbreviation for "intelligence," but it is actually a contraction of "integrated electronics."

"It was one of the few times that I helped start a company that I absolutely knew in my own mind that it was going to be a big success," Rock later said of Intel.

The new company made a name for itself early, with the introduction of usable memory products, including the DRAM (Dynamic Random Access Memory) chip, which launched another branch of electronics. However, the company backed into its hallmark product, the microprocessor, when two engineers on assignment for a company that made calculators designed a chip that could actually perform functions. Containing 2,300 transistors, the thumbnail-size chip was initially directed at the watch business. It soon spread anywhere that a really miniature computer could be used.

Intel thrived with its two lines, memory chips and microprocessors. But all at once, in 1984, it was forced to withdraw from the market for chips. Japanese manufacturers had underpriced Intel's products. In response, the company didn't dally, but to its credit saw nowhere to go but forward—as fast as microprocessor development could take it. Under the leadership of Andy Grove, Intel's notoriously impatient president, the company set a goal of remaining at least eighteen months ahead of the competition. That was at least the company's position in 1989, when it introduced the 486—a chip containing 1.2 million transistors and the power to operate Windows, due out the following year.

The Intel Decision

Long-term investors applauded Intel's nimble turnaround from 1985's memory chip loser to 1990s dominant force in microprocessors. However, those with a shorter attention span, who swarmed all over the stock in the late 1980s, didn't see that Intel

was a very different company from what it had been five years
before. Most of them were doing a dangerous thing: they were looking at the past to judge the future of a high-technology company.

Despite its description as a high-tech company Intel didn't
command the p/e's that we've become used to of late. Instead, it
enjoyed a relatively modest price-to-earnings ratio in the 10 to 13
range. The stock price was held in check by the volatility of the
market for computer chips, so only in periods of strong run-ups
did the p/e rise beyond the teens. Usually, it hovered well below
the average p/e ratio of the larger S&P 500.

In terms of profitability, a healthy company is one that's not
only growing but growing more profitable. Intel's return on shareholders' equity was an impressive 21.8 percent as of 1989. Some
investors would have been satisfied with that figure as a measure
of the company's viability. More impressive and even more important was the improvement shown in the company's average return
of 8.4 percent over the previous five years.

Intel's technological advancements may have been at the core
of its success, but its strong finances were the object of nearly as
much admiration in business circles. Even with a few bad years in
its recent past and in the midst of a worldwide expansion program,
Intel had a tidy $2 billion in cash assets in 1990. Any company that
can make the same claim—that its cash reserves are healthy
enough to withstand downturns and simultaneously fuel future
growth—is in a position to make decisions for the right reasons,
without the warping influence of monetary constraints. Usually,
that is quite a luxury for a growth company.

In 1990, the word on Wall Street was that Intel's golden age
was over. In its place, companies like Advanced Micro Devices
were coming into the picture with products equivalent to Intel's
bestsellers. Even while Intel kept a battalion of lawyers at work
fending off AMD and other encroachers, it was depending most of
all on its designers. Intel's stated goal was to remain at least eighteen months ahead of all others in product introductions. By the
time competitors caught up, according to Intel's reckoning, the
product price would have decreased—along with the profit mar-

gin. The only way to make real money was to get out in front of Intel, technologically. In the 1990s, that proved impossible.

Though Apple may have invented the personal computer, it was not until mighty IBM introduced its version in 1982 that a major industry was launched. Whether a PC was an IBM or merely IBM-compatible, it was built around two characteristics: Microsoft's operating system and Intel's microprocessors. At a time when customers could buy a new car for the price of a PC, the demand was not always steady, but Intel banked its future on the market. "If there isn't a new generation, there isn't an Intel," said company president Andy Grove in 1989. Investors who bought Intel in 1990 were quite specifically buying the future of the personal computer.

Chips Ahoy!

Before 1989, Intel had licensed manufacturing rights to its chips, but it denied licenses for the potent 486 microprocessor, introduced during that year. At first the new chip was regarded as an interesting failure: highly capable, but too sophisticated for the average customer. Then, in early 1990, Microsoft launched Windows 3.0, an instant hit that forced computer owners by the millions to upgrade their old machines, even as it invited many millions more to buy computers for the first time. The Intel 486 was the engine that opened and shut Windows in practically every one of those PCs.

While competitors scrambled to make a chip equivalent to the 486, Intel concentrated on the microprocessor that would leave them all behind. To be named the Pentium, it would have four times the power of the 486, and with computers trying to run more and more complex programs, power translated into speed. And speed into sales. Even while computer "box makers" battled over the expanding market by slashing prices, Intel was safe from pricing pressures. It was one of the essentials.

Intel didn't know bad news in the mid-1990s. Its market share was climbing, as it supplied chips for 85 percent of the PCs sold in America. At the same time, sales since 1989 had grown by nearly one-third *per year*. More important, profits had grown annually by just short of two-thirds, thanks to constantly expanding and improving production facilities all around the world. In fact, the largest private employer in Ireland was Intel, which helped lead a high-technology boom in that country.

And yet, Intel's stock remained the bargain it had been at the beginning of the decade. The price shot up, but failed to outpace earnings, with the result that the price-to-earnings ratio failed to crack into the teens, remaining at about 12. Many analysts were using a formula developed specifically for Intel: when the p/e for the coming year's earnings dipped below 12, they bought stock; when it rose above 16, they sold off.

While some people in the market continually fretted about competitors stealing Intel's market share, Intel itself worried how it could keep up. The world had developed a burgeoning appetite for microprocessors. The Internet phenomenon induced computer users to roll over into stronger PCs, with new generations of chips, and at the same time cellular telephones and portable music players added vast new markets for microprocessors.

By the mid-1990s, Intel stock was a perennial most active stock, a bellwether for the high-tech/computer/Internet sector. It was ranked as the third most popular stock among Merrill Lynch investors, for example, but even more important, studies showed that it was inordinately popular among online investors. That made sense; most of them knew enough about computers to appreciate the importance of microprocessors and the wonder of Intel's dominance. As online investing invited a horde of new money to Wall Street, Intel was among the prime beneficiaries. The company's advances had taken chips out of the commodity category, and the computer market's growth had removed the perception that Intel was a cyclical stock.

Epilogue

Slowly, the stock price lost its status as an underpriced bargain, as the price-to-earnings ratio crawled past 16 in 1995. For most stocks related to e-*anything*, $115 a share was considered mundane by that stage in the high-tech rally, but for Intel, the move signaled a disheartening change. After years of sternly rational stock pricing, investors were attaching a kind of *certainty* to Intel's hold on the market. And why not: a $100 investment at Intel's IPO was worth $155,764 thirty years later. The price shot forward ahead of earnings, until the p/e ratio hit 45 in the summer of 2000.

Intel dominated the chip market, but not the stock market, so when the reversal of 2000 swept the froth out of the high-tech sector, Intel was as vulnerable as the rest. The stock price hit a lull, not so much because the business was decreasing, but simply because it wasn't as fantastic as the high p/e ratio had predicted.

Lessons

Management, management, management . . . *No question that this company had a talented leader in Andy Grove. Why should investors care? Because his hunger transformed Intel from a commodity producer to a manufacturer at the cutting edge.*

Being trendy . . . *Intel was a big-time beneficiary of the excitement surrounding high tech. Just look at their techy investor base.*

Valuable . . . *Intel was always attractive to investors because its p/e ratio was under control. It was only after that number rose sky high that the stock had trouble fulfilling its promise.*

TIMELINE

1968 Intel incorporates as NM Electronics.

1970 Brings out first successful product, the 1103 chip.

1971 Creates the first microprocessor, the 4004.

1971 Sales of $9.4 million.

1972 Introduces the 8-bit processor.

1973 Sales reach $66.17 million.

1975 Corporate reorganization.

1979 Revenues are nearly $661 million.

1980 IBM chooses the Intel 8088 microprocessor for its upcoming personal computer.

1988 Revenues soar to $2.9 billion.

1990 Intel launches the 486 chip.

1990 Approximately 14 million PCs worldwide include an Intel microprocessor.

1993 Launch of the Pentium processor.

1995 Sales of $16.2 billion.

2000 Revenues of $33.7 billion.

NINE
EXPANDING THE MARKET

BUILDING A FORTUNE: HOME DEPOT (1992–2000)
THE "EXPERTS" AREN'T ALWAYS RIGHT: AMERICA ONLINE (1996–2000)

If the nineteenth-century political economist Thomas Malthus had been right, the world wouldn't have withstood the population explosion of the twentieth century. Malthus *was* right that natural resources were in finite supply, but he woefully underestimated humankind's adaptability. The human race, happily for all of us, became more productive and efficient, thereby postponing its day of reckoning for many centuries to come.

Doomsday logic also has its shortcomings in the stock market, because limits aren't always what they appear to be. It's easy to assume that companies grow either by increasing their market share in existing markets or by creating brand-new markets. Fair enough, but there is a third possibility: companies can grow by expanding the very markets in which they participate.

Anyone who has ever downloaded a computer file (with a slow connection) knows the following situation: your computer displays its little "thermometer" and says 123,456 out of 140,000 bytes (or whatever). Great, you think. I'm almost done. But the next thing you see is 234,567 out of 250,000, or something similarly irritating. The numbers have changed before your very eyes. No fair!

It may not be fair, but it's life. And many successful start-up enterprises have become multibillion-dollar businesses not by attaining a 98 percent share within their perceived market, but by enlarging the market's scope. Home Depot and America Online became sensational stocks for the 1990s by doing just that, and both were automatic entries in the top 25 list.

However, to build on the Malthusian tradition, our time frame for both of these stocks starts not with the IPO, but when modern-day Chicken Littles were shouting that the companies' growth was coming to an end. We will discover that "market saturation" is a terrible excuse to avoid a stock, especially one that's trying to include *you* in its market.

BUILDING A FORTUNE

Home Depot

1992–2000

Every house can stand some improvement. That—in a nut-shell—is the basis of Home Depot's business. With this same philosophy, the company adopted the concept of warehouse retailing, fine-tuned it, and used it more successfully than any other chain. At the same time management was also constantly revamping its own house. And what did all this improvement lead to? Phenomenal growth for Home Depot. For many savvy investors, the late 1990s will be remembered as Wall Street's high-tech—and Home Depot—rally.

No one enjoys missing out on a winning stock, especially when the company in question is expanding nationwide, reminding you of your missed opportunity every time you pass the store. But sometimes you can make money even as a Johnny-come-lately. All you have to do is stop feeling sorry for yourself, give the numbers another look, and realize that even the best growth stocks offer buying opportunities.

If you missed Home Depot in the 1980s, your funk would be understandable. But note that this story begins in 1992, even though you could say that Home Depot from 1981 through 1992 was itself one of the twenty-five best stocks of all time. If you don't let your analysis be colored by what might have been, you'll be able to join the rallying cry "better late than never."

Anyone who bought $1,000 worth of shares in Home Depot during its IPO of 1981 would have had $246,406 ten years later and a staggering $1.4 million in 1999. Though there was hardly a bad time to buy the stock, there were lulls when the price stalled, as in the mid-1990s, when retail stocks as a group were out of favor—"Flat as a two-by-four," in the words of one smug analyst. Perfect time to buy. While prevailing opinion classified Home

Depot with all other retailers, who were puttering along, the smarter view started with what made Home Depot different.

The Building Blocks

Throughout most of the twentieth century home improvement was hardly considered a booming area. People fixed up their homes, sure, but getting the materials often involved many trips to many various types of places to find supplies. For example, the do-it-yourselfer types went to hardware stores for tools, to lumberyards for wood, and then to plumbing, electrical, or painting stores for more specialized items. In the 1970s, a new breed of store, popular especially in the South and West, combined all these handyman specials under one roof. Future Home Depot founders, Bernie Marcus, then forty-nine, and Arthur Blank, thirty-six, were ranking executives at one such place, a Southern California chain called Handy Dan. Unfortunately—for Handy Dan, as it turns out later—management abruptly fired the duo in 1978, accusing them of plotting secretly against a union, an offense at a publicly held company. (The charge never went to court.)

Ken Langone, a friend in business, looked on the firing of Marcus and Blank in a bright light. As he so eloquently put it to them at the time: "You've just been kicked in the ass by a golden horseshoe." Indeed. After a few months, Marcus and Blank joined forces again. They reentered the retail fray with a new concept conceived in the coffee shop of a Hyatt Hotel in L.A. Langone was an initial investor.

Workshop Atmosphere

Home Depot had the radical idea to stock merchandise directly from the manufacturer. Where other hardware stores were stocked by one distributor or co-op, such as True Value or Ace, and so favored certain manufacturers, Home Depot offered as wide a selection as possible and in as many categories as possible. By design, the aisles looked like overstuffed closets. The busy workshop atmosphere has been a hit.

Home Depot stores may have looked different, but they retained one quaint aspect of the old-line hardware store: the relationship between customers, clerks, and the clock. "It's very important to us that when a homeowner comes in with a leaky faucet," Bernie Marcus once said, "our salesman can spend a half hour with that person explaining how to fix it, and then be able to sell them a fifty-cent washer that will solve the problem."

Out to Prove Something

Marcus and Blank would speak sincerely over the following twenty years about the quality of basic decency ("Do what is right") that they wove into the company credo at Home Depot. However, the smoldering anger they felt after their firings at Handy Dan stayed with them; indeed, it became part of the fabric of their new company. Those firings transformed Marcus and Blank from stable, upper-tier executives with fairly predictable gold watch–types of careers into the leaders of a company known for its take-no-prisoners rapacity. Long after Handy Dan went out of business, along with most other regional home improvement centers, Home Depot still acted like a company out to prove something.

Case in point: store size. In 1979, stores like Handy Dan looked enormous at about 33,000 square feet (the size of a medium-size supermarket today). Early Home Depot stores averaged 75,000 square feet, and would soon grow to a staggering 125,000 square feet. The company helped to pioneer the discount warehouse, known in retailing as the "category killer" as it stomped into me-too niches including food, toys, auto parts, and office supplies.

The first Home Depot store opened in June of 1979 in Atlanta. For the five years following, the company could do no wrong, opening stores on a march through the Sun Belt and with a special attack reserved for California. However, in 1985 the grand plan caught up with Home Depot when earnings came in dented. Painful as it was, management learned a great lesson: never try to grow by more than 25 percent per year or, as Marcus put it, "what we can handle intelligently." So, the company held itself in check and it paid off. By 1990, Home Depot stores averaged $30 million a year in sales, while other home improvement stores averaged $4 million—if they were still in business after Home Depot moved into town.

Taking Stock

"The great secret of success in business of all kinds is a liberal division of profits among the men who help to make them, and the wider the distribution, the better," said Andrew Carnegie in a speech delivered in 1903. "There lie latent, unsuspected powers in willing men around us," he added, "which only need appreciation and development to produce surprising results." Was Carnegie speaking about the business plan for Home Depot, founded seventy-five years later?

Home Depot is an example of a modern type of capitalism that depends on stock not merely to raise money but to bind the factions of management and labor. Stock gives the people associated with the company a reason to trust one another. At most corporations, stock represents a way to raise money—without having to pay it back. At Home Depot, stock is also used that way, of course, but to its employees it means even more. Fundamentally, common stock is the very currency of the company. Instead of paying commissions or bonuses to its sales associates, Home Depot furnishes them with stock. The value of the employee "bonus" is reported every day in the newspaper, listed for all to see under the share price for HD.

"Everybody is motivated to get rich," Marcus said of this methodology. Indeed, approximately 96 percent of Home Depot employees own stock through the company's plan. In the 1999 book *Built from Scratch*, about the history of the company, Arthur Blank explained that the plan was intended to introduce an aura of shared growth, not speculation. So, while employees can benefit from a rise in stock price, they are protected from losses by the store's guarantee to buy shares back at the purchase price. "Receiving company stock further deepened the loyalty," Blank wrote of the employees.

It is easy to see why: Home Depot stock had increased in value by an annually compounded 48 percent since its IPO. That kind of commission made millionaires out of about a thousand early Home Depot employees. Also, it encouraged them to make billionaires out of Marcus and Blank, owners of about 5 percent and 3.5 percent of outstanding stock, respectively.

LIKE A SMALL-TOWN SOCIAL CLIMBER

Stock was not an obsession at Home Depot, mind you, but it certainly mattered. From the beginning in the early 1980s, HD pushed its way into the in-crowd on Wall Street like a small-town social climber whose sights are set on the penthouses of Park Avenue. In 1984, after only six years in existence and just three years of public trading on the NASDAQ exchange, Home Depot yearned for what was then considered the big leagues: the New York Stock Exchange, with all the increased exposure and prestige that it offered. However, to be traded there at that time, a company had to fulfill certain requirements, one of which was at least seven profitable years. Home Depot had only four. But in its short history, it had already given investors a whale of a ride in the market: at the end of 1983, its stock was up 160 percent for the year.

Home Depot convinced the NYSE, and in turn asked it to convince the Securities and Exchange Commission that the rules should be changed. And they were. Home Depot started trading on the New York Stock Exchange on April 19, 1984.

Company Stalls—Buying Opportunity

After ten years of appreciation, Home Depot stock started to stall in the mid-1990s. However, though it would have been a good idea to buy Home Depot early on, when all signs pointed toward growth, the mid-1990s also proved a smart, ripe time to accumulate shares. The breather proved that a growth stock often accused of getting ahead of itself can also lag behind its recognizable value.

In midyear 1992, Home Depot was celebrating a streak of twenty-six consecutive quarters—over six years' worth—of record sales and earnings. To extend the earnings momentum, analysts calculated accurately that the company would have to increase sales at a 35 to 40 percent clip in coming years. At the time, Home Depot was consistently reporting sales increases of 33 percent. It wasn't in a growth industry and that made a difference to certain investors: overall, home-improvement retail sales were only growing at a dull 6 percent. As technology was gaining momentum, the bulls of the day figured it was better to be the tenth-biggest PC-maker than the number one retailer in staple guns.

A smarter way to look at the stock, however, would have been to examine Home Depot's position within its niche. Even as the biggest chain in the business, it accounted for only 4 percent of the $105 billion home-improvement market, meaning that it had 96 percent in which to grow. Sure, sector growth is easier to spot, encompassing a whole gaggle of stocks, but company growth is none the worse for being solitary. In fact, a stock can certainly buck a trend, chalking up growth of 20 percent or more while competitors dawdle.

To boot, the fact that Home Depot had yet to expand into the northern United States worried some investors, who thought that the store might find differing customer attitudes outside the sunny South. Again, this aspect signaled to the astute that there might just be plenty of room to grow: Home Depot had thirty-five states left to conquer. But it wasn't called "the next Wal-Mart" for nothing. In 1992 the chain announced plans to open one new store per week, upping its roster of 195. Competition was next to nil. The second-biggest player in the sector was Lowe's, which counted more stores, at 308, but 60 percent less revenue.

No matter how well a company is doing on the balance sheet, for its stock to succeed a growth stock needs attention within the institutional finance community. A whopping twenty-six analysts were tracking Home Depot (with only two of them rating it a "sell"). Another sign of attention was in the percentage of shares held by institutions: just over 50 percent in Home Depot's case. That figure is high for any firm, but in a relatively young company it was also a sure sign that it had been noticed. Institutions—pension funds, investment houses, and insurance companies—trade massive numbers of shares and can move a stock price markedly.

Throughout most of the 1990s, a knock against Home Depot, however, was its price-to-earnings ratio, which hovered around 61 in 1992, when the average for stocks in the S&P 500 was 7. On top of that, in the year before, the investment house Kidder Peabody had released a study showing that Home Depot had the second-highest price-to-earnings ratio of all companies with a market capitalization over $200 million. For many investors, this solidified a perception that Home Depot was a gamble. For example, Robert Stovall of Stovall/Twenty-First Advisors said the company was "vulnerable to a downside earnings surprise that might interrupt its string of 28 quarters of record profits."

Just Rewards

Investors who persevered through Home Depot's doldrums from 1994 to 1996 were rewarded, however, when the stock dislodged and went from 10 (split-adjusted) to 70 from 1996 to 1999.

In 1997 investors rediscovered the Home Depot stock. A big reason was that earnings had continued to rise while the stock price remained stationary. This made the price-to-earnings ratio drift downward, from the lofty 68 of 1993 to a veritable bargain (in the bargain-retailing biz, that is) of 24 in late 1996. This decrease made the stock more attractive to a more conservative investing crowd. With all this popularity, it's no surprise that within two years the p/e ratio had bounded up again, with the price of the stock. As the company began international expansion in 1998 with a major initiative in South America, sustainable growth obviously became the priority at headquarters. Other types of retail outlets, including mail order, were added to Home Depot's "big box" home centers.

By 1997, home improvement had grown to a $157 billion per year industry. By then, Home Depot had a worthy competitor in the refurbished Lowe's chain, perceived on Wall Street as another growth company with a well-rewarded stock price. On the shopping strips, competition may have been annoying for Home Depot, but in investment circles, the presence of Lowe's and a few other aggressive chains livened up the home-improvement sector (ever heard the saying "a rising tide lifts all boats"?) without affecting Home Depot's sales or stock performance.

During the 1990s, HD was the thirteenth-best-performing stock within the Standard & Poor's 500. A $10,000 stake in Home Depot taken in 1990 would be worth $370,120 at the end of the decade, making the annualized rate of return a jaw-dropping 43.8 percent. For the employees each glance at the HD stock price was a ringing incentive to sell even more of those 50-cent washers, or any of those 29,999 or so other products.

Epilogue

From 1999 to 2001, Home Depot's shares took a hit in the midst of a difficult stretch for the entire stock market. During this breather, investors were able to look up and notice that other companies in the home-retailing sector, notably Lowe's, were increasing sales at the same rate as HD—yet had lower price-to-earnings ratios. For aggressive investors, the switch was a tempting one.

Regardless of which horse folks ended up putting their money on, it appeared that the outlook for the whole home-improvement sector remained good despite—or rather because of—talk of recession. "That doesn't mean we're recession-proof," Marcus once said. "But when things get tough and people tighten up, they are much more likely to do that home-repair job themselves than hire someone else."

Hidden in Marcus's words was the final lesson of the Home Depot saga. The superstore concept worked brilliantly in the home-improvement sector not just because of cost efficiencies and superior sales tactics. The other vital ingredient was that people will always be improving their homes, through thick and thin. There were many success stories in the superstore arena, from Staples and Office Depot in office supplies to Circuit City and Best Buy in electronics. But the hardware franchise proved the most valuable of them all.

Lessons

On a mission . . . *Not just anyone can expand a market. This management was capable* plus *felt they always had something to prove—a lethal combination.*

Nothing in the rearview mirror . . . *By redefining its category, Home Depot had virtually no competition, but always acted as though it did.*

Give 'em the benefit of the doubt . . . *Home Depot had years of consecutive growth before it took a breather. With that kind of track record it's wise to see if the glitch isn't just temporary.*

TIMELINE

1978 Executives Bernie Marcus and Arthur Blank fired from Handy Dan.

1979 Home Depot is founded.

1981 Goes public on September 22, with 16 stores.

1982 Sales of $118 million.

1984 Stock begins trading on NYSE (April 19).

1985 Earnings fall, largely due to overexpansion.

1992 Sales of $7 billion, 6.7 percent of $105 billion home-improvement market.

1996 Sales of $19.5 billion, 14 percent of $140 billion home-improvement market.

1998 Begins a major initiative in South America.

1999 $1,000 invested in HD in 1981 is worth $1.4 million.

2000 In July, opens its 1,000th store.

THE "EXPERTS" AREN'T ALWAYS RIGHT

America Online

1996–2000

*For a time in the 1990s investing in AOL seemed to be syn-
onymous with investing in online computing. Where one
evolved, so did the other. Until one fateful six-month stretch
in 1996, making money in AOL shares seemed like a no-
brainer. Then it all turned upside down—the stock price
most of all. Predictions about the company's demise were
everywhere on Wall Street. Investors couldn't miss them if
they tried. But anyone who paid attention to those sentiments
without listening to AOL users missed something else entirely:
the stock's steepest climb yet.*

Hope is a most peculiar state of mind. We can't live without it, but
deep in our hearts we know that the real world can rarely live up
to the standards of our hopefulness. And the stock market is no
different. Stocks can move up on hopes rather than realities, so
when reality intrudes, watch out!

It could be argued that during America Online's first years as
a public company, the share price was based on hope and not reality. The company, after all, had never really earned a dime. Those
who invested on hope had done sensationally well in those first
years. But even when some harsh realities struck in 1996, the
stock was just getting ready for its second big jump.

First Internet Blue Chip

In the mid-1980s, Steven Case was logging time as a mid-level
marketing executive with PepsiCo. Hard to imagine that only fifteen short years later, he would be the chairman of a media conglomerate that swallowed the mammoth Time Warner in a gulp.
Case's rise in the media world marched in line with the standing

of AOL. It wasn't a computer company. It wasn't a high-tech company. The people who turned America Online into one of Wall Street's most consistent moneymakers in the 1990s understood that it was simply a way to reach people.

As the guiding force of the online services industry, Case didn't just ride the information superhighway, he paved it. Compared with other services, AOL was almost defiantly easy to use, and that alone gave it a distinct niche in the early 1990s. The company worked actively to remove extraneous steps, so subscribers didn't have to understand technology in order to jump into it. In the early years, AOL may not have been granted much respect from industry observers, but it did attract paying customers.

Even while AOL's growing success added momentum to the Internet craze, it was receiving its own fresh impetus from Wall Street. Adventurous investors picked out its stock right from the IPO in 1992 and kept it moving higher. AOL became the first blue chip among Internet stocks, with only one crisis of faith in the decade.

Logging On

In 1992, when seven-year-old America Online went public, it was a closed circuit of chat rooms, with a limited amount of other content. Subscribers could send e-mail, but couldn't go to other sites or surf the Internet.

The northern Virginia–based company had 180,000 subscribers and a talent for forming alliances with other companies (such as Chicago's Tribune Co.) or institutions (such as SeniorNet) that could provide it with either content or subscribers, or both. Running a weak third behind Internet service providers Prodigy and CompuServe, both of which were extremely well capitalized, AOL was constantly struggling to stretch its own paltry financing. With a successful IPO, the company found a source for money. It learned how to nurture its stock with analysts and investors, using (literally) street-smart charms to dress news and dole it out so that, as one analyst said,

"They always have a new story, a new feature, a new alliance to keep AOL hot."

Two years later, in 1994, AOL was still number three, but it was the fastest-growing online service. Its subscriber list had quadrupled and its stock price went up eight times, from the original $11.50 to $92. However, the company kept getting hit by complaints about service glitches and even billing practices. For example, if a client logged on for one minute and 46 seconds, the session was charged as three minutes under AOL's policies (rounding up to the next minute after a 15-second charge just for logging on).

Even with these complaints, AOL seemed poised to take over the lead and dominate the business of online services. Increasingly, though, the multitude of naysayers was questioning whether that business was even worth the effort. "A novelty that will drop off" was what the *ComputerLetter* called online services with their bland news and typed conversations. Others compared such services to citizen's band radio, the great person-to-person fad of the 1970s, and predicted that these too would die out when the chatter did.

Strategies and Underwear

In 1996, 11 percent of U.S. households were online, up from 3 percent in 1992. And more were signing up at the rate of one every four seconds. Although AOL had five million subscribers around the world, the company reported an unexpected lull in subscriber sign-ups during the summer.

Many online subscribers who grew bored with their electronic communities graduated to the Internet, that is, the World Wide Web, which offered exciting sites but required an advanced level of technical sophistication. Analysts began to couch the coming battle as AOL versus the Internet. It didn't exactly turn out that way.

By early 1996, AOL was offering a connection to the Internet *along* with its proprietary community of services. "Case changes strategies more often than most chief executives change underwear," wrote Allan Sloan, *Newsweek*'s Wall Street editor. For the first time, investors were not impressed with Case's tack. He had joined the Internet, but he had not beat it. And in May a sell-off in the heavily traded AOL stock began on fears that inexpensive Internet service providers would obviate the need for AOL and its hefty monthly bills.

These ISPs, like Earthlink or PSINet, didn't generate much content, but gave subscribers access to the Internet at a reasonable cost. Some of the country's richest corporate citizens, notably the Baby Bell telephone companies and Microsoft, were readying to launch ISPs. In addition, though AOL had passed its head-on rivals, Prodigy and CompuServe, in the proprietary online service business, they were all still gunning hard for the same customers. Those in the know were considering AOL inches from the grave.

AOL responded by offering an unlimited service plan at $19.95, but in the short term that only made things worse. Subscribers responded by using it—a lot. Chaos ensued. The service sputtered to keep up with demand. It finally shut down under the strain for 19 hours in early August. AOL stock fell by 12 percent, part of a descent that would lead it from about $75 to well under $30 by autumn.

America Online may have helped to launch the general public onto the Internet, but even that worked against it in 1996. In one of AOL's own stock market chat rooms, a member summed up the outlook: "As a shareholder, I'm concerned about my investment because, as a customer, I know that I would switch in a flash if an option became available." AOL had been a good stock pick in the past, but in a fast-changing industry the past is of limited value as an indicator. "The real question," said Kate Delhagen, an analyst for Forrester Research, "is whether there'll be a place for them in a year or three when the Internet gets to the next level."

Accounting Shocker

In the third quarter of 1996 all the negative news canceled everything once considered appealing about AOL and its outlook. The big revelation came from AOL itself, with the announcement of revised accounting. Not only did AOL have no earnings for fiscal 1996 according to the new annual report, it hadn't, in fact, had any earnings during the previous three years, when it was widely touted as the "only Internet stock in the black." Investors ran. In late 1996, AOL attracted the wrong kind of investor: the company had more short-sellers than any other stock on the NASDAQ exchange. The share price dropped by 50 percent.

Late 1996 was a difficult time to make a decision about AOL. Experts in finance and high technology were practically unanimous in the opinion that the company was faltering and on course to becoming obsolete. This assessment directly contradicted AOL's still expanding slice of a vast potential market. It was, after all, at the center of a fast-growing utility, one equivalent to power or running water for many people.

To Buy or to Sell?

Despite the ambiguity in AOL's earnings reports, overall income was undeniably charging ahead. Revenues were up more than 110 percent in fiscal 1996 (year ending in June), rising from $394 million in 1995 to more than $1 billion. However, a report that the subscription base had a turnover rate of about 50 percent coupled with the high cost of recruiting new subscribers seemed to underscore AOL's vulnerability and dampen the outlook. The company waged a successful marketing battle, albeit an expensive one, which ate up one-third of revenue. Until it established a huge, loyal base, the struggle over subscriptions would continue to unplug profits.

By almost any measure, America Online was an expensive stock. In May, when the company was valued by the market at $6.8 billion, the price-to-earnings ratio was 110. And that figure was based on projected earnings for 1997; in other words, a foreseeable degree of growth was already assumed. Investors buying AOL, or any stock, at over one hundred times forward earnings are anticipating a rate of growth that is rare.

In the midst of AOL's long, bad summer, Case hired a former FedEx executive to serve as president. The new man lasted only four months. AOL wasn't a logistics company, like FedEx. It was a media company, a fact underscored by the entrance of the new president, Bob Pittman, a cofounder of MTV. Investors, constantly alert for new directions at AOL, discerned one in a man who was not only tuned in to pop culture, but knew creative ways to strike advertising contracts.

NEW CRITERIA: BEYOND EARNINGS

The accounting switch had confused the earnings situation, but the decision to buy AOL stock had to be based on factors more qualitative than earnings. Rising earnings will always be the first and most reliable indication of a growth stock: no one should ignore them. Even in a year without earnings, AOL still had strengths, including market share, cash flow, and business affiliations—all of which can support aggressive growth as well. However, they were all dependent on something that no one could predict with certainty in 1996: the expansion of online communication and AOL's role within it. That was the point that set a value on AOL in the stock market. If it prevailed, few doubted that it would make money. The best-informed opinion was that AOL was the wrong company to anchor the new online universe. The shifting focus toward the Internet in 1996 forced a new assessment of AOL, but investors who believed that it was down for the count missed one of the best picks of the late 1990s.

Hanging On

Between May and November 1996, AOL's stock dropped from $70 to less than $27. The company was threatened on all sides, derided as "America On Hold" for its service problems, and called "Online for Cro-Magnons" because of its pandering ways toward members. For a company in a cutting-edge industry, AOL seemed, well, passé.

Over that winter, individual investors insisted on carrying the Internet rally forward, however, and many of them could hardly help noticing something unexpected. AOL wasn't going away. Alive and well, even after the crush of bad omens the previous year, the service was surging ahead, carried on the crest of the Internet wave. The "problem" of too many people trying to use the service looked as silly as Yogi Berra's skepticism about a popular restaurant: "Nobody goes there anymore. It's too crowded." As the nation—and the world—embraced a new obsession with the Internet, investors looking for a pure Internet play had a choice of hundreds of stocks, but AOL was still the blue chip, with real income and real growth.

Millions of people seeking a foothold on the Net in 1997 were bound to hear that AOL was the easiest service to use. "The cognoscenti," said one analyst, "wonder why anybody would spend any time on America Online with all the free content on the World Wide Web. But the truth is that when they're on America Online, they don't feel as lost in space as they feel on the Internet."

If their friends didn't tell them, AOL's unending advertising certainly did. The company added close to three million subscribers that year, accounting for more than half of online households in the United States. As a percentage of sales, the cost of marketing began to ease. Advertising revenue increased. At the same time, Bob Pittman turned the content equation around. AOL no longer paid producers; no, instead, they paid AOL for the honor of appearing on the world's most popular portal. More revenues resulted, and AOL began to look for similar sources of income in every corner of its service.

Reboot

AOL's stock price started to rebound in January 1997 from a low of 29 and passed its old high of 76 in September, when the company had the satisfaction of buying its former nemesis, CompuServe. That year, the company also purchased Mirabilis, a little-known Israeli company, to gain rights to the software responsible for Instant Messaging: private, real-time online chat. It has been especially popular with young people, who are advertisers' favorites. More than any other feature, Instant Messaging gave new life to AOL's proprietary community and succeeded in retaining members.

In just over two years, from early 1997 to 1999, AOL stock grew from $5 (split-adjusted) to more than $138. AOL had more than 14 million subscribers and was reporting earnings—real ones, without footnotes (!)—that increased every quarter. The company had taken advantage of the rising price of its stock to make a major acquisition in 1998 of Netscape, the company responsible for creating the first browser, which made the Internet easily accessible.

Within the hierarchy of high-tech companies, Netscape was known as the company that had embarrassed Microsoft by easily beating it in what should have been a much tighter race toward introducing an Internet browser. Purchasing Netscape brought AOL into contention as a direct rival to Microsoft, at least on the Internet front. Investors liked its new role and bid the price up 586 percent in just one year, 1998.

Epilogue

With a market capitalization of $150 billion, AOL could do as it liked. And in January of 2000, it did just that by announcing that what it wanted to do most was buy Time Warner, the publishing–broadcasting–cable television conglomerate. AOL didn't pay cash, but used its high-priced stock instead. The timing was good from AOL's point of view, attaching it to an "old economy" company that helped protect it from the ravages of the Internet stock meltdown of late 2000.

After the acquisition, many investors lost their enthusiasm for the stock. They worried about the proportions of the deal and were especially concerned that Time Warner's primary industries, including publishing and cable television, were growing more slowly than AOL had been. The announcement of the AOL–Time Warner merger is now seen by many as a symbolic end to the Internet bubble—the day when investors finally placed Internet valuations next to real-world valuations and decided they didn't make sense.

Nonetheless, those believers who had purchased $10,000 worth of AOL shares in late 1996 could cash out the day after the announcement for a tidy little profit of $548,000. For a company once dubbed "on hold," things certainly got back on track.

Lessons

Hitch yourself to a winning industry . . . *As the Internet took off so did AOL. Sometimes it even seemed like the other way around!*

Experts? Ha! . . . *AOL is a perfect example of the wisdom of looking beyond the expert opinion to see what was happening in the real world of friends, coworkers, and neighbors. A lot of them couldn't have made the leap to the Internet without AOL.*

Earnings aren't everything . . . *When earnings were nil, AOL had some other great things going for it, like market share and cash flow.*

Pricing is all-important . . . *When AOL offered unlimited service at $19.95 a month, fears of a price war dissipated, and the naysayers gave up.*

TIMELINE

1986 America Online founded.

1992 AOL goes public in March.

1993 Rumors of a takeover attempt by Microsoft cofounder Paul Allen.

1995 Revenues of $394 million.

1996 Revenues pass $1 billion.

1996 New pricing plan instituted in June.

1997 Buys CompuServe.

1998 Buys Netscape and its browser.

2000 Merges with Time Warner.

TEN
THEN AND NOW: THE ROAD WE'VE TRAVELED

INVESTING IN THE TWENTIETH CENTURY: AMERICAN TELEPHONE &
TELEGRAPH (1900–1984)

DOUGHNUTS TO DOLLARS: KRISPY KREME (2000–2001)

In case you're keeping count, we've got two stocks to go to complete our quota of twenty-five. Rather than creating yet another category, it made sense to use those final two selections to show just how far investing has come in the last century.

One hundred years ago, not many households owned shares of stock, and those that did frequently left buy-and-sell decisions in the hands of a professional advisor. Turnover was low, goals were long-term, and the most important number a stock could offer was a high dividend yield. Today shareholders are engaged, informed, and, as often as not, responsible for their own welfare. Growth now comes first and income a distant second, with dividend yields a mere footnote. And time horizons? For better or worse, those have changed as well.

The bottom line—with investing, there's always a bottom line—is that you will be a better investor if you understand the lessons of history. Our final top two stocks send you on your way by illustrating the "then" and "now" of common stocks in no uncertain terms.

In the far corner, representing the twentieth century, is the granddaddy of all common stocks, AT&T. Here is a company that earned its place in the pantheon of great stocks simply by increasing its dividend for an absurdly long period of time. Old-fashioned, yes, but also immensely profitable.

In the near corner, in keeping with this book's tradition of strange bedfellows, is the most recent success story among our twenty-five selections, Krispy Kreme. It is not a stock for nostalgia buffs, but it surged to market stardom by incorporating many of the themes we have talked about, from broadening the market to shining during difficult times. It was arguably the first real success story of the twenty-first century. Here's hoping you buy all the success stories yet to come.

INVESTING IN THE TWENTIETH CENTURY

American Telephone & Telegraph

1900–1984

> *AT&T was the pillar of Wall Street—and Main Street—for more than eight decades, perhaps because it was so unusual for a common stock, since it acted more like the preferred variety with the legal obligation to deliver dividends. AT&T had no such duty, guided only by its own no-investor-disappointment attitude toward earnings and dividends.*

If you had to name the single most important stock of the twentieth century, which would it be? At first glance there are too many candidates and no obvious winner. But a second look shows that one company stands out above all others, simply because it was dominant for so long. It is a company that could be taken for granted, and often is. More people owned this stock than any other in the world. You don't hear much about the stock anymore, but maybe that's because its glory days have passed. We can only be talking about AT&T.

Permissible Monopoly

AT&T was a company that loved to bandy statistics. The number of telephone conversations per day, the proportion of stockholders from New England, the number of telephones as a percentage of population: these are the numbers that filled the pages of weekly press releases and probably constituted the easiest way to understand America's largest corporation. Deep down, though, there was only one statistic that really interested AT&T's presidents: the number of times the company missed or lowered its quarterly dividend—zero.

For most of the twentieth century, AT&T was America's permissible monopoly, building a utility operated by governments in every other industrialized country. It was a private company with a public mission, and for four generations its stock—the most trusted on Wall Street—constituted what was undoubtedly America's favorite savings plan. Hotshots on the street may have disparaged it as a "widows and orphans" stock, but AT&T was more than merely safe. Within its conservative, highly unique finances lay the chance to grow in *direct relation* with telecommunication, one of the two or three fastest-growing industries of the whole era. In 1930, leading financiers, asked how they might invest a hypothetical $500,000, mentioned AT&T first. The consensus was that $200,000, or 40 percent, of the whole portfolio should be represented by AT&T. It was by all means a stock for widows, orphans— and anyone else who wanted to make the century's easiest money.

Building a telephone system across thousands of miles is a complex business, but also an overwhelmingly expensive one. The American Telephone & Telegraph Company set a formula early on. The plan was to borrow only a third of its capital needs, in the form of bonds, relying on equity markets for the rest. To attract investors, the company paid an annual dividend that grew from $7.50 to $8.50 during its first twenty-two years, 1900–1922.

In those days, investors expected companies to do anything and everything they could in order to post huge profits. In fact, a bonus profit was known as a "melon," because shareholders expected it to be cut up and distributed immediately. AT&T's managers showed that their company was different by announcing that the annual dividend would be the only one—excess profits would be saved for a rainy day, or reflected in future rate cuts for telephone users. The company wanted to return a fair profit to shareholders, but absolutely no more than that.

Under the circumstances—with a company claiming that it didn't want to make *too much* money (imagine!)—AT&T stock didn't fluctuate very much. Over the course of the same twenty-two-year span it moved between a low of 88 to a high of 186 (with no splits). Yet shareholders didn't have to be satisfied with the respectable dividend they received on their shares, an average of 5 percent depending on the purchase price. Money came in other ways, too.

Back to the Well

Whenever AT&T needed more capital, it issued more stock, just as companies do today. However, AT&T returned to its most reliable source, current shareholders, typically offering them the chance to buy one new share for every five or six shares already owned. The stock wasn't offered at the market price, as secondary offerings usually are. Instead, AT&T rewarded its shareholders by selling stock at par value. "Par value," the determined price, is a figure barely considered today. Yet AT&T gave its stockholders a bargain deal, selling the shares at their par value of $100, even though the market price was nearly always above that by $20, $40, or even more. The deal was, in effect, a valuable stock option, accorded to the shareholders every two or three years. Ninety-eight percent of shareholders accepted the offering, or else chose to sell the purchase to someone else for cash. In one way or another, AT&T stockholders could boost their annual dividend rate to 10 or even 13 percent annually.

The AT&T stockholder made money three ways: by an increase in the share price, by raking in some very serious dividends, and by accepting the largesse of the home office in the form of cheap stock. The formula worked for the corporation, too, since it built a reliable source of capital. Most large companies inevitably become beholden to banks or large shareholders, but not AT&T, which used the stock market to tap the power of the people. It was a covenant that would be tested as times turned hard after the crash of 1929.

"Built Upon a Prime Human Necessity"

No one ever made a fortune on AT&T, or so the business writers always marveled. There were people who did fine, but it is a fact that no single robber baron or cadre of insiders walked away with a million times their fair share, as was often the case with many other business successes of the last quarter of the nineteenth century. After Alexander Graham Bell demonstrated the telephone in

1876, he and two backers agreed to split the proceeds. Yet they were forced to fight off interlopers on one side and naysayers on the other. Eventually, they emerged with some nice profits, but neither they nor anyone else dominated the growing enterprise. In the 1878, National Bell, the antecedent of AT&T, was incorporated in Massachusetts and joined a nation full of scrambling phone companies, some serving whole regions, some only small towns.

Since Bell owned the patents, it remained at the center of the industry, a position it consolidated in 1900, when it was incorporated as the American Telephone & Telegraph Company. AT&T was primarily a holding company, owning or controlling almost two dozen regional phone companies. Those companies paid AT&T a dividend of about 6 percent per year, and the parent, for its part, acted as a bank, lending the subsidiaries money. While those early "Baby Bells" operated independently, AT&T also controlled its own moneymaking operations. Called Bell Labs, it originated the technology that took the phone from the age of the crank to the push-button and well beyond: Western Electric, the manufacturing arm responsible for handsets and other equipment, and the Bell System, the long-distance service.

The telephone industry was a business "built upon a prime human necessity," as John Mumford wrote in the *New York Herald* in 1923. That year, AT&T passed U.S. Steel as the nation's largest industrial company. Americans had more telephone conversations than any other people in the world, though Canadians were a close second, serviced through AT&T's Canada Bell subsidiary. Over the course of AT&T's first eighty-four years, the telephone never stopped evolving as an essential element in business and social affairs.

The Investment Rationale

Today, many of the most ambitious growth stocks don't pay any dividend at all, returning all profits to the extension of the business. (A bigger company is presumably worth more, so investors wait for returns in the form of increased share prices.) The AT&T idea was quite the opposite. Investors bought it hoping for an increase in the price, but they were more intent on the dividend as a reflection of the company's success. In other words, AT&T is an example of a stock that people bought on the basis of its current prosperity, not its future prospects.

But its future market certainly looked limitless. From 1902 to 1907, the number of telephones in use more than doubled to 5.5 million. Telephone use continued at that pace over the eighty years, when there were more than 136.3 million telephones in the system.

Though it was huge, this wasn't a business without competition. AT&T faced hundreds of "independents" around the country and made several attempts to combine them. The going was tough for independents, with names like the Citizens Telephone Company of Terre Haute (Indiana) or the Los Angeles Home Telephone Company. They often failed, either from promising lower rates than they could deliver or from providing service at rates that didn't cover their costs. As of 1902, AT&T was only slightly ahead of the independents in aggregate, but by 1912 it counted 5.2 million phones in use to their 3.6 million. From there the difference only continued to increase.

An Institution of American Life

The person who bought 180 shares of AT&T in 1900, when the new company was formed, would have paid $18,000. By 1928, the value of the stock would be almost double at $34,740 and dividends of $42,300 would have been paid. Moreover, if the stockholder decided to sell the rights to subsequent par value offerings, another $14,770 would have been realized. The original $18,000 yielded a straight $73,810—with minimal risk and without compounding. Both of the latter points indicate why AT&T was so popular as a savings instrument. First of all, the company was among the most conservatively managed in any industry and its stock was—rightly so—considered rock solid. Second, many AT&T

investors did not reinvest (or otherwise compound) their dividends. While dividend reinvestment is a sound strategy, it wasn't always possible. Fact was, many people relied on the AT&T dividend as a means of support.

During the first thirty years, the number of AT&T shareholders increased from about 7,000 to more than 469,000, on the way to one million in 1951. By 1920, women already outnumbered men among shareholders, as they would ever after. Some commentators saluted the telephone company's populist ownership: the average holding during the 1920s was 27 shares and no person or institution owned more than one-fifth of 1 percent—hardly a voting block. There were others, though, who felt that AT&T's management could and did protect their own power behind the mob of docile shareholders. The "virtual monopoly," as the company president Walter Gifford termed it in 1936, did have the hallmarks of a dangerous institution.

Yet even the most aggressive investigations were hard-pressed to find any abuse of that power. During the 1930s, when hundreds of people in the movie industry would consider themselves cruelly exploited at salaries of less than $100,000 per year, only three executives in the entire telephone industry earned more than $62,500. Only one worked at AT&T: Walter Gifford. His salary was far from the highest in the land, never mind that he headed the largest of all industrial companies.

Other interests were always well represented in the AT&T shareholder roster. For example, about 20 percent of the shareholders were AT&T employees. (Looked at from the other direction, more than 80 percent of eligible AT&T employees owned stock in their company.) Nearly all shareholders were telephone users, of course, and on that basis they were satisfied, since rates generally decreased with each technological advance. Decade after decade, AT&T stockholders were indeed a docile lot, largely because they judged the company by the arrival each quarter of the sacred dividend. That dividend was by itself an institution of American life, steady at $9 per year per share after 1922.

Dividend Payment

"Telephone," as the company was known on Wall Street, used most of its earnings to pay the dividend. For example, from 1907 to 1920, when the dividend was $8 per year, the company earned on average $10.31 per share. During the early years of the Depression, though, AT&T didn't make enough money to cover the dividend. The subsidiaries, which provided a large part of its income, were flagging. "Holders of the common stock of American Telephone and Telegraph Company have become increasingly nervous about the continuance of the $9 yearly dividend rate," observed *Newsweek* in 1933, "with successive announcements this year of dividend cuts by operating company affiliates." To pay the dividend, the company would have to dip into its own reserves. After three years of doing so, 1930–1933, the expectation was that it would bow to hard times and cut the dividend in 1934. That, of course, would fail the investors, as well as the future.

"Sighs of relief went up from the American Telephone & Telegraph Co.'s 680,000 stockholders," *Newsweek* followed up in May 1934, "as the directors declared the regular quarterly dividend of $2.25 a share. On July 16, uncounted postmen, as usual, will blow whistles and slip checks totaling almost $43,000,000 into mailboxes of stockholders." While other people suffered through the Depression, AT&T shareholders were receiving the same amount of money they had in the best years of the 1920s. During the Depression, one thing seemed stable: AT&T's $9 dividend.

Part of the reason the company could continue its dividend uninterrupted was that in its conservative fashion, it had never conceded to cutting up the "melon" in good times. The money was saved for just such a contingency. The reason it *did* pay the $9 out of savings was that future expansion, according to its own reckoning, depended upon it.

In the first four years after World War II, the company increased its assets by $4 billion—a figure more than the *total* assets of the country's second-biggest nonfinancial corporation (Standard Oil of New Jersey). By then one in every forty-five American households owned AT&T stock, and even more people depended on it through trusts and mutual funds. The stock remained between $100 and $200 in price until 1960, when it began to move higher, perhaps influenced by a stock split.

Normally, stock splits are of dubious influence in affecting share price, but since Telephone was the choice of so many small investors (more than half of whom owned ten shares or less), the difference between a $50 stock and a $150 stock loomed large. The $9 dividend continued through 1959, when it was raised, continuing upward through 1984. That year, AT&T's long run as America's favorite stock ended, with the breakup of the parent company. AT&T turned into eight companies, all of which have followed their own serpentine paths. This couldn't have been more different from the steady, straight path taken by the stock of old Ma Bell. But then again, these were modern companies. AT&T was a hard-nosed business, built unsentimentally on a promise to pay the dividend.

Epilogue

What makes a great racehorse even greater? Siring a stable of stakes champions would be a good place to start. As if AT&T hadn't already proved its greatness by 1984, it went on to sire septuplets of "Baby Bell" companies, which became stock market winners in their own right: Southwestern Bell, Bell South, Pacific Bell, and so on across the country.

Lost in the confusion of 1984 was that the Baby Bells came to market attractively priced, with dividends in the 7 to 8 percent range. Growth prospects were reasonable as well, once people figured out what these companies could and couldn't do. Ironically, what several of them ended up doing was merging. It seems that when it comes to making money for shareholders, AT&T covered every possible angle.

Lessons

True blue . . . AT&T kept up its loyalty to investors by paying its dividend through good times and bad.

Know the importance of selling to buyers . . . AT&T kept selling shares back to its customers, its current shareholders. You don't see deals like that anymore.

Grow with a trend . . . "Telephone" grew in relation to, well, the telephone. And we all know how popular that is. When you control the most important household item for an entire country for the better part of a century, you're going to make a lot of money.

TIMELINE

1876 Alexander Graham Bell invents the telephone, for which he receives two patents. With the support of two financial backers, Mr. Bell founds the company that becomes AT&T.

1877 Bell Telephone Company, the first AT&T predecessor, is formed and issues stock to its seven original shareholders.

1882 American Bell Telephone Company acquires a majority interest in the Western Electric Company, securing a supplier for telephone equipment.

1885 American Telephone and Telegraph Company is formed as a subsidiary of then-parent American Bell Telephone Company,

1899 In a corporate reorganization, American Telephone and Telegraph acquires the assets of its parent, American Bell Telephone, and becomes the parent of the Bell System.

1913 AT&T settles its first federal antitrust suit with a document known as the Kingsbury Commitment, which establishes AT&T as a government-sanctioned monopoly.

1959 On April 24, AT&T completes a 3-for-1 stock split. Shareholders receive two additional shares for each share owned.

1964 On May 28, AT&T completes a 2-for-1 stock split. Shareholders receive one additional share for each share owned.

1982 AT&T and the Justice Department agree on tentative terms for settlement of an antitrust suit filed against AT&T in 1974. AT&T agrees to divest itself of its local telephone operations.

1984 On January 1, the Bell System ceases to exist. In its place are seven regional Bell operating companies and a new AT&T that retains its long-distance service, manufacturing, and research and development operations.

DOUGHNUTS TO DOLLARS

Krispy Kreme

2000–2001

Even while Krispy Kreme was delighting customers all over the country with melt-in-your-mouth doughnuts, it was presenting Wall Street with something even more tasty. The financial books of this bakery chain featured plus signs in all the right places, most notably under revenue growth. To gauge whether those numbers would hold, investors would have to appreciate the company—without sentimentalizing it.

The twenty-first century isn't quite over, you might say. But the single biggest sensation of the first years of the new century seemed like a throwback to the old: a doughnut company. Yet a look at the story shows just how much has changed since AT&T's launch of a hundred years ago.

One Tasty IPO

The surprise bright spot of the bear market of 2000–2001 was, of all things, a doughnut maker. Krispy Kreme's initial public offering, on April 5, 2000, coincided with the end of the great 1990s high-tech rally. One day before, the Dow Jones Industrial Average fell 400 points, and the NASDAQ dropped 600. The high-tech rally, which had been barreling forward for four years, stopped short that day and started to move in reverse. Many companies were not only on their way down, but out—for good. All of a sudden it was apparent that this wondrous "new economy" had grown too fast. The market turned with a special vengeance on those "nonprofit" institutions known as Internet start-ups.

As though it were intended to make a mockery of the "e"-obsessed market, Krispy Kreme came along with an IPO that performed as well as anything that had barreled out of Silicon Valley. One of the oldest doughnut makers in the South, Krispy

Kreme opened for business on the NASDAQ even as some IPOs scheduled for that same day were canceling their issues.

Other investors may have been reeling, but anyone who got in on Krispy Kreme at $21 was ecstatic. In one day its stock price rose 74 percent, finishing at $37. The stock snatched headlines as though it alone had vanquished the Internet bubble.

Krispy Kreme had two big things going for it, especially in the climate of April 2000. It was not only well known, but *beloved*. In line with the teachings of Peter Lynch and Warren Buffett, these doughnut-loving investors thoroughly understood the company in which they held stock. Also, investors weary from (and now wary of, for that matter) untested companies found that Krispy Kreme offered a second attraction: a history of profitability.

Star Quality

Since the 1960s, restaurant industry stocks have been notorious. Many seem to pull in investors who have more hunger than sense. One of the worst, Boston Chicken, cashed in on the rotisserie chicken trend. Although its 1993 IPO was one of the most successful of all time, the stock was pretty much worthless four years later. Companies launched on other eating trends, like bagel chains, yogurt shops, micro-breweries, and coffee houses (remember those?), followed roughly the same ill-fated course. Yet anyone who compared Krispy Kreme with the likes of Boston Chicken was in for a big surprise.

Like McDonald's in the 1960s (see chapter 3), Krispy Kreme had a track record long before it had an underwriter. Investors knew what they were buying. This, of course, is crucial for any stock purchase, but nowhere more so than with an IPO. In addition, Krispy Kreme had some sort of star quality that propelled it onward and upward.

Both Sides of the Side Door

With his last $25, Vernon Rudolph rented a building in Winston-Salem, North Carolina, and launched Krispy Kreme in 1937.

Besides space, he had a secret recipe for a tender, tasty raised doughnut developed by a Cajun chef in New Orleans. Though Rudolph intended to produce the doughnut only for wholesale distribution, he had to throw that plan right out the window when local residents near his factory in Winston-Salem got wind of just how tasty the doughnuts were when hot. From that moment they started buying Krispy Kremes fresh at Rudolph's side door.

Krispy Kreme still works both sides of that side door. The company is building factories that can turn out up to 12,000 doughnuts an hour, either for distribution to grocery stores or sale direct to the customer. For the first fifty years, Krispy Kreme was limited to about three dozen locations, just under half of them franchises, and all of them in the Southeast. Because the locations were full-fledged doughnut factories, few cities had more than one Krispy Kreme.

In 1994, Krispy Kreme started to groom itself for national or even international growth. It experimented with a smaller shop, dedicated to the retail trade. Moreover, it made its first foray outside the South, opening a location in Indianapolis. The brooding fear that no'th'ners wouldn't appreciate Krispy Kremes was dispelled by the sight of cars lined up for six blocks on opening day.

The news that Krispy Kreme was on the move may have been exciting to aficionados, but meant nothing to stock market investors, since the company was privately held. However, management at Krispy Kreme was either supremely cunning or simply lucky as hell, because long before it went to Wall Street, it made the critical move to West 23rd Street. In 1996, the first New York Krispy Kreme opened up as a winner. The sophisticates of Manhattan hardly knew what hit them as they found themselves fawning all over the treat with the "kitschy" appeal. No wonder the *New York Post* declared "Dixie Donuts Take New York."

"In every market, we've gotten a lot of attention," said Jack McAleer, vice president of Krispy Kreme. "But New York translated beyond local media to national media and we had never had that before."

Anyone who has ever seen a Krispy Kreme operation in full cry—with thousands of doughnuts marching determinedly off the line, purchased by people who seem grateful for the privilege of buying one—has yearned to own a piece of the action. So it was one thing to fill Indianapolis with such converts. It was another to fill the investment capital of the world with them.

It's Not a Technology Company

In late 1999, rumors of a public offering started circulating. "Krispy Kreme has a retro appeal and is a familiar name to those who grew up in southeastern United States," said institutional investor Kevin Callaghan of Berkshire Partners. "It can awaken old loyalties." He was talking about the product, but he might just as well have been speaking of the IPO. It seemed the market was primed for Krispy Kreme—most of it, anyway. "It's not a technology company," squawked one analyst, aghast at all the attention this non-dot-com IPO was receiving, "It's a food company." In any case, Krispy Kreme was ready to try the market.

The Ingredients

"The cornerstone of our growth," said company president Scott Livengood, "was repositioning the company from a wholesale bakery strategy to a specialty retail strategy. From 1996 to 1998, we began implementing a variety of programs consistent with this repositioning. The positive effects of these programs positioned the company for an IPO."

The new business model, with more accelerated openings, resulted in profits that increased from $180,000 in fiscal 1996 to $5.9 million in 2000. One of the ways that Krispy grew so fast was through careful selection of regional partners to develop franchises in major markets, selling rights to firms experienced in the restaurant business. In addition to initial fees and a 4.5 percent royalty on franchise stores, Krispy Kreme received revenues by selling franchisees the mix for its doughnuts and the complicated equipment that produced them.

The doughnut industry was growing at only 4 to 5 percent per year in the United States—not enough to give much of a push to Krispy's 25 percent annual growth rate. So instead the company had to take business away from its competitors, or develop a new niche. Part of the appeal of Krispy Kreme stock was that, if anything was recession-proof, doughnuts certainly were. In terms of doughnut-to-doughnut competition, Krispy Kreme, with its 144 locations (58 company stores and 86 franchised ones) was up against 3,600 Dunkin' Donuts stores, 300 Winchell's, just under a hundred LaMar's shops, not to mention the thousands of independent doughnut makers. Of the three, only Kansas City–based LaMar's purported to compete head-on with Krispy Kreme in the connoisseur market. Krispy Kreme was, as one executive put it, "all about volume." Most businesses are, if they can manage it, but Krispy sold more doughnuts per location, on average, than its competitors—at the highest price and profit margin. As a result, its operating profit was 40 percent, versus 25 percent for industry leader Dunkin' Donuts.

However, the gamble was also contingent on whether Krispy Kreme was really special enough to expand the doughnut universe. Analysts often compared Krispy Kreme to Starbucks (which actually carry the doughnuts). Sure, there were certainly other coffee shops in the world, but few anywhere had quite the same panache. Krispy's believers felt the same way about their brand.

Defying Pure Reason

Although investors may have been smitten by Krispy Kreme's retro image, the fact is that the company is as automated in turning out doughnuts as Intel is in stamping out computer chips. Krispy's proprietary doughnut-making equipment accounted for $200,000 of the $850,000 cost of a new store. The equipment not only made doughnuts but a show that inspired the company to refer to its locations as "doughnut theaters."

The IPO show didn't slow down either after the excitement of that first day in April 2000. After fourteen months, the stock price was up sevenfold and was on the way to its second two-for-one split.

Not long after the IPO (probably no more than a few hours later, in fact), analysts and others began to insist that Krispy Kreme was overpriced. Even in the dreary bear market, this stock forced investors to wonder whether the valuation was in line. The question was not whether Krispy Kreme was a good stock but whether it was worth the premium included in its *triple-digit* (!) price-to-earnings ratio.

As the stock rose, naysayers took it upon themselves to note than according to the details of the offering, only one-quarter of the company's outstanding stock had even arrived on the market in April of 2000. The balance would be available for trading the following April. Obviously, according to this logic, the influx of new shares would water down the intense interest in the stock and force down the price. Nonetheless, April 2001 came and went and Krispy Kreme shares did not fall. In fact, by June the common shares had added another 40 points.

SHORT-SELLING

Short-sellers, the gleeful pessimists of the market, hovered around Krispy Kreme, borrowing blocks of shares, selling them, and then hoping to buy replacements after disaster struck the price. A year after the IPO, fully 10 percent of the shares was attached to short-sellers. Disaster didn't strike, at least through the middle of 2001. Time and again, it was the short-sellers who actually boosted the price of Krispy Kreme, at least temporarily, as they raced into the market to buy stock—at any price—in order to cover their positions (or buy shares to repay the borrowed ones). Some short-sellers eventually gave up on Krispy Kreme and scurried back to stumbling high-tech stocks, where the take was far more rewarding.

For every high-flying stock, there are always the naysayers and short-sellers. In Krispy Kreme's case, however, they had a point. Krispy Kreme was in a precarious situation, with its price-to-earnings ratio in the 90s—ten times the average for restaurant stocks. Even its fans admitted that much. They also recognized that the national fad was subsiding somewhat, as were same-store sales figures.

All along, much of the enthusiasm surrounding Krispy Kreme was stoked by knowing that the company managed to beat analysts' expectations, quarter after quarter. That could not exactly be said for many stocks in 2000–2001.

A key reason for Krispy's quarterly surprises was the high rate at which same-store sales increased. However, as that figure began to shrink, fears rose that Krispy Kreme was maturing into something, like, *gasp*, predictability—a wretched thing for a growth stock to do. Whatever the reason, what was happening with the stock was a cause for concern. And what was happening was that the stock was still going up. "We cannot remember a big-expectation story in the restaurant industry where the stock's multiple [its p/e ratio] expanded as the same store sales decelerated," wrote Peter Oakes, an analyst at Merrill Lynch in the spring of 2001. Indeed, John Ivankoe, analyst at J. P. Morgan (one of Krispy Kreme's stock underwriters for its IPO) had to admit the shares were defying pure reason. "This is a case where people's love of the product is helping the company's stock achieve a high multiple," he said.

All growth stocks carry a high level of emotion along with them, that mixture of hope and excitement at which detractors scoff. A degree of it is a natural part of the market. Too much, though, is perplexing at best. Krispy Kreme is a prime example of a stock that is forcing investors to decide just exactly where the love leaves off.

Epilogue

It's far too soon for a Krispy Kreme epilogue, but we can say the following: the odds on Krispy Kreme being the AT&T of the twenty-first century are, to use a word not usually associated with the doughnut business, slim. Great long-term picks often begin quietly, not with the tremendous splash accorded Krispy Kreme's debut, and a few years' success do not a century make.

If there is a stock of the twenty-first century, we hope it's one that you select yourself, having seen the lessons in this book. It's time to simply say, "Good luck!"

Lessons

History repeats itself . . . *Looking back on the Krispy Kreme story, just because we're in a new century doesn't mean the lessons of the past are outmoded.*

Expanding the market . . . *Though the doughnut market wasn't growing so fast, the appetite for newcomers to try Krispy Kreme was huge.*

Thriving in bad times . . . *Krispy Kreme's successes came as the NASDAQ was cratering. There's always a shining light in the market, if you look for it.*

Remember 1972 . . . *Keep your eyes on a stock whose p/e is sky high—no matter how well the company is performing.*

TIMELINE

1937 Krispy Kreme launched by Vernon Rudolph in Winston-Salem, N.C.

1994 Grooms itself for national or even international growth.

1996 First Krispy Kreme opens in New York; company reports sales of $151 million.

1999 Company reports sales of $318 million.

2000 IPO, April 5, where stock was priced at $21 a share.

Acknowledgments

As a magazine editor, I value the power of collaboration. No great magazine is ever the work of just one person, nor is this book. First, I must thank the person who was the soul of this book—Dinah Dunn of Byron Preiss Visual Publications, whose iron-tough yet gentle encouragement was a constant inspiration. Thanks also to her big boss and my friend Byron Preiss for believing in me and the power of the *Worth* message. I've often believed that great things come in threes: I was one of three sons brought into this world by the world's most supportive parents; I've been blessed with three sons of my own thanks to the most beautiful and caring wife a man could ever have; and over the last ten years I've been involved with the creation and nurturing of three great magazines. In the case of this book, the power of three once again has proven the axiom. The three stars who breathed life into this book with their brute intelligence and masterful wisdom were Julie Fenster, Caroline Waxler, and Derrick Niederman. Having authored six books herself, Julie, with her deft hand and keen insight, was the bedrock of this project. I salute her knowledge and understanding of how the market really works. Caroline Waxler brought style and grace to the prose and a "can do" attitude that I greatly admire. And Derrick Niederman, who has been my friend and investment hero since the early days of *Worth*, helped me find the lessons in each one of the greatest stock picks of all time that can help every investor navigate today's tricky markets.

I would also like to thank my invaluable colleagues at *Worth*, who stood by me every step of the way, so often doing the heavy lifting while I was juggling this project and so many more. Alison Parks, our president and COO and the steel magnolia of *Worth*, is the best business partner a CEO could ever have. Nancy Holmes,

Worth's editor-at-large, who helped put *Worth* on the map through her dogged passion and belief in me and the *Worth* mission, is a national treasure. Susan Feldman, John Koten, Gretchen Morgenson, Jane Berentson, Susan Goodall, Michael Peltz, Gary Walther, Dan Ferrara, Jim Rogers, Nelson Aldrich, Walter Russel Mead, Andy Tobias, Todd Buchholz, and Jim Jubak have all added their master craftsmanship to *Worth*. But *Worth* would never have been possible without my friends at Fidelity Investments, most especially Ned Johnson, Jim Curvey, Peter Lynch, and Laurie Watts, who gave life to this enterprise when it mattered most— the beginning. Ned Johnson is the most intriguing man I have ever met. Jim Curvey was the godfather of this exciting enterprise called *Worth* and continues to be my mentor and friend, and I will always be grateful to him for his constant championship even after Fidelity was no longer involved as an investor. I learned more in five years from the Jim Curvey school of management and life than I did in seventeen years of formal education. Laurie Watts has the keenest insight into people of anyone I have ever known, and of course, even though Peter Lynch has retired from writing his column, he continues to be the soul of *Worth* magazine.

And then there are my handpicked ambassadors of *Worth*, who are gems of generosity and were abundantly helpful in the early days of *Worth*: Lee and Walter Annenberg, Nancy Brinker, Betsy Bloomingdale, Nancy Hamon, John and Noreen Drexel, Denise Hale, Norman Brinker, Nancy and Jerry Tsai, Ann and Bob Hoover, Mary and Reese Milner, Yvette Mimieux and Howard Ruby, Joan Collins and Percy Gibson, Alyne Massey, C. Z. Guest, John and Susan Gutfreund, Martha Hyder, Nolan Miller, Aaron and Candy Spelling, Oatsie Charles, Joan Snitzer-Levy, Joan Rivers, Tommy Corcoran, Mario Buatta, Evelyn Lambert, Mary Lou Whitney, John Hendrickson, Fleur Cowles, Terry Allen-Kramer, Lucky Roosevelt, Charlie and May Jane Wick, Ann Alspaugh, Ann Slater, and Brooke Astor.

My journey down the road of journalism began principally because of one man—Phillip Moffit, who was my mentor, boss, partner, and friend during the turnaround days of *Esquire* in the

'80s, and it is thanks to this incredibly insightful man that I developed an almost insatiable passion for publishing and the power of the written word and the "big idea."

While I'm on the subject of big ideas, the man who embraced this big idea from the start, my editor, John Mahaney of Crown Business, has been the dream partner. Never intrusive, but always supportive—his watchful eye and gift for packaging ideas have been the glue of this book.

In the category of those who believed in me most, I have to give special thanks to the folks who have deprived me of a lifetime of in-law jokes—Marion and Woodfin Cole, who have been my second parents and my greatest champions. Also, I have to thank Uncle Robert and Aunt Connie Gunter for always being there for me. If I live a life half as rich and full as these four incredibly generous people, I will have succeeded beyond my wildest imagination.

This book also belongs to my dear friends who have stood by me and urged me on through the process of building the *Worth* brand. I can't possibly name them all, but I have to single out Keith Abell, Tim Collins, Paul Mucci, Stan Shuman, Joe Armstrong, Adam Hanft, Janie Sides, David Kahn, Chris and Michael Boskin, Missy Godfrey, Bente Strong, Bob Lessin, Vin Cipolla, Dick Stolley, Dorothy Kalins, Tom Ryder, Della Van Heyst, Nick and Jackie Drexel, Todd Berman, Sande Finkel, Sandi Mendohlson, Leo Dworsky, Bob Clark, Michael Braun, Fred Nelson, Jim McCabe, Larry Diamond, Fran Cohen, Jennifer Hillis, Carol Layton, Ina Saltz, Stephanie Koenke, Phillip Raygordetsky, Damir Perge, Cheryl Hammer, Ravi Kumra, George Green, Debbie Himmelfarb, Laurin Sydney, Deborah Norville, Nini Ferguson, Annette Tapert, and Angelica Hall.

In writing this acknowledgment, I realize how truly blessed I've been to have had so many truly special people in my life. Life is good.

Index

About the Authors

W. Randall Jones (editor in chief of *Worth* magazine) is the founder, chairman, and CEO of Worth Media LLC, the parent company for *Worth* magazine—the financial lifestyle magazine for active, wealthy investors. Mr. Jones founded *Worth* in 1992 and has been the guiding force behind its growth to 500,000 circulation in just three years. An industry maverick, he became the youngest publisher of a major magazine at 29 when he took the helm of *Esquire*. Randy is also the voice of the ABC News radio program *A Minute's Worth*, syndicated daily to 4,600 ABC radio affiliates. He is a frequent commentator on numerous television shows, including *The Today Show*, CNBC's *Power Lunch* and *Business Center*, CNN's *Business Unusual*, and Fox News programs. Mr. Jones currently sits on the board of the National Council of Economic Education and recently was honored as Philanthropist of the Year by the Leukemia and Lymphoma Society of America. Mr. Jones resides in Manhattan and Bronxville, New York, with his wife Connie and their sons Cole, Chancellor and Chip.

Julie M. Fenster has written several books on personal finance and business history, including *In the Words of Great Business Leaders* and *The Yahoo! Book of Personal Finance and Money*. She is also a columnist for *American Heritage* magazine.